Race, Redevelopment, and the New Company Town

SUNY SERIES IN URBAN PUBLIC POLICY
RICHARD RICH, EDITOR

RACE, REDEVELOPMENT, AND THE NEW COMPANY TOWN

Daniel J. Monti

STATE UNIVERSITY OF NEW YORK PRESS

Rn

Published by
State University of New York Press, Albany

© 1990 State University of New York

For information, address State University of New York Press,
State University Plaza, Albany, N.Y., 12246

Library of Congress Cataloging-in-Publication Data

Monti, Daniel J.
 Race, redevelopment, and the new company town / Daniel J. Monti.
  p. cm. — (SUNY series in urban public policy)
 Includes bibliographical references.
 ISBN 0-7914-0325-4. — ISBN 0-7914-0326-2 (pbk.)
 1. Urban renewal—Missouri—Saint Louis—Case studies. 2. Inner
cities—Missouri—Saint Louis—Case studies. 3. Relocation
(Housing)—Missouri—Saint Louis—Case Studies. 4. Afro-Americans—
Missouri—Saint Louis—Social conditions—Case studies. I. Title.
II. Series: SUNY series on urban public policy.
HT177.S33M66 1990
307.3'4216'0977866—dc20

                89-21829
                  CIP

10 9 8 7 6 5 4 3 2 1

*To Nip, Danny and Chris without whom little matters
and virtually nothing is much fun.*

CONTENTS

ILLUSTRATIONS

TABLES

PREFACE

The last forty years, with few notable exceptions, have not been particularly kind to St. Louis, Missouri. It lost half its population and many employers. This had many predictable and bad consequences for the city generally and for the people and companies that did not leave. The people who stayed behind tended to be both younger and older than those who left. They also were more likely to be black and have modest incomes. All manner of employers and jobs were lost to the city during this period. The losses were especially severe in manufacturing jobs and other areas requiring less formal training. This was bad news indeed for the people who still lived in the city, because many were not well suited for other kinds of work. It was not especially good news for the companies and institutions that remained, either. They conducted their business in a place that was deteriorating quickly and severely.

St. Louis was hardly the only city having a difficult time, though it often was cited as an example of how bad things could be. Similar changes occurred in many cities. Everywhere people fought over what could be done to deal with these changes and soften their impact.

Much of this fighting had a distinctly racial flavor to it. Minority people, especially blacks, had a hard time adjusting to new urban realities. Much public debate and private discussion centered on what could be done to relieve minorities of at least part of their burden. St. Louisans were not immune to these struggles. Although the city had no major outburst of civil unrest during this period, there was much tension and no small amount of conflict. In St. Louis, as in other places, it was not unreasonable for people to link problems faced by blacks with the problems of the whole city. Blacks were becoming a more prominent part of the city's life just as conditions in the city reached a low point. A similar connection was made when people discussed ways to solve urban problems. Whatever people did or even thought about doing to help one was considered in light of how the other would fare.

Whether this was an entirely accurate or fair connection to make is quite beside the point. People saw the two connected in a variety of ways and organized their effort to build a new St. Louis with this joint theme in mind. This cross-fertilization occurred most prominently and consistently in debates over school desegregation and urban development. My first book dealt with school desegregation in St. Louis. This book deals with the redevelopment of St. Louis.

The debate over desegregation unfolded in a fairly predictable way, notwithstanding the amount of discord it caused. Implied in the plans that eventually were implemented was a promise that people of African-American descent would receive a better education and, in the long run, occupy a more secure niche in the area's economy. Amid all the public rumbling for and against this reform, however, several important things have been successfully overlooked. First, more black children in the city are left unaided than are helped. Second, it is not clear that children who are helped are doing better academic work or enjoying a healthier social life. Third, and finally, black people are being encouraged to see their future as laying more in the suburbs than in the inner city. The schools they attend in the city are not highly regarded and usually are segregated. A concerted effort is made to entice black families to send their children to predominately white surburban schools. White and black people who support desegregation have seen this as the best way to ensure minority children a chance of succeeding in St. Louis' future.[1]

This idea was reinforced by much of the redevelopment work that took place in the city. St. Louisans took advantage of federal programs intended to help older cities rebuild, just as people in other cities did. Over the last forty years, St. Louisans have been relatively successful at transforming the central city into the heart of a modern, postindustrial metropolitan area. Yet much of this work also had the effect of moving many low-income, often black, residents from one area in the city to another or out of the city altogether. People held different views about all of this moving around, but few would think that it did much good for those who moved. Many believe that the city also was hurt by it, even when they agreed that St. Louis needed to be rebuilt. No matter how one stood on the issue of tearing down old neighborhoods and moving around their inhabitants, it seemed evident to many observers that black people did not fit into the plans for the new St. Louis. Similar events in other cities led people to reach the same conclusion about the future of their own communities.

It was not an unreasonable conclusion to draw, given the general thrust of public policies over the last twenty years. Cities and their residents could count on some direct assistance; but minority persons would be better served if they found places other than the older cities in which to live.[2] Part of the defense for this approach was that it would help to integrate American society. There also was a less high-minded reason for taking this approach: People who were not likely to help in efforts to rebuild cities and who could actually set them back should be spread around.

The corporations and institutions expected to play a prominent role in rebuilding cities were thought to be covetous of the land around them. The neighborhoods and people on that land often did not fit in the corporation's plans and were removed. It was assumed that business leaders could do pretty much what they wanted, because modern corporations were thought to be mobile and not terribly committed to the places in which they were located. Thus, no one was too surprised when big institutions promoted ambitious expansion programs for themselves and were not turned away by public leaders.

More conservative observers of urban redevelopment found such behavior acceptable, if only because it helped cities to adapt better to a changing economic world. More liberal or "radical" observers bemoaned this rapaciousness and fretted over the poor people and small businesses that were displaced. Neither thought that modern corporations and institutions could behave differently. The way urban areas were organized all but guaranteed that corporations and institutions would behave that way. Or so it was commonly believed.

Some thirty years ago, at least one person thought that the situation could have turned out differently. Political scientist Norton Long had hoped that business leaders would find a responsible way to reassert themselves in the daily affairs of cities. He viewed the modern corporation as competing with the city itself for the loyalty of its personnel; and he worried about the loss of civic-minded stewards who could help guide the city. He thought that if unions and corporations found an agreeable way to invigorate the political process, it might be possible to build a more united community and a set of ethical standards everyone could adopt. Long's view of citizenship and politics was borrowed from the Greeks and more recent urban reformers. They all worried about how to build a community from a mass of people who had very different backgrounds. Long resurrected the nineteenth century American idea that the city's business leaders could be instrumental in drawing everyone else together.[3]

Today, few students of urban politics and economics would hold such a view. Most would reject it outright. There is little in the recent history of U.S.

cities to indicate that business leaders are much interested in doing this. There is more evidence to suggest that quite the opposite is true.

In this book, we will see that Long's vision was neither impaired nor destined to turn cities into a plutocrat's playground. Considered here is the redevelopment of five parts of St. Louis, Missouri, and the role that major corporations and institutions played in that process. Today, these areas not only look better, but they also have a racially and economically mixed resident population. The political debates inspired by redevelopment work did not ignore the problems inherent in building a more pluralistic neighborhood. Indeed, the behavior of public and private leaders fueled such arguments. The lessons learned in these areas have yet to be widely shared with other parts of St. Louis. Nevertheless, they are readily available for others to adopt as they see fit.

Not everything done in these areas turned out well, or as well as it might have. On occasion, rather serious mistakes were made. Only part of the time were people able to overcome the problems they created for themsleves. *Race, Redevelopment, and the New Company Town* tells the story of what they did, why they did it, and how it turned out in the short run. Others will have to decide whether it worked out well enough to be held up as a model for people in other places to consider.

What is offered here is a case study of how people in one city tried to combine good business with better politics. As such, I make no broad claim to having tested one or another theory about the way cities are rebuilt. What I have done is to lay out several ways in which social scientists look at urban redevelopment. Each has its own peculiar strengths and weaknesses. None alone provides a complete explanation of what *really* is going on when people try to rebuild cities. Yet one approach does help me make better sense of what apparently was occurring in St. Louis. I try to make clear why this is the case and how the other approaches can help to clarify some things I cannot explain satisfactorily.

Much of what I learned about redevelopment in St. Louis was told to me by persons involved with one or another part of its rebuilding. These were people who did the work or saw to it that work was done. They lived in the areas before redevelopment occurred, and some lived there afterward. They were corporate officials, politicians, developers, small businessmen, reporters, bureaucrats, young urban professionals and elderly people, real estate agents and activists, priests and ministers, cops and robbers. Some supported redevelopment work; others resisted it. Some provided big pieces to my puzzle; others filled in the details. Some were candid and informative; others avoided answering questions. Only a few tried to lie, and they were not especially good at it.

Most persons were interviewed more than once. The first meetings were relatively formal affairs. Subsequent visits were often quite informal. After a while, it was not uncommon for people to answer specific questions over the telephone, at a public gathering, or during a chance meeting on a street corner. The interviews usually lasted for at least one hour. There were times, however, when they lasted three and four hours. I conducted several hundred interviews lasting many hundreds of hours.

There was understandable reluctance on the part of some persons to talk with me. Much controversy had enveloped efforts to rebuild St. Louis, especially in the areas described in this book. Potential informants were concerned not only with how they might be characterized but also with the confidentiality I was willing to guarantee them. The politics and economics of redevelopment are taken seriously. No one was willing to provide information, if they suspected that something might be shared with a competitor, opponent, or prospective client. The rules I followed in conducting interviews for this book were the same that I had used in speaking to people about school desegregation, another sensitive issue. No one would be quoted or even have an idea attributed to him, or her, unless the material in question had come from a public source such as a newspaper.

Assuming they were willing to speak with me, they had the right to put what they told me into one of two categories: things I could write about and things that were to be considered only as "background material." It was assumed that these latter things would not be published. The respondents understood that something they wanted kept out of the public record might be offered by someone else with no such restriction. I can think of only one instance in this book where a piece of information acquired in this way was used. My general rule for accepting a piece of information as valid went something like this: The first time I heard it I took it down. The second time I heard it I took it seriously. After hearing it three or more times from different people, I believed it.

Notwithstanding these rules of engagement, some people were still a bit uneasy about talking to a college professor. Several proponents of redevelopment assumed that I had to be a Marxist who wanted to write about developers who pushed poor people from their homes. Several critics of redevelopment assumed that I was a "closet conservative" who wanted to make a lot of money writing a steamy novel about urban redevelopment. They themselves confessed to be negotiating with a Chicago firm to produce a movie about their exploits. Eventually, most persons talked to me and were quite candid.

There is a real bias in the social sciences against the kind of research described in this book. Most persons do not do case studies, thinking that these are not especially "scientific" and cannot be easily generalized to other settings. These persons prefer to do larger pieces of research covering many places or involving many individuals. Often, they rely on demographic and survey data to make their arguments. Such data allow one to perform sophisticated statistical analyses and make some statements that can be more easily generalized to other settings or populations. Case studies do not lend themselves so readily to this kind of "scientific" handling.

Case studies based in part on unstructured interviews with informants who remain anonymous are looked upon even more suspiciously. This is unfortunate, because such case studies often provide insights into the way the world works that escape researchers who prefer more mathematically precise ways of examining that world. The case study is a tool uniquely suited to ferret out things most social scientists never see or care to search for. It is especially useful when the object of the research is to examine something that may be novel. On such an occasion, researchers have no hope or intention of testing a theory about the way the world works. They are engaged in a rather more modest, and in some ways more interesting, enterprise. Their intention is to make persons reconsider what they had come to accept as established dogma. The object of such work is to develop an alternative way of viewing something that most everyone thought had been explained. They are in the business of creating new hypotheses for others to examine more widely. They do not test them themselves.

This is precisely what I hope to accomplish in this book about inner-city redevelopment. It may be that previous researchers described the rebuilding of cities as accurately and thoroughly as they could, given the information available to them. It also may be, however, that what they looked for and saw in the redevelopment of cities was conditioned by their views of how the world works. Researchers may not have been led astray by their theories; but they might have found it easier to overlook some things that did not fit in their ordered explanations of redevelopment because of these theories. Case studies such as the one presented here can help to balance the picture a bit and, with any luck, provide some fresh insights into sensitive matters.

This is all well, but it does little to help combat the feeling that the information provided in case studies and by anonymous informants may be pretty shaky. Several things have been done in this study to deal with the problem. First, I review what is known about redevelopment in different places. This will provide some basis for judging just how unique are the places described here. It also will determine how easily the lessons learned in the present case could be applied elsewhere. Second, I make a serious effort to check the stories I heard against published and unpublished reports about specific redevelopment projects. Archival materials acquired from news-papers, both citywide and neighborhood publications, supplement these reports and provide good background information. Census materials, crime statistics, and other hard numbers on the demographic, business, and social profiles of the areas described in this book and the whole city help to reveal the broad context within which redevelopment efforts took place.

One other type of information was used to acquire a sense of what happened in these areas and what it means: Information was obtained by walking through the areas at various times of the day or evening, striking up conversations with neighborhood residents and business persons, attending public meetings, and visiting people in their homes. This takes a good deal of time, but it is the only way one can learn what is happening in a neighborhood short of living in it.

The fieldwork for this book was begun in January 1984, and it continued through August of that year. I have kept up my visits and contacts since then, though on a more intermittent basis. I received no outside funding to defray my expenses for this project. On the other hand, I was attacked by one large dog with sharp teeth, tailed by three surly men who were sizing me up for an assault and robbery, and learned of plans to murder a neighborhood activist. The dog tore a large hole in my briefcase, which I managed to put in front of my chest just before he performed a crude surgical procedure on me. I escaped the three surly men with some creative, albeit quite illegal, driving maneuvers through residential neighborhoods. And I met with federal law enforcement officers on the matter of the proposed murder. The shooting did occur, and one person was seriously injured.

All told, it was an interesting and worthwhile experience. I hope you think the same after reading the book.

ACKNOWLEDGMENTS

This book contains some of what I have learned about the thorny problem of rebuilding American cities. That I learned anything at all is a tribute to the many St Louisans who took the time to teach me and the researchers whose work I was able to consult. I do not doubt that in both sets of persons some will find a little to a lot in this book with which to disagree. This is to be expected. One who attempts to summarize so much history and so many complex ideas in a relatively few pages is bound to miss something. Events are compressed. Important dates, persons, and ideas can appear to have been ignored or, worse than that, misrepresented. These possibilities nothwithstanding, I made a conscientious effort to present as complete and unbiased a picture of attempts to rebuild parts of St. Louis as I could. I apologize in advance to anyone who thinks that his or her contribution was somehow treated less seriously or fairly than it deserved to be.

In excess of 100 persons were interviewed for this book, a number of them several times. I promised them that I would not mention their name—and I have no intention of reneging on that pledge. I thank them all for trying to fill the empty vessel between my ears. Particular thanks need to be extended to several well-placed persons in St. Louis who reviewed the final draft of the book and helped me to sharpen some of my thoughts and to clean up some of my more obvious errors. I deeply appreciated their efforts. Some of my students at the University of Missouri and Missouri East Correctional Center also reviewed early drafts of some chapters and offered their suggestions as to how the book might be improved.

It is possible to thank in a more public way several persons who helped to improve the quality of present book and see to it that it was published.

Professors Robert Whelan of the University of New Orleans and Bryan Jones of Texas A&M University were instrumental in this regard. Without the considerable talent and patience of series editor Richard Rich of Virginia Polytechnic Institute and State University and general editor Peggy Gifford, however, it is unlikely that the book would have made it into print. Only time will tell whether they should be roundly praised or condemned for their efforts, but I am grateful for the job they did.

It is customary to thank the persons who helped to prepare the manuscript. In this instance, no fewer than four women nursed my drafts into something resembling a manuscript: Celeste Hazley, Sandy Overton-Springer, Mary Hines, and Donna Palmer. Part of the time that I needed to conduct the original study and to prepare these drafts was provided by the University of Missouri, its two research centers—Metropolitan Studies and International Studies—and their directors: Don Phares, Dennis Judd, and Ed Fedder. I thank them all for their assistance.

CAN CITIES BE REBUILT
FOR RICH AND POOR ALIKE?

A serious though uncoordinated campaign to rebuild United States cities was initiated forty years ago. Much work has been accomplished; much remains to be done. We know that it is possible to rebuild large portions of a city. We do not know whether it is possible to do so in a way that satisfies the needs of diverse elements within that city's population, however.

On most occasions, urban redevelopment favors the more prosperous and powerful. Less prosperous and powerful groups are not as likely to benefit directly from such efforts and are more likely to be discomforted. There are exceptions, of course. Low-income or minority groups occasionally have stopped a particular project or shaped its eventual outcome. So-called progressive municipal leaders sometimes manage to tack programs benefitting the whole community onto a developer's project. Most of the time, though, this does not happen. Usually, no accommodation is reached between those who benefit from redevelopment efforts and those who do not.

That such an outcome occurs much of the time upsets some persons but surprises few of us. There is much evidence documenting the way redevelopment campaigns typically unfold and much thinking that suggests this is either quite acceptable or all but inevitable. It has not seemed possible to rebuild cities in ways that serve a diverse community of interests.

Explored in this book is the possibility that urban redevelopment can serve a diverse community of interests. Nothing said here will contradict the conventional wisdom that urban redevelopment usually does not work this way. What will be said is that there are conditions under which a rough accommodation can be reached between those who ordinarily benefit from efforts to rebuild cities and those who do not. Given the continuing deterioration evident in most U.S. cities and the real needs of many persons who live in them, this is a possibility well worth considering.

To provide a balanced treatment of this subject, three related problems will be addressed: Of course, the basic question is, Why and how are cities redeveloped? Can cities accommodate new kinds of industries and residents, and how? Finally, can low-income minorities benefit from urban redevelopment?

Much has been written on these subjects. To see how this thinking can inform our own search for ways to rebuild cities for a diverse population, I offer a description of redevelopment efforts in St. Louis, Missouri. Analysis of those activities will show that a more complex view is needed of how cities can be reclaimed and who can benefit from the reclamation. I will argue that accommodation is possible between a city's existing minority population and newer industries and residents. Under certain conditions, urban redevelopment can proceed in a manner that helps corporations *and* builds more racially and economically mixed neighborhoods. Moreover, modern industries and unorthodox mixes of people can occupy the same neighborhoods in relative harmony.

Prior to introducing St. Louis and its redevelopment, however, it will be necessary to do a little academic housecleaning. This chapter reviews what generally is known about rebuilding cities and the parts played in that process by modern corporations, more well-to-do persons, and the poor. It will provide both a basic introduction to the problem addressed in this book and a basis for judging how unique and praiseworthy is the work accomplished in St. Louis.

Building A Postindustrial City

The United States is in the midst of its second industrial revolution, and nowhere have the effects of this great change been more pronounced than in the nation's cities. Skylines are spiked with tall buildings, as manufacturing plants and warehouses are replaced by banks, corporate headquarters, and convention centers. Instead of producing goods, the city's new industrial tenants produce primarily information. Smokestacks have been removed in favor of stacks of paper.

To better appreciate the significance of this second industrial revolution, it would be useful to recall briefly what the first one did to and for cities. The introduction of heavy industry and manufacturing plants to cities during the nineteenth century changed the face and character of urban America. The commercial or trade economy that had given cities life seemed almost overwhelmed by numerous manufacturing facilities. The number of cities increased and their populations grew. Millions of immigrants came to American cities from Europe and, on the West Coast, from parts of China and Japan.

Living conditions for these people often were harsh. Their opportunities for employment tended to be limited, even though factory production was increasing. Poverty was as commonplace as it was mean; and efforts to soften it were not nearly so pronounced as they are today. Decent housing was hard to find. Thousands of people found shelter in tenements on blocks surrounding industrial sites or elsewhere in the city. The neighborhoods in question were crowded, but often the effects of crowding were mitigated to an extent by an intimacy based on the residents' common ancestry. Despite their obvious problems, these neighborhoods had a gritty resilience that defied the best efforts of moral reformers and scientific planners to clean them up.

The same probably could be said of the people who lived in the neighborhoods of industrial cities. Nevertheless, many of their number were able to find enough work to survive. It might have taken a generation or two, but gradually many of these people improved their material and social standing in the community.

This did not happen for the people who eventually took the place of earlier European immigrants. Just over a century ago, newly freed black slaves were discouraged from moving North and taking advantage of the industrial jobs that were becoming available. They remained agricultural workers in a regional economy that had yet to be mechanized or give them much chance to become more self-sufficient. By the time they finally began moving to northern urban and industrial centers, the period of rapid industrialization was near its end, and the cities they inherited already showed signs of being worn thin.[1]

The number of Europeans coming to the United States decreased sharply after the imposition of immigration quotas following World War I. Only during this period did black Americans begin to leave the South in large numbers and move to northern cities. A second wave of black immigration occurred after World War II, and these people eventually were followed by Hispanics and Asians.

Their skills may have been comparable to those of many earlier immigrants to northern cities, but these people arrived at a bad time. Many economically secure white families were moving to newer suburban communities, and this created lots of empty space in neighborhoods that were rundown. Many industries either closed altogether or moved from the central city, and this created big holes in the job market for minority laborers.

The combined effect of these factors was devastating for cities as a whole and especially their increasingly minority and poor populations. Without new capital to reverse their physical deterioration, cities crumbled even as they emptied. Services provided by city governments decreased. The tax base of cities eroded. Minority people came to be identified with this deterioration and often were seen as contributing to it.

A second industrial revolution, promoted in part by the federal government, held some promise for changing this situation.[2] Large urban renewal campaigns were initiated in many cities. Much of this work took place in and around the city's central business district. Abandoned or rundown blocks were cleared of buildings, making space for newer industrial tenants. These tenants were professional, technical, and service corporations rather than manufacturers. Efforts were made to attract new residents to the central city as well. These residents were more well-to-do persons who had professional training or simply wanted to enjoy the life-style available in central cities.

All of this rebuilding and moving around often compelled minority people to leave the areas being rebuilt. This compounded whatever housing and employment problems they already had. It also contributed to a debate over the consequences of urban redevelopment that has been going on for nearly forty years.

The debate has focused on three parts of the inner city: the downtown or central business district; so-called gentrified neighborhoods; and neighborhoods being reclaimed by descendants of earlier settlers.[3] In none of these areas has much consideration been given to retaining minority citizens. If anything, an effort usually has been made to keep them out of the area once it has been improved.

This tendency is clearest, perhaps, in projects designed to modernize and expand the downtown areas of central cities. These areas often had good-sized populations of low-income and minority residents. (Most of the time the minority people were not well-to-do.) These persons were moved out and the buildings where they lived were razed. The displaced persons might find themselves new residences, but they often were relocated by government agencies into public housing and neighborhoods some distance from the downtown area. The places receiving these people usually had problems of their own. The arrival of the displaced residents typically exacerbated these problems.

Those persons who moved downtown or into neighborhoods contiguous to it were different from those who had been displaced. The new residents tended to by younger, white, single or childless couples who held white-collar jobs. They often found housing that was rundown but had historical significance, and they carefully rehabilitated these buildings. These are the kinds of neighborhoods that one customarily calls *gentrified.*

Other neighborhoods, somewhat removed from major commercial and institutional hubs, also have been improved. Neither these neighborhoods nor the person leading their comeback, however, are likely to be as fancy as those in gentrified areas. Typically, long-term residents and others who have the same ethnic and religious background lead the revitalization effort. What is appealing about these neighborhoods is their connection to some established group of people and its traditions. It is not the housing, which can be fairly modest.

In both the gentrified area and the ethnic preserve, it generally was assumed that the people living there had a great deal in common. They would have similar values and traditions, or at least a roughly comparable style of life. They also shared two important attitudes toward housing. It should be maintained well and owned by its occupants.

Private institutions, corporations, and individual citizens take an active part in redeveloping both the downtown areas of cities and residential neighborhoods. However, their work often is subsidized or protected by government actions. Public officials have granted broad and far-reaching authority to private developers who want to rebuild an area. Public money can be used to acquire and hold property for a "suitable" developer, who then purchases it at discounted prices. Taxes may be deferred on the value added to a property by an approved developer. Public money can be used to improve the physical appearance and amenities of an area. It also can be used to help finance approved projects. City housing and zoning codes may be adhered to more strictly or waived in the interest of promoting redevelopment. There even have been occasions when city governments ceded to private parties the authority to approve who can or cannot stay in an area being redeveloped. In these and other ways, public officials have supported redevelopment work undertaken by private parties.

Nothing said thus far suggests that minorities are likely or supposed to find good places to live and work inside the postindustrial city. At least in terms of housing, however, there are a few signs that minorities sometimes can be accommodated. Observers have noted that a degree of racial and economic integration may occur in some neighborhoods, though no one is certain how long it can last. There also are cases where rental housing has become available in a redevelopment area.[4] This would be important for many minority residents, who often cannot afford to buy a house or condominium. Promising as such things are, it remains to be seen just how widely they will spread or benefit minorities.

Nevertheless, the question of which neighborhoods become redeveloped or who has the opportunity to stay may not be as easy to answer as it once was. The same could be said of how modern corporations and institutions fit into the picture. It has been known for some time that neighborhoods being redeveloped often are found near large institutions or commercial centers of secondary importance to a city.[5] With the exception of some early research on urban renewal projects, though, there has not been much study of how commercial redevelopment might complement neighborhood revitalization. This is something that will be described in detail in the present book.

The possibility that new industrial development can help to create more economically and racially mixed neighborhoods is even more attractive. Assuming it could be shown that this can occur, one still would have to face the uncomfortable fact that most of the time urban redevelopment does not work out this way. Critics could argue, and no doubt will argue, that redevelopment usually does not benefit the whole community in any obvious way. Corporations, developers, and relatively well-to-do white people usually seem to benefit from it. They acquire new or improved buildings, and the real estate taxes they might pay may be reduced or waived for a time to attract them back to the city or to keep them from moving away. Minority and poor people often are portrayed as "victims" of redevelopment, and city residents who do not live in redeveloped areas ordinarily receive no direct benefit from such improvements. For these reasons, it is not clear that urban redevelopment can serve a well-defined public interest.

Views About Redevelopment

This is not much of a concern to those who rebuild cities. Nevertheless, many ideas used to promote or dismiss urban redevelopment are based on bigger notions about the way society works. There is no "theory of urban redevelopment" as such. Competing views of human society have been borrowed to explain how cities grow and decline. Parts of these different views will be used here to explain how cities are redeveloped.

Peter Steinberger provided a concise statement of the three ways that social scientists explain "the urban crisis"[6]: human ecology, Marxism, and the city as polity. This book builds on Steinberger's analysis but uses terms more familiar to students of urban redevelopment when describing his ideas. The first of the bigger schools of thought that I will address is human ecology. The second is Marxism. The third approach, for want of a better label, will be called *the city as polity*. The first two approaches—ecology and Marxism—

are better known and provide a useful starting place for an assessment of how cities are rebuilt and who benefits from the rebuilding. The city-as-polity approach will be used as a counterpoint to these better-established schools of thought.

It should be noted that a thorough discussion and test of these alternative perspectives on urban redevelopment will not be presented in this book. There is a rich literature describing these perspectives,[7] and the reader can consult the bibliography or references at the end of the book for a partial list of works using one or more of these approaches. This book contains a case study of one city's experiences with redevelopment. As such, I am more concerned with generating ideas that can be reexamined in other places than I am with laying to rest some heated theoretical argument between already committed partisans. Throughout this book I will borrow liberally from each of the three major explanations of how and for whom cities are rebuilt. None provides a full or fully satisfying way to account for the way St. Louis was redeveloped after 1950. Each makes a contribution and raises important questions.

At times it seems that these competing explanations have more in common than their advocates acknowledge or recognize. This is especially true in the case of human ecology and Marxism, which have been portrayed, respectively, as the "old" and "new" theories of urban growth and decline.[8] In both approaches, for example, changing economic conditions outside the city have a big impact on what happens inside the city. The change from an industrial to a service economy or the mechanization of agriculture in the South, for instance, had a major effect on the ability of persons of African-American descent to succeed in cities. Consistent with this is the idea that business persons have a disproportionate amount of influence on what happens in cities. Their decisions to stay or leave, for example, would make it easier or harder for officials to provide services and for minority residents to find work. Both ecologists and Marxists suggest that this influence is one reason why plans to rebuild cities usually favor corporations or more well-to-do persons.

No matter how well planned they are, redevelopment efforts do little to reduce the aggregate level of suffering endured by low-income residents. Indeed, a redevelopment program actually can undermine the effects of other programs that are supposed to help such people. Expenditures for public education are going to suffer at least a bit, for instance, when a developer does not have to pay all the taxes on an improved piece of property. And when persons are removed from a building scheduled to be rehabilitated, more pressure is likely to be put on the existing stock of public housing in the community.

Government officials cooperate with business people who want to do redevelopment work. It is a tenet of both Marxism and ecology that government officials respond to initiatives from the private sector. The political and fiscal constraints under which they work are so severe that theorists generally believe officials have little choice but to act favorably toward business people.

These are important areas of agreement; and much of what was said earlier about the building of postindustrial cities reflected the ideas of Marxists and human ecologists. Yet there also are important issues on which ecologists and Marxists would disagree. These generally are of a prescriptive nature and deal with what ought to be accomplished by redevelopment and who should have a hand in shaping such accomplishments.

Persons using an ecological approach to redevelopment believe that such work should help a city better meet the challenges of a new economic order. Private investors also are viewed as being in the best position to rebuild cities in efficient and profitable ways. Beyond this, it probably is foolish to talk about urban redevelopment serving a public interest. The best that government can do is to help smooth out some of the bigger bumps obstructing the work of private investors. Among the things it could do is relocate and train poor and unskilled city residents for new jobs. This accomplished, developers could put more useful things in the space vacated by low-income people and outdated businesses.

The difficulties experienced by low-income residents and small businesses would be accepted as an unfortunate but unavoidable result of rebuilding efforts. Providing better relocation assistance to them would satisfy any claim they might make for fair treatment. Holding unskilled people where there are no jobs would be considered irresponsible. It also would discourage more modern corporations from moving into the city. In general, however, there is little that anyone can do to halt the introduction of these newer employers to the city and no good reason to try.

Marxists believe that some transcendant good can be served by urban redevelopment. Yet, they are vague on precisely what form redevelopment work should take to satisfy the "public interest." It seems that they are more interested in the process that leads to a decision about work being done. They advocate regional planning and suggest that it be coupled with more effective citizen participation and local governmental review. Marxists are far more inclined to say that politics does have a bearing on how cities are rebuilt, though they take strong exception to the way politics usually is played.[9]

It is reasoned that planning on a regional basis would allow resources to be distributed more equitably. It also could help make more even the uneven rates of development occurring among different cities and between different parts of the same city. Creating more opportunities in the decision-making process for less powerful groups would help in this regard. Areas inhabited by persons from those groups would likely receive more assistance because their needs could be less easily ignored. The process of redevelopment would have been "democratized." The benefits of rebuilding would have been passed to all segments of the community, and the work could be viewed as serving a broad public interest.

This abridged treatment of the ecological and Marxist perspectives does not do full justice to the range of opinion within each camp. There is a little to a lot of debate on some of the points summarized here. At the same time, the present discussion does no violence to their basic views of how urban redevelopment works and whom it benefits. Thorough enough information about each has been provided so that comparisons between the two are possible and will be made throughout the book.

One must acknowledge an intellectual debt to the proponents of ecology and Marxism. They show that many of the problems that redevelopment was to address were created by decisions made earlier by private corporations. Particular attention often is paid to the decision to move jobs from the city or not to invest in city real estate. The cumulative effect of such decisions over many years was to create an economic and political crisis in cities that public leaders could not resolve satisfactorily. Ecologists would not argue that private corporations have an obligation to remedy these problems or to rebuild the city in a way that its citizens deem responsible. Marxists would argue that private corporations should do this, but rarely do. In neither case does it seem that theorists offer an especially hopeful view of cities or the ability of persons living in cities to shape the world in which they live.

Actually, there is good historical precedent for such a view. The seed for the idea was planted by earlier city leaders who failed to bring the diverse and sometimes feuding elements of population together in any lasting or meaningful union. It was easier to imagine a city as a vital and viable community than it was to build one. More contemporary thinkers simply built their theories on the shoulders of these disgruntled nineteenth century reformers. They did not think it possible to build an integrated and civil community, or polity, within a city.

In what remains of this chapter, I will explore why they took this position and how the redevelopment of modern cities might offer some hope that they were wrong. This discussion constitutes my treatment of the city-as-polity approach to urban redevelopment.

If earlier reformers failed to build a polity within cities, it was not for lack of trying. They had hoped to guarantee the prosperity of cities by creating a common set of values—a shared understanding of the common good if you prefer—for everyone in the city. To this end they labored long and hard, reforming or trying to reform most everyone and everything that was part of the city during the nineteenth and early twentieth centuries.

Cities continued to grow, if only in a haphazard way; but the great reforms that were supposed to provide us with that clear vision of the common good did not accomplish their stated purpose. In many instances, these reforms merely reinforced the differences between one or another group and made it easier for more privileged persons to make their escape behind a puff of patriotic smoke.[10] These were confusing times. Everything was growing bigger faster. Even if they really had wanted to, no one could find a way to bring different people together long enough to decide what that vision might be.

The dispersion in this century of people and jobs over much broader metropolitan areas has not made that task any easier. The urge to own a house in a less crowded and more pastoral setting was carefully nurtured by persons who could make money by persuading others that the suburbs were a place where old problems could be avoided and new solutions tried out.[11] It was not hard for contemporary theorists to ignore the city as the most important place to begin one's search for the common good.

This intellectual bias gained a broader public audience in 1933, when Roosevelt was in his first term as president and the New Deal had just been initiated. Many persons were deeply concerned about the economic situation in our cities and the potential for political unrest. Reforms inititated at the federal level were to have been copied at the local level. Specifically, the federal government began to assume more responsibility for mapping out an economic recovery plan and renewing the public's faith in itself and a common purpose. Notable persons such as sociologist Louis Wirth argued persuasively that a shared sense of community required new forms of social organization at the local level as well. They did not appreciate reformers who looked upon neighborhoods as the foundation of a new, more cosmopolitan moral order.[12] They proposed instead newer metropolitan forms of governance that, if put into place, would have complemented changes being introduced on a national level.

Local communities had been unable to provide a vision of the common good, fractured as they were along sectarian, racial, and class lines. Agencies representing broader segments of the urban population were the key to creating a sense of the community as a whole within metropolitan areas, whereas the federal government provided a similar vision of the nation as a whole. These complementary visions of ourselves as part of a bigger, more inclusive community where people shared the same values made sense in a world that appeared chaotic.

The search for answers to the cities' most pressing problems grew beyond the warrens of the poor to include the whole city and, by the 1930s, gradually were redefined as public concerns, subject to government action. Finally, as the geographic breadth of the search for solutions to urban problems grew to include whole metropolitan areas so, too, did the quest for a moral vision that might unite a divided urban population. Urban reformers tried to establish institutions that would help persons realize a common sense of purpose. Failing that, more well-to-do citizens continued their outward trek to the suburbs or protected inner-city neighborhoods. As we will see at the end of this chapter, there are important parallels between this line of reasoning and contemporary arguments about the best way to integrate minorities into American society.

The New Company Town

In the meantime, it would be prudent to reconsider whether an accommodation between "old" and "new" ways of organizing our urban world might be found. Our predecessors left us with two unpromising solutions to the problem of creating a more workable moral and social order in urban areas. Pulling them from one side was the neighborhood, little "natural areas" into which people were attracted or driven by virtue of their income, customs, jobs, and the like. Against these pockets of parochialism stood the institutions of a modern urban society: schools, various media, voluntary srvice organizations, political parties, unions, and big government. These institutions allegedly pulled urban residents in the opposite direction, toward a broader vision of their place in a bigger community. Until contemporary Marxists combined these strategies, no compromise seemed possible between these very different ways of organizing and thinking about the modern urban community.

Earlier urban residents and critics were unable to reconcile what seemed to them contradictory ways of organizing and thinking about a modern urban world. Today, we know that these two approaches to securing a workable social and moral order are less antagonistic than was once supposed. The modern, postindustrial city has room for many small neighborhoods where persons from the same background or who share a similar style of life can be comfortable. Nevertheless, it is difficult to advance a new vision of ourselves as part of a more integrated and cosmopolitan community in the absence of something that shows us how this vision works out in everyday life. We have yet to create a bridge between that postindustrial world and the many small neighborhoods that fill our cities.

The idea to build such a bridge was behind George Pullman's famous attempt to construct a model industrial town outside Chicago in 1880. Pullman's idea was to defuse the tense relations between labor and management that characterized industrial relations after the Civil War by building a new town for his workers and their families. His fortune already secured by virtue of a near-monopoly in the construction and leasing of railroad sleeping cars, Pullman was convinced "that paternalism wisely administered would make labor more amenable to the interests of his corporation."[13]

The corporation loomed over everything that was built or done in the town, and that was the major problem. Especially troublesome was the unwillingness of the corporation to allow its employees to own property in the town. The management of the town—its newspaper, stores, bank, school board, and government—was equally undemocratic. Officials were appointed in most cases or, when elected, still were in the employ of the company. Pressure was put on all employees to vote the way Mr. Pullman desired, and no labor agitators or radical speakers were allowed to rent or use the town's "public halls." The intended effect of these rules had been to create a solid little industrial community, a place where the connection between one's work and private or public lives was explicit and strong.

The contrived social and moral order he hoped would be created in his town, one supposes, was to have mimicked but refined that which had grown somewhat more naturally in the ethnic villages of industrial Chicago. There, too, a connection existed between one's place of work and one's more private and public lives; but it was an imperfect connection, untidy and usually not too well thought out. No such inefficiencies were to have been tolerated in Mr. Pullman's town. His was to have been a town free of personal or civil improprieties and imperfections. It had no hospital, cemetery, almshouse, orphanage, jail, or system of public charity. Persons like "paupers, orphans, and the aged poor had no place in the town, and an individual who lost his job. . .[were] ordinarily expected to leave."[14]

The town of Pullman was to have been neat, clean, and ordered. This would have made it very different from the industrial, working-class neighborhoods common to cities of that time. Despite its obvious shortcomings, the town of Pullman provided some important clues in the search for a solution to the problem of order in urban areas. First, it may be possible to build a relatively small community or neighborhood that complements the needs of the prevailing industries in an urban area. This community also may grow to a fairly good size. Second, in such a community, it will be difficult to muffle much less suppress the conflicts built into the larger society. Instead of avoiding or ignoring such stresses and strains, it probably would be better to use "the right kinds of tension" in a "creative rather than destructive" way.[15]

Giving expression to such problems in small communities makes sense. It allows persons to work out their own solutions to the problem of order on a relatively manageable basis unencumbered by some big public institution whose caretakers must worry about big territories, big solutions, and the possibility of making big, well-publicized mistakes. Finally, the community's members—both individual and corporate—can receive a moral education by virtue of their struggle with the tensions inherent in the larger society. New ways of viewing the world and one's responsibility to it emerge from such contests. Glimpses might be caught of a new moral order being fashioned, while both the practical and ethical lessons learned in small places work their way through the larger society.

Left unanswered by the Pullman experiment are three equally important questions. First, is it really feasible for corporations to build or rebuild communities in urban areas? We are not accustomed to thinking of corporations as much interested in a small urban community or neighborhood beyond their need to secure cheap land, good public services, and maintain decent relations with the local residents. The growth of suburban industrial parks in this century has all but removed the corporation from the day-to-day concerns of townsfolk, separated as such parks frequently are from residential areas. However, the modern professional, technical, or service corporations located in a central city may be different. Cities as well as small towns have long enjoyed the services provided by interested business leaders. Such efforts by business persons today hold the potential to be quite significant, as government spending on domestic programs at all levels is cut.

Today, business persons representing one or more companies are engaged in a range of projects that not too long ago might have been undertaken by one or another government agency. Included among these projects are training programs, technical assistance for small businesses, neighborhood economic development, home and business financing, work-study programs for students, and efforts to develop policies that local governments can pursue. Sometimes specific neighborhoods are helped, though how much is not known. On most occasions the assistance is targeted for a larger area or more diffuse clientele, or it has no specific geographic area as the object of its attention. Only rarely do we see companies deal with the gritty problems of the neighborhoods surrounding them or do much more than simply annex property to feed their own expansion programs. Corporations that make an effort to rebuild a specific geographic area complete with permanent residents, sociologist Gerald Suttles tell us, are creating a "contrived community."[16]

The second unanswered question is, Would such a community be a tolerant place? Social philosopher Alasdair MacIntyre, who has made an impassioned plea for the reconstitution of local forms of community, does not think so. Our creations might be no more tolerant and no less exclusive than the town created by Mr. Pullman. Indeed, MacIntyre believes that "when a moral community is in good order, relatively little will be open to question." It might even find "quite legitimate uses of exclusion and repression."

A healthy moral community, in this view, probably "would be more intolerant than liberal democracies are now."[17] Among the bigger sources of intolerance built into societies like our own are those tied to racial and social class differences among our people. To the extent that MacIntyre is correct, there would seem to be little reason to break down the barriers that separate one race or class from another in our society. Such forms of intolerance would be viewed as having some value.

This brings us to our third question: Could these new communities provide an opportunity to create a viable and vital civic culture? The small communities envisioned by MacIntyre and created by Pullman would produce a viable public, at least in the sense that persons had well-defined political roles and an orderly setting within which to practice their citizenship. Whether such communities would make much of a contribution to the larger society's civic culture is another issue. Pullman showed us one way to merge the politics of the workplace with that of the community. His town provided an example of how to develop a coherent civic culture that would take in all the various parts of a person's life. Unfortunately, the public that was created was terribly parochial and reactionary. It provided nothing in the way of new ideas or tricks to better organize large urban areas. In this sense, it did not make a vital contribution.

All the big moral lessons were negative. We learned that paternalism was ineffective, if not wrong, in an urban, industrial world. We also learned that the viability of its public, like that of Aristotle's polis, was predicated on the exclusion of certain classes of persons like the elderly and poor. Not only should we reject this as an operating premise in our own communities but we would be hard pressed as well to carry it out in a large urban area. The civic culture produced in a place like Pullman may work on a small scale, but it would offer little hope to those searching for ways to draw a very diverse population together. Various reformers and social philosphers have thought this an important thing to do. To create a vital public or civic culture, they reasoned, one must have viable communities where different people live, work, and engage in politics together. It is clear in the case of Pullman, Illinoise, that this did not happen. Whether it is possible to build a city as a polity in our postindustrial world is one of the issues considered in this book.

Criteria are available to help us judge how successfully a city's politics can be reinvigorated as parts of the city itself are rebuilt. Several already were mentioned in relation to Pullman's failure to accomplish a similar goal. The first criterion is the preservation or enhancement of *pluralism*. Redevelopment may be said to serve a common good to the extent that it compels us to face more forthrightly those things that divide and trouble us most. Surely, the way we separate ourselves on the basis of ethnicity, wealth, and skin color is a challenge to our ability to build a world where different people can be accepted and respected. Contemporary ecologists and Marxists would not expect such issues to carry much weight in deliberations over urban redevelopment.

The second criterion is *enhanced political equality,* defined here as the ability of groups ordinarily excluded from important public deliberations to be included. It is one thing to have sensitive matters raised before the public. It is quite another to make room in the political process for those who have an immediate and compelling interest in those discussions and are antagonists. Contemporary ecologists would not expect such parties to be involved. Contemporary Marxists would anticipate some resistance to redevelopment efforts by poor and minority people, but they would predict that such efforts would fail. That would be the extent of less powerfull persons' involvement in the redevelopment process.

The third criterion is *efficacy,* defined here as the ability of minority groups to secure redevelopment projects more to their liking. Neither contemporary ecologists nor their Marxist counterparts believe that most important decisions are made inside cities. The big decisions are made by outsiders. Local folks generally are not expected to be able to alter the basic conditions that shape life in large cities. This would be especially true for less powerful groups. They would not be expected to realize any appreciable rewards by virtue of their involvement in politics.

Contemporary Marxists expect most efforts by neighborhood groups to resist redevelopment to fail and segregation to persist. Corporations and politicians who cater to business leaders are expected to win most fights over how land in the city is recycled, and neither is expected to be sympathetic to the interests of low-income residents. Evidence to support this line of reasoning is fairly strong. Much of the research cited at the end of this chapter indicates that victories by grassroots activists in the redevelopment game are rare and short-lived. It is harder to come by evidence that neighborhood groups influence rebuilding projects or that redevelopment reduces residential segregation for low-income and minority residents.

The fourth criterion is the *evocation of a moral discourse* through local politics. If redevelopment is to serve some transcendant good, Steinberger says, the deliberations need to operate and appeal to us on the basis of some well-defined sense of what is good and what is bad. The idea of efficacy implies the ability to put ideas into practice. For such a process to evoke a moral discourse requires that people base their decisions and actions on principles. It is not enough that something work. Its working must inform a broader dialogue on what we mean to be as a people and whether what we mean to be is deemed good.

The goal here, Peter Steinberger tells us, "is to view the problems of the city as moral problems and to insist that the effort to deal with them...be undertaken in terms of ethical principles."[18] More is expected here than a grudging agreement among antagonists that something will be deemed in the public's interest at a particular moment. This aspect of "the common good," political scientist Clarence Stone rightly suggests, is worked out over time and need not be agreed to by all members of the polity.[19] What is required in a moral discourse is at once more enduring and difficult to apprehend.

In the case of urban politics, it is the ability to resolve a question first posed by Aristotle some 2,000 years ago: How does one build a community composed of different people who are able to practice politics together? The building of such a community was considered a good thing in its own right—a moral imperative if you prefer—and a problem that was distinctly urban in nature. Generations of social philosophers, scientists, critics, and reformers have addressed it in their work and have yet to rediscover a satisfactory answer.

Conclusions: Redevelopment and the Underclass

Their failure should not discourage us from trying to fashion a city for everyone. On the other hand, it should sober us to the hard realities confronting any people who would try. Each generation of would-be city builders had to face its own particular challenges and hard-to-fit-in populations. That is no less true today.

Today's most difficult population is the so-called underclass, those low-income minority persons who seem unable to be brought into the mainstream of American life. They are the ultimate challenge to contemporary city builders because so much of what can or cannot be done in cities hinges on what happens to the underclass. It is appropriate, then, that we conclude this chapter with a brief assessment of how the underclass fits into a broader discussion about urban redevelopment.

Several of the bigger economic and social factors that conspired to create the underclass were described earlier. One other factor contributing to its existence and plight was the movement of stable working-class and middle-class minority families from the inner city. Such families, argues William Julius Wilson, were important social anchors in ghettos prior to 1950, and their absence has been keenly felt.[20]

Wilson acknowledges the bittersweet progress made by many black persons since the 1960s. Changes in American society and law made it possible for stable families with employable adults to find better housing or often just newer housing away from their old city neighborhoods. Those same changes had virtually no impact on many poor and often single-parent households that had no means to leave. Conditions for this latter group grew worse as job opportunities for unskilled laborers inside cities declined.

Wilson's primary interest is in prescribing what should be done to dismantle the underclass. Central to his proposals is the idea that the social isolation of the underclass must be ended. The individuals in it must be integrated more fully into American society, if they are to enjoy anything more than a minimal level of subsistence. Given their overwhelming presence in cities, what Wilson suggests would have profound implications for future efforts to rebuild central cities. The problem becomes where best to integrate them.

Wilson could have looked to the city as the crucible in which minorities will grind out some solutions to their problems. Instead, he argues, as many others have, that the postindustrial city is essentially a hostile environment for most minority group members. It would be better for members of the underclass to move out than to stay. They should be relocated to places where they could find employment and be given training for available jobs. One supposes these places would be most any suburban community where less skilled industrial and service jobs have become available. These places even could be in states other than the one currently resided in by the prospective emigree.

Persons whose primary interest is the redevelopment of cities would find much to favor in Wilson's proposal. After all, the presence of low-income people in rundown areas has long been a serious impediment to redevelopment schemes. On the other hand, critics of urban redevelopment could see this as just a nicer way to remove minorities from city property that was about to become valuable. Against this argument stand two important points. First, tangible and significant rewards are promised to those who follow the relocation rainbow. Second, it is customary in the United States to think of social mobility and geographic mobility as tied. Wilson and others simply suggest that all minority groups should have a chance to embrace this custom.[21]

Wilson's argument has stirred a lot of interest for all these reasons. Unfortunately, it is based on several questionable assumptions about what is to be gained or lost by a large-scale movement of minority groups away from central cities. The integration of minority groups into suburban job and housing markets would be extremely difficult, certainly more difficult than proponents of this strategy are acknowledging at this point. It might not even be a good idea.

The kinds of jobs that probably are best suited to members of the underclass are in industries not so far removed from existing minority communities. In fact, they are jobs that keep a modern urban complex running. Government at all levels has need of unskilled workers. There also is great need for sales personnel, maintenance workers, and people to work in the food service industry.[22] Even if these jobs held much promise for professional advancement, it should be possible for many suitable minority applicants to reach them without moving. They certainly would not have to move far from the central city to reach them. It would be easier and cheaper to subsidize the transportation costs of low-income workers who needed to commute to work.

Many minority persons in the near future are likely to remain unqualified for more sophisticated service jobs. Yet, such jobs will continue to figure prominently in the future of the central city economy. It seems decidedly short-sighted to move minority persons away from places where the future will be shaped, unless one does not want them to participate more fully in it.

One need only recall the devastating effect being kept in the South had on earlier generations of African-Americans. They were discouraged from moving north when heavy industrial jobs were becoming available. They were denied an opportunity to be part of the first industrial revolution. Moving them to places where they can find low-skilled jobs would remove them from places where the second industrial revolution is being fashioned. The long-term effects of such a policy might prolong the existence of the underclass rather than shorten it.

Were minorities not removed from cities it would be even more important to improve the faltering public school systems in which they are enrolled. There is no compelling evidence to suggest that suburban school districts would help large numbers of minority young people. There is evidence to suggest that valuable resources are denied to city school districts when some minority children are sent away to suburban schools.[23] This makes it more difficult to prepare minority children remaining in city schools for the jobs becoming available in their community.

Even if such problems are overlooked, the disquieting effects of racial discrimination in the rental and purchase of housing would still have to be dealt with. Despite much hard work to overcome housing segregation, most minority persons still live in racially segregated neighborhoods. Suburban communities are only slightly less segregated that the central cities.[24]

Residential segregation persists for several reasons. One may be that white and minority residents are more willing to support integration verbally than with their actions. Another reason involves the timing in this century of minority immigration to cities. Yet a third reason concerns the actions of public and private institutions, which have the effect of limiting interracial contact.[25]

Public officials may have said they wanted to encourage residential integration; but government programs and spending have not been designed or implemented in a way that made integration much more likely. At least more attention has been paid to cleaning up rundown neighborhoods and building large public housing complexes for low-income persons in the cities.

Many critics, however, have argued that neither program has done much to improve the qualtiy and amount of housing available for minority residents or to increase residential integration. Indeed, a case can be made that these programs had quite the opposite effect.[26]

Attempts by the federal government to build low-income housing in the suburbs have not worked. Most public housing is viewed negatively by local municipalities, even when it is set aside for the elderly. People do not like to have apartment complexes, even low-rise buildings, set in or next to a neighborhood with detached houses. This is especially true when the prospective tenants are members of racial minority groups. Many municipal officials and suburban homeowners are only slightly less upset to see minority persons who can pay their own way move into their community. Integration has never been a high priority for them, except as something to avoid.

Many minority persons, especially those with low-incomes, have great difficulty finding descent, affordable housing. They also tend to live in segregated communities. There is every reason to believe that this will remain the case for most minority citizens in the forseeable future. Legislation, legal suits, even the improved economic fortunes of many minority persons have not dented too much a pervasive pattern of residential segregation. Persons who propose moving large numbers of minority people to places where work might be found for the underclass ignore this fact.

None of this is to say, of course, that efforts to increase minority representation in the suburban job and housing markets are wrong or bound to fail. It is to suggest, however, that the obstacles to doing so are greater than advocates suspect or are willing to admit and that the benefits would be less far-reaching than they suppose. It would seem wise to take another look at what can be accomplished *inside* cities. There may be conditions under which residential integration can be pursued where America's second industrial revolution is being created. This would be in the long-term best interest of minority citizens. In the chapters that follow, we will see how feasible this is.

THE DECLINE AND
RECLAMATION OF ST. LOUIS

The Decline of St. Louis

S t. Louis lies in the center of a large metropolitan area spanning eight other counties in Missouri and Illinois, just south of where the Missouri and Mississippi Rivers join. The city once enjoyed the status of being both the population and employment center for the whole region. Today, it holds less than 20 percent of the region's 2.5 million residents, and the population and employment center of the metropolitan area has shifted west into St. Louis County.

City officials identified the first signs of central city abandonment as early as 1936 and tried to alert the public to its likely consequences in the years ahead. Issuing its report in the midst of the Depression, the city's planning commission warned that "if adequate measures are not taken, the city is faced with gradual economic and social collapse. The older central areas of the city are being abandoned, and this insidious trend will continue until the entire city is engulfed. Shall we gradually abandon St. Louis?" they wondered.[1]

The answer to this question seemed clear to many persons after 1950, when people and employers began to leave St. Louis in large numbers.[2] Few observers were prepared for the mass exodus that occurred. The city's population dropped by nearly 50 percent between 1950 and 1980. Many of these people moved to St. Louis County, just west of the city. The suburbs closest to St. Louis city absorbed what additional people they could, but they, too, began losing people as early as the 1960s. Most of the growth took place in the outer suburbs of St. Louis County and eventually spilled over into the counties west of them.[3] Virtually all of the early emigrants from St. Louis city were white. Minority residents did not begin to emigrate until the 1960s, and they did so in much smaller numbers than had whites. In general, black emigrees followed the paths laid out by whites. Most headed to the inner suburbs of north and central St. Louis County, but few have ventured much farther west.[4]

The city's racial composition was changing, too, during this period. It was becoming blacker. Although the number of black persons in the city had dropped off a bit between 1960 and 1980, their share of the population relative to whites had increased dramatically. Blacks had constituted only 18 percent of St. Louis's 1950 population, but that figure grew to nearly 45 percent by 1980. Most of these persons lived in the northern third of the city, which represented a big change from the situation in 1950. Back then, most of the black population had been concentrated in parts of the Near Northside and the Central Corridor. Many whites left northern St. Louis over the next three decades, however, and blacks took their place. By 1980, approximately 90 percent of the population in North St. Louis was black.

The population of South St. Louis, in the meantime, had remained largely white. It was 99 percent white in 1950 and 97 percent white in 1980. Between the increasingly homogeneous population of black North St. Louis and white South St. Louis lay the Central Corridor, substantially emptier than in 1950 but with a population more racially balanced than anywhere else in the city. Approximately 20 percent of central St. Louis's 1950 population had been black. Nearly 43 percent of the area's resident population was black in 1980.[5] There was not too much residential integration, however; most neighborhoods remained largely white or black.

The types and quality of housing in St. Louis city and county had some bearing on where people moved. Areas that had newer housing and less rental property tended to be settled more by white people. Black people tended to settle in areas that had more older housing and rental property.[6] The respective incomes of white and black people no doubt contributed to their decisions on where to move; but discrimination and public policy also played a part in determining where blacks were able to move. After all, the housing in south St. Louis city was nearly as old as that in north St. Louis city, and nearly half of the available units in south St. Louis city were rental properties.

Blacks simply were excluded from most neighborhoods in south St. Louis city until the early 1980s. That was not the case in the central and northern sections of St. Louis city. Blacks already were there, and they increased their presence as whites moved to the suburbs. Their movement into more city neighborhoods was encouraged, even compelled, by changes in public policy that led to the dismantling of predominately black areas in the central city. Much older housing was demolished and the availability of rental housing in the middle section of St. Louis city declined after 1950.

The loss of residents from the whole city was compounded by the loss of many employers and jobs. As late as 1970, St. Louis city still had more businesses and employees than St. Louis County.[7] This situation changed by 1977, and the reversal in the economic fortunes of the city and county continued into the 1980s. Today, St. Louis County contains more businesses employing more people in nearly every part of the economy.

The redevelopment of St. Louis has not stopped the erosion of its economic base. There is some indication that the erosion has slowed, however, and even a sign or two that a mild reversal in the city's fortunes may be at hand. The drop in the number of businesses and employees between 1977 and 1984, for example, was much smaller than it had been between 1970 and 1977. The number of construction businesses and people employed in some service businesses actually increased between 1977 and 1984. Perhaps even more important, the portion of the city's work force employed in more "post-industrial" businesses such as finance, services, and communication technologies increased between 1970 and 1984. Indeed, by 1984 nearly half of the employees based in St. Louis worked in such businesses.[8]

Similar changes are reflected in census data that show where people live and work inside the metropolitan area. In general, available evidence indicates that the city is being transformed into a postindustrial center despite the stiff competition provided by St. Louis County. On one level, this validates the hard work of many city leaders to rebuild St. Louis into such a place. At the same time, it creates new challenges and opportunities for city leaders to find ways to accommodate those people living in St. Louis who have not yet benefitted from its revival.

St. Louis city and County dominate the area's economy. In excess of 70 percent of all workers living in the metropolitan area are employed in the city or county. Although people of all ages find work in both places, younger workers are becoming a less important feature in the city's economy and more important in the county. More mature workers, on the other hand, are becoming relatively more important to the city's work force and less important to that of the county.

The problem for cities such as St. Louis is that they have so many younger minority residentes who cannot find entry-level jobs that offer prospects for advancement. Such people also tend to be unprepared for the more sophisticated service jobs becoming available in central cities. Jobs for which they are more immediately qualified and that offer hope for advancement increasingly are found outside of the central city or the metropolitan area altogether.

An increasing portion of available jobs are going to more educated and higher-paid workers. The city has fewer such workers, but the portion of its work force fitting that description is growing a bit more quickly than it is in the county. Just the opposite is true for workers in less well-paying jobs. Their number is decreasing, and they are becoming a less prominent feature in the city more quickly than in the county.

These changes notwithstanding, black people have become a more prominent part of the city's work force. It is likely that some are employed in the growing professional, technical, and service sector of the city's economy.[9] The possibility exists that an even greater share of such jobs could go to them in the future.

Black people who live in St. Louis County became a bigger part of the county's work force between 1970 and 1980. Yet, the county exported more of its black residents and fewer of its white residents to work in the city during the same period. Those St. Louis County residents working in the city have changed in other ways. The number of county residents working in the city barely changed between 1970 and 1980, whereas the number of residents in St. Louis County was able to hold onto as workers generally increased. However, the city increasingly attracted more mature, better educated, higher-paid people employed in professional, technical, and some service occupations.[10] Black people undoubtedly held at least some of these jobs.

The situation inside St. Louis city was different. The city lost approximately 13,000 black workers from its resident population between 1970 and 1980, if the census reports are to be believed. Among those black workers who remained, however, fewer were being exported to the county. The percentage of black people who lived and worked in St. Louis actually increased between 1970 and 1980. These changes were occurring at the same time that the city's working residents were becoming more educated, highly paid, and concentrated in professional, technical, and more skilled service occupations.[11]

The redevelopment of St. Louis city that took place after 1950 did not stop people or businesses from leaving. These losses may have slowed, but the city's population has been depleted of many married couples and working people in their peak earning years. The results of such losses are clear enough. There are more single-parent households and higher rates of unemployment among St. Louis residents than was once the case.[12]

Every section of St. Louis has some people who fall into these categories; but today such people are much more likely to be found in the predominately black sections of North St. Louis. This was not always the case. Back in 1960, neighborhoods in both North and South St. Louis had large juvenile populations and relatively low per capita incomes. By 1980, neighborhoods in North St. Louis still had relatively large juvenile populations and low per capita incomes.[13]

Three decades of inner-city redevelopment have not helped many low-income black people in North St. Louis, or many low-income white people in South St. Louis for that matter. It is by no means clear, however, that all blacks have been uniformly hurt by the planned and unplanned changes occurring in St. Louis city and County since 1950. There also are signs that the economic fortunes of working black people in the city have been improving to some extent.[14] Many white people in St. Louis city have been adversely affected by all the changes taking place around them, but their situation is still relatively better than their black counterparts in North St. Louis.

Two questions need to be asked at this point. First, what encouraged such changes to take place? Second, is it possible for people who benefitted least from these changes, and were perhaps hurt worst by them, to participate more fully in the city's future recovery? An answer to the first question will be offered in the present chapter. A partial and tentative answer to the second question will be advanced in the remainder of the book.

The Reclamation of St. Louis

The basic outline for a revitalized and updated St. Louis city was set well before the federal government initiated urban renewal programs in the 1950s. The midsection of St. Louis always had been the focus of development efforts in the city, and by 1950 it already held most of the city's major commercial and institutional tenants. North and South St. Louis already held most of the city's residents. North St. Louis had a large proportion of black residents, and South St. Louis was overwhelmingly white long before redevelopment began.

Thirty years of redevelopment helped to sharpen these differences. The Central Corridor lost half it its population and one of the city's worst slums, and it began to experience dramatic improvements in its commercial base and in some of its residential neighborhoods. North and South St. Louis became the undisputed population centers of the city. The north side became overwhelmingly black, while whites retained their dominance on the south side. Few neighborhoods in either area came unscathed through all of the population losses and changes affecting the city. Some were devastated. Efforts have been made over the last thirty years to undo some of this damage. These efforts have been more successful in South St. Louis than in North St. Louis; and persons from each part of town have different explanations for why this has been the case. Whites and blacks do agree, however, that the Central Corridor has been the primary focus of the city's redevelopment efforts.

Critics of redevelopment believe that there was a "plan" to rebuild the city in a way that benefitted only certain classes of citizens. Rebuilding the city's midsection constituted the guts of this plan. A close inspection of the various redevelopment schemes pursued in St. Louis does not reveal a very well-conceived plan to rebuild that part of town, however. The general idea of revitalizing the Central Corridor more closely resembles a theme to which many builders and city leaders consistently returned over the course of four decades. Sometimes the idea was executed well. On other occasions, it was bungled miserably. Yet it always was returned to, dusted off, revised, and reasserted as the most crucial element in efforts to recast St. Louis as a postindustrial city.

Two Periods of Redevelopment

There have been two distinct periods in the city's redevelopment. The first period spanned the years 1950-1974. During this period, urban renewal plans proposed and carried out by the Land Clearance for Redevelopment Authority, with the consent and cooperation of local leaders, dominated efforts to rebuild the city.[15] The LCRA was created in 1951 by the state of Missouri in order to conform with the 1949 "slum clearance" law enacted by the federal government. Before any federal money could be allocated for local renewal projects, states had to establish public redevelopment authorities "with broad powers" to plan, acquire property, construct and rehabilitate buildings, and finance redevelopment efforts. The state law also held that the local municipality must "afford maximum opportunity" to private developers to actually carry out the projects.[16]

This 1951 statute complemented another state law passed in 1943 that was supposed to have encouraged developers to rebuild the state's two largest cities: St. Louis and Kansas City. This latter statute, called the Urban Redevelopment Corporation Law, is more commonly known as Chapter 353. It was an ambitious thing, and until recently few states had anything like it. Through this law, local government could grant real estate tax abatements for up to twenty-five years for any development project designed to improve "blighted, substandard and insanitary areas." In practice, this authority could be ceded to an approved development corporation that, for instance, might reward persons rehabilitating commercial or residential buildings in an area for which it was responsible. More impressive, perhaps, the same development firm also was allowed to exercise the power of eminent domain. A developer, and not the government, could acquire someone's property so that it might be used in a way more in keeping with the "public interest."

Housing, commercial, and industrial projects all could be inititated under this law, though its use had been limited until the federal "slum clearance" statute and funds became available in the 1950s. It was too risky, many argued, to invest so much in a rundown city. Prior to the availability of urban renewal money, the cost of acquiring properties, demolition, and site improvements had been thought to be too high. Now, with the federal money available, these costs to the private developer could be greatly reduced. For more than two decades, those funds passed through the LCRA.

LCRA's domination of redevelopment campaigns ended in the early 1970s. It was then that the city of St. Louis established the Community Development Agency (CDA) to help determine how and where the new federal dollars going directly to the city would be spent. Charlie Farris, the LCRA director, wanted to fold this new agency into his own, but Mayor John Poelker rejected that idea. Many people had tired of projects that destroyed so much housing and left so much space vacant for long periods. The CDA became the local agency through which new federal funds passed.

The LCRA (which became the St. Louis Redevelopment Authority, or SLRA) survived, nonetheless. Indeed, it was able to expand its services to private developers in the city by helping them acquire tax-exempt financing for their projects. It also was assigned major responsibility for providing public improvements in redevelopment areas, despite the fact that the city already had a public works department.

The remodeled LCRA was able to survive because Farris had many influential friends. He also had a good and loyal staff. Most important perhaps, the SLRA had a good deal of money in its accounts that persons were anxious to share with the agency.

It seems Farris had been able to recapture some $9 million "spent by the city to provide new lighting, streets, sewers and other city improvements" when the new stadium was built in the early 1960s.[17] The LCRA also owned the land for that project. As developers came in at each stage of the project, they leased different parcels from the LCRA. All of that money was to have been turned back to the federal government. A good portion of it, however, went into the agency's private accounts, certificates of deposit, and the like.

Former U.S. Senator Harrison Williams, an old friend of Farris, I was told, had attached a rider to a federal housing bill in the early 1970s. This rider allowed the LCRA to hold on to its "profits" from the rents it was receiving. These profits were invested wisely over the years and grew to nearly $20 million. It was expected that this would be Farris's "rainy day money," I was told. Farris thus was able to remain an important actor in the city's redevelopment efforts.

The original purpose of organizations like the LCRA, of course, was to funnel federal money to projects that would replace slums with new commercial and residential developments. To help secure that end, the federal government would allow three important things to be done. It would allow private property to be turned over to new owners who promised to recycle it in a manner thought to be in the public's best interest.[18] It would defray some of the costs of "upgrading" properties in such risky areas by purchasing and clearing large tracts of land. These properties—whether empty or with buildings still on them—then could be sold or leased to the new owners at a greatly reduced price. Finally, the government would facilitate the successful completion of such projects by improving some of the public amenities— streets, curbs, parks, and the like—surrounding the chosen site. In essence, the government would create and subsidize a redevelopment industry quite distinct from the individual companies and persons who eventually moved into a cleared slum area. The CDA would assume many of the same responsibilities after 1975, but its backers learned important lessons from the LCRA's successes and mistakes.

Commercial Slums: The Stadium Project

The LCRA "worked best," one developer said, "on projects like the convention center or stadium, where someone could see the possibility of making some money on his original investment, as long as the thing was kept up." The stadium project showed the LCRA at its wheeling and dealing best. The thirty blocks on which the project was to be built were in pretty bad shape and filled with little more than old warehouses and parking lots. When Charlie Farris brought his plan to rebuild this part of downtown to the Chamber of Commerce in 1958, there was a lot of skepticism that the area could be refilled with a new sports stadium, two parking garages, a riverfront hotel, two large office buildings, and a pedestrian mall; but leaders thought it worth the risk.

A corporation was formed. It acquired $20 million from local businesses and an additional $31 million loan from the Equitable Life Insurance Company to help finance the project. It leased the land from the LCRA, which had purchased all of the property. The original project was completed by 1970.

The notion that a project should have strong corporate sponsors and sound financing certainly made sense. The stadium project showed what could be done for commercial redevelopment when local businesses pooled their resources. The idea that the same strategy might work for residential projects was a bit slower in coming; but the strategy was fixed in St. Louis's corporate culture as a result of this downtown redevelopment project. Several other features to this deal also came into play in corporately sponsored residential projects somewhat later. Foremost among was the way in which the LCRA, a public body, played the role of entrepreneur and brought local businesses together to support the project.

The LCRA put together a development "package." It showed the project's corporate sponsors how to plan and execute such a plan. It also demonstrated how state and federal laws intended to promote redevelopment could be used to sponsor privately initiated building programs. Corporations provided the seed money for this project. These funds were used to "leverage" additional public money to support the project. The city government successfully pushed for the passage of a $6 million bond issue in 1962. This money was used to fix the streets, sewers, and lighting for the area and to do the landscaping for the pedestrian mall. Such improvements were held out as an attractive carrot to the sponsoring corporations. This lesson would not be lost on developers who came along later and wanted to rehabilitate older or gutted neighborhoods.

The final positive lesson to come from the stadium project involved the "recaptured" public improvement funds from the federal government. The city, through the LCRA, eventually received a $9 million reimbursement for improvements to the public amenities within the project area. Portions of these funds and the lease money became the basis for the LCRA investment portfolio. The money earned by this portfolio in turn became an important source of discretionary income for future redevelopment projects. For instance, some of this money came to be spent on the convention center and a new downtown mall that was opened in the mid-1980s. Both projects were located on the northern edge of the central business district and figured prominently in the overall plan to rebuild the DeSoto-Carr area just north of downtown. The availability of these discretionary funds also anticipated and supplemented the federal government's Community Development Block Grant program that was introduced in the 1970s and provided cities with discretionary income.

Cities used this new federal money differently. Many used it to maintain selected public services or to sustain urban renewal projects when that pot of money emptied. St. Louis officials used a lot of the CDBG money to create, feed, and promote the work of a class of entrepreneurs who would help fill some of the residential holes left in the city's landscape as a result of property abandonment and demolition. Charlie Farris's "rainy day" fund contributed to these efforts, just as the old LCRA had helped to create some of the holes now in need of filling.

Residential Slums: Mill Creek

Among the holes that proved most difficult to fill are those that once were residential areas or still are. The LCRA showed itself to be an effective slum buster in old commercial areas, but it failed when working on residential projects. Urban renewal projects designed to transform rundown residential areas into a revitalized mix of commericial and residential properties created problems in many cities. This also was the case in St. Louis. It was the approach that was to be used throughout the DeSoto-Carr and LaSalle Park urban renewal areas. By some fortunate combination of luck, bad timing, and bureaucratic befuddlement, the plans for these areas never were carried out completely. St. Louisans still talk about what happened when the LCRA did have its way in the area known as Mill Creek.

The Mill Creek area of St. Louis lies just west of the central business district. It is a large, rectangular piece of land covering nearly 100 city blocks. The LCRA reserved about 454 acres of this area for renewal activities in 1958. Back then, it was a horrible slum. It was home to thousands of poor, black persons who only recently had moved to the city from rural areas in the South. The families were large, and they were unfamiliar with the fine and not-so-fine points of urban living.[19] Most important, perhaps, they and their slum stood in the way of plans to expand the central business district westward. They would have to go.

Some 3,700 new housing units were built in Mill Creek. Most were in apartment buildings, reserved for middle-income or elderly tenants. Less than 20 percent of the renewed Mill Creek area was saved for residential purposes. More than a third of the area holds commercial and industrial businesses brought in by the renewal program. Another 40 percent of the land is carpeted with major roadways intended to speed traffic through the city's midsection. It was the largest redevelopment project ever undertaken in St. Louis, and it took fourteen years to complete.

This was urban renewal at its biggest and most ambitious. It was expensive. Nearly $150 million was poured into the area. Federal and local governments put up $50 million. Private investors put in the rest. Critics referred to the whole area as *Hiroshima Flats* in mock honor to the hundreds of barren, wasted acres that laid empty for many years and the estimated 1,700 families and 600 single individuals the LCRA said it moved out of Mill Creek. Nothing done by a developer since Mill Creek has had as devastating an effect on the public's reaction to redevelopment projects as the forced relocation of these people. Blacks and whites alike still speak with considerable bitterness about the way these people were picked up and unceremoniously dumped into neighborhoods that were having their own problems. There is great irony in this because a new development, LaClede Town, was built in the middle of this area as an integrated neighborhood. Today it is a deteriorated public housing site and home to one of the city's nastier street gangs.

The original Mill Creek residents who were displaced only made matters worse in the neighborhoods to which they were moved. According to a report submitted to the city planning commission in the early 1970s, "the income level of the newer residents...was generally lower than that of the previous residents; resident ownership decreased, maintenance levels sank, and school enrollments increased beyond the capacities of existing facilities."[20] The rate of abandonment and blighting in these areas accelerated. This led other neighborhoods around the relocation sites to become less stable.

The LCRA eventually conceded that its relocation practices had a substantial and bad impact on these receiving neighborhoods. Beginning in 1965, the agency initiated a renewal project in one of these neighborhoods that was supposed to feature housing rehabilitation, a more gradual clearance policy, and more attention to relocating persons within the area. By 1968, however, the whole project was in danger of collapsing. Agency officials simply were unable to rehabilitate housing in a timely and economical way.

The Legacy of Early Redevelopment Efforts

In general, the early commercial projects were successful. The middle of the city was opened up and its major commercial and institutional centers were encouraged to grow toward each other. It was equally apparent, however, that projects intended to restore some viability to residential areas reeling under the effects of racial changes, property abandonment, and a depressed real estate market had failed miserably.

Efforts to refill abandoned areas with new homes or apartments for low-income people failed to stop the migration out of these neighborhoods and proved an inviting target for vandals. There simply was no stable institutional or communal anchor in these areas that might provide some support for a new settlement. Everything was in disarray in these areas, and the new residential buildings were an insufficient and expensive response to the chaos. Federal projects designed to mix low-income people into established working-class or middle-class neighborhoods also failed.

CDA and The Plan

This, in general terms, was the legacy of early redevelopment efforts in St. Louis. Two notable events in the early 1970s marked the passing of this phase in the city's redevelopment efforts. The Nixon administration's insistence that local governments assume greater responsibility in providing leadership in this area was one. The other event was the creation in St. Louis of the Community Development Agency, a government body designed to funnel the new block grant and revenue sharing funds from Washington into local development projects.

The general philosophy of the CDA that was laid out in the early 1970s has been embraced by three successive Democratic mayors: John Poelker (1973-1977), James Conway (1977-1981), and Vince Schoemehl (1981-the present). If the process of building the CDA, and more generally a new redevelopment program, can be likened to that of building an automobile, then Poelker was responsible for designing its body and pushing the chassis down the assembly line. Conway took that chassis and equipped it with a jet engine. And current mayor Vince Schoemehl ought to be credited with adding the car's fancy grillwork, sticking sparklers up the exhaust pipe, and taking it on a national tour. Each made a different and useful contribution, and each carried out the basic redevelopment policy first envisioned for the CDA. The CDA has its defenders and detractors. Its defenders say that leaders were trying to undo the damage caused by disinvestment and the LCRA. Its detractors say that there was a plan to take back some parts of the city for buisness persons and more well-to-do white people. Less attractive and more rundown parts of the city were to be left to minority citizens and the poor. Critics of redevelopment can even fix the date when the politicians and business people let their secret get out to the public—March 1975—and word of the plan was said to have been contained in a "secret" report to the city planning commission.

A small urban planning firm named Team 4 had been awarded a contract in 1973 to help the commission work out a general approach to redeveloping different parts of the city. The Team 4 report was finished by July 1974, and the timing could not have been worse for the firm. Jim Conway was beginning to mount his challenge to incumbent John Poelker, and Conway's staff was searching for an issue. Poelker, who by this time had decided not to run for reelection, was in the process of working out the final details for the birth of the Community Development Agency, while letting the planning commission and its chairman Charlie Farris pass quietly from the scene. Someone leaked word of the report to the press. Neither Poelker, who reportedly had no interest in creating comprehensive development plans for the city, nor Farris, whose agency had thrived on such grand schemes, would release it. Team 4 could not release it or discuss its contents and was allowed to take a public thrashing.

The press eventually obtained the report from the Department of Housing and Urban Development in Washington. The essential points in the report were these. Redevelopment is a costly and time-consuming process. Officials will never have enough money to do everything that could be done. Nor do they have the luxury of waiting around for someone else to take care of the city's problems.

Officials must make tough choices the authors argued. They have to decide where the city's limited development capital can be spent so as to increase the chances that any given project will succeed. The key to any successful project, the authors of the report suggested, was the ability to attract "long-term, private sector investments." The private sector could not be expected to carry the burden of redevelopment alone, they argued. The public sector would have to do things to strengthen the market potential of the area in which a project was being built. Granting developers the authority to carry out their projects under the state's 353 statute was an example of something that could be done. So, too, was the targeting of public improvement funds for new curbs, streetlights, and parks, and stricter code enforcement in the approved redevelopment area.[21]

The approach to redevelopment outlined in the Team 4 report sounded reasonable, but critics of redevelopment thought otherwise. They objected to the idea that public funds would be used to subsidize projects whose primary beneficiaries, they maintained, would be private investors. More important, perhaps, was their objection to the parts of the city where these redevelopment dollars would be spent. Most of the money, critics maintained, would go to projects in the Central Corridor. A little new spending would occur in South St. Louis. Virtually nothing would be done for neighborhoods in North St. Louis. The plan was to save St. Louis for businesses and white people, it was alleged.

Conway's people capitalized on this perception. They said that the report was used "as an organizing gimmick to beat up on John Poelker and get their man into city hall." They did this directly by connecting Poelker, as the mayor, with Team 4, the planning consultants hired during his administration. They also did it indirectly by promising northside blacks that Conway would remove John Roach as head of the Community Development Agency. Persons close to the Poelker administration stated that no such strategy existed. Rather, elements from within the black community promoted the controversy with the help of a nonprofit organization that had been trying to demonstrate how banks were refusing to provide loans in city neighborhoods.

Moving Toward Neighborhood Redevelopment

The specifics of this controversy aside, many white and black persons still see much of what has been done to redevelop different parts of St. Louis as part of the Team 4 "plan." The 1979 closing of a public hospital in North St. Louis, for example, was seen as just another step in the campaign to destabilize the black community. The closing was promoted by the mayor, James Conway. Conway was tarred as the man who stole an important part of black St. Louisans' culture. Many blacks threw their support to mayoral aspirant Vince Schoemehl, who promised them that he would reopen the hospital and restore that important institutional anchor to North St. Louis. Schoemehl did not fulfill that pledge, and many people are not sure whether he ever intended to or simply did not understand the great finanical costs involved in running a public hospital system. In any case, Schoemehl used the hospital closing to attack Jim Conway just as Conway had used the specter of a "secret" plan to empty North St. Louis to attack Schoemehl's mentor John Poelker.

No one forsees a quick resolution to the debate over who lost North St. Louis. The important point to all of this intramural fighting is that the debate has not led to any basic changes in the redevelopment philosophy conceived along with the CDA, now more than fifteen years old. The philosophy was laid out in the Team 4 report issued in the mid-1970s. Subsequent mayors departed from that philosophy only to the extent that changing economic conditions and federal policies compelled them to alter their immediate redevelopment plans.

After 1974, for instance, there was much less demolition and more rehabilitation. Greater attention was paid to restoring older neighborhoods, a number of which were located some distance from the Central Corridor. Finally, a number of institutions and corporations began to apply techniques used successfully in commercial projects to the residential areas surrounding their headquarters. Changes in local and national politics facilitated these initiatives, but most of the redevelopment work conducted during this period still took place in and around the Central Corridor just as the Team 4 report predicted.

These were substantial changes in the way redevelopment programs were carried out, and by no means were they warmly received by all St. Louisans. The approach to redeveloping St. Louis laid out in the Team 4 report was consistent, however, with the concerns and priorities of a new generation of city leaders. The Community Development Agency was an institution created to give expression to that redevelopment philosophy in the same way that the Land Clearance for Redevelopment Authority had been set up to enforce an earlier view of how best to save cities.

In principle, the reclamation of old buildings and neighborhoods has much to recommend it. The same could be said of working with the people who live in a neighborhood to improve their community rather than displacing them. Both strategies, one might think, would increase the chances of building stable neighborhoods or reducing the trauma associated with revitalizing an old city.

In practice, these two strategies have proven rather difficult to implement together. Those people who worked with the early federally sponsored redevelopment programs did not seem to worry about salvaging either the neighborhoods or the residents. Those people who have worked with the CDA have had to worry about such things, if only because they are haunted by the ghosts of the ealier clearance and demolition projects. More often than not, however, they have recycled the buildings and not the people living in them.

The Five Redevelopment Areas

To some extent this was unavoidable. This can be seen in Table 1, where the major features of each area's redevelopment history have been summarized. Plans to rebuild DeSoto-Carr and LaSalle Park, which lay just north and south of the central business district (see Figure 1), were approved during the urban renewal phase of St. Louis's rebuilding campaign. Yet, substantial work in these areas did not begin until after a change had been made in the city's redevelopment philosophy and the agency coordinating such work. The new emphasis on rehabilitation made little difference in DeSoto-Carr because most of the old buildings already had been cleared. The only housing left was public housing. LaSalle Park, on the other hand, did not lose all of its homes because work in it began later than in DeSoto-Carr.

The remaining three areas benefitted from the new emphasis on preservation. Plans to demolish every structure in the Washington University Medical Center area had been made, but the plan was not formulated until the early 1970s. By then, this traditional urban renewal approach was falling from favor, and there was much negative reaction to the WUMC plan. A new plan featuring rehabilitation was drawn up and approved.

Backers of the Pershing-Waterman area were adamantly in favor of recycling old buildings. When plans for the area's redevelopment were made in the mid-1970s, this philosophy was just being adopted. Some old structures in the area had to be razed to make room for parking lots or because they were simply too delapidated to be saved. The vast majority of older apartment buildings were spared, however.

This was not the case in the Midtown Medical Center area. It had contained

TABLE 1

Highlights in the Redevelopment of Five Areas Assisted by Major St. Louis Corporations and Institutions

	Late 1950s and 1960s	1970s	1980s
DeSoto-Carr (plan approved in 1959)	Gradual, but near-total clearance of rundown properties. Many persons are displaced. Only public housing and several truck depots are left. The public housing rent strike occurs in 1969.	The public housing groups begin to manage their sites and clear out disruptive families. Plans to redevelop the area. Public housing rehabilitation begins and a new turnkey public housing development constructed.	The rehabilitation of public housing continues. New apartments built. Some have subsidized rents; others do not. New townhouses for middle-class homeowners built. Some commercial construction begins.
LaSalle Park (plan approved in 1969)	Construction of a highway and public housing complexes isolate the neighborhood. Already showing signs of wear, the area continues to decline and many persons move away. Ralston Purina sponsors a plan to rebuild the area.	All the residential population is cleared out. Much housing is demolished. Work to rebuild finally begins with the construction of low-rise public housing. Home rehabilitation begins. St. Raymond's Church is constructed.	Home rehabilitation continues. Apartment rehabilitation and condo conversions begin. Apartments for elderly persons built. Some office rehabilitation begins. New town-houses for middle-class persons built.
Washington University Medical Center (plan approved in 1974)	Some deterioration is evident. Demolition of select buildings, but new apartment construction quickly fills in the holes. Two hospitals leave the area. The WUMC formed.	No redevelopment work is initiated and conditions grow worse. Selective demolition continues. By the mid-1970s, some new townhouse and condo construction. Some private rehabilitation of individual homes.	Commercial rehabilitation and new construction throughout the area. Work in the Ranken neighborhood initiated but only in a limited way.

TABLE 1 (continued)

Highlights in the Redevelopment of Five Areas Assisted by Major St. Louis Corporations and Institutions

Pershing-Waterman (plan approved in 1976)	General deterioration in commercial and residential properties. Apartments split into efficiency units. Many families leave the neighborhood.	Deterioration continues. Individuals displaced from other parts of town are moved into this area and add to its problems. Some selective demolition. Substantial apartment rehabilitation and condo conversions.	Townhouse construction proceeds slowly. Some commercial rehabilitation begins but does not attract a stable mix of shopowners. The residential portions of the area stabilize.
Midtown Medical Center (plan approved in 1978)	Deterioration throughout the area. In some spots, substantial abandonment and demolition. The population begins to drop in a dramatic way.	Abandonment and demolition continue. Individuals displaced from other parts of town are relocated here. The resident population becomes predominately black. The level of deterioration increases.	MMCRC initiates apartment and home rehabilitation. Some privately sponsored rehabilitation. Some commercial rehabilitation and condo conversion, but no new construction.

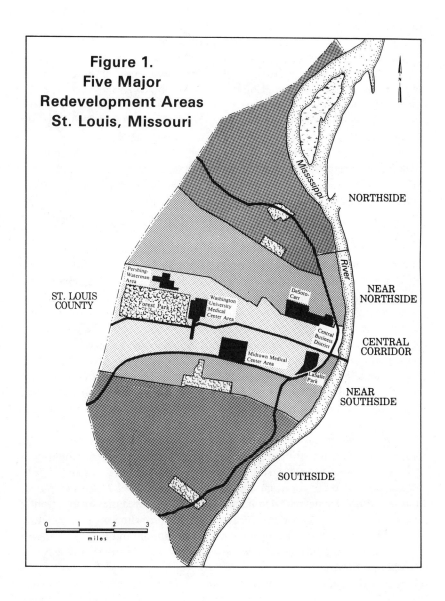

Figure 1.
Five Major
Redevelopment Areas
St. Louis, Missouri

a variety of smaller residential and commercial structures. Most of the buildings in the eastern half of the area were demolished before a plan was created for the area in the 1970s or were too shabby to be rehabilitated. Those in one neighborhood in the western half of the area were in good enough shape and in sufficient number to make rehabilitation an attractive option.

The kind of projects undertaken in each area varied considerably. Part of the variation, naturally, was attributable to the preferences of those in charge of each area's redevelopment. Some of the variation can also be explained by the number and types of developers around when work began. Early in the 1970s, for instance, few companies had any experience in rehabilitation work. By the late 1970s, dozens of companies were doing such work.

One problem they all faced was what to do with the persons living in the buildings awaiting repairs. Most of the time these persons were not well-to-do, and sometimes they also were troublesome. Whether such persons would be invited back once buildings were repaired was a sensitive matter. In none of the five areas discussed in this book was this issue handled as well as it might have been.

Supporters of the tenant-managed public housing sites in DeSoto-Carr note with considerable pride that they "rehabilitated the people along with the buildings they lived in." Indeed, DeSoto-Carr has kept more low-income persons than any of the other areas discussed in the book. Two things should be noted, however. First, many persons could not be "rehabilitated" and were not invited to stay by their fellow tenants. Persons causing trouble continue to be helped, if they are willing to change their behavior. Otherwise, they are helped off of the public housing sites by their neighbors. Second, much of the people-rehabilitation work was subsidized, albeit indirectly, by the federal government. Most of the residents were receiving one or more types of assistance—welfare, social security, and the like—while they were teaching their neighbors how to improve their behavior.

Low-income black people did not live in LaSalle Park before it was redeveloped. Ralston Purina executives were convinced that it would be a good idea, however, to rebuild the neighborhood as a racially and economically mixed area. The corporation sponsored the building of a low-rise public housing complex in its redevelopment area and supported the construction of another complex for the elderly. Middle-class persons who were rehabilitating houses, renting apartments, or buying a condominium in the neighborhood knew that low-income black and white persons were living there, and they still moved into the area.

The residential blocks immediately contiguous to the Washington University Medical Center did not have low-income minority families living on them, but students and many elderly persons, who often were alcoholics. WUMC staff worked hard to relocate these persons. Many elderly residents still are in the area. If the WUMC is to make a contribution to building a racially as well as economically mixed residential area, though, it will have to be done in a small neighborhood that was grafted onto the redevelopment area because of political pressure. Many poorer minority families live there, but a good number of middle-income whites do as well.

The Pantheon Corporation was more interested in stability and bringing the middle class back to the city than it was in integration. Its work in the Pershing-Waterman area reflects that idea. Some black people live in the neighborhood today, and some low-income people, too. The former are not young or poor, however, and the latter usually are white and elderly. One cannot look to this area for many lessons on how to integrate the underclass into the postindustrial city. Nevertheless, the area has retained an economically and racially mixed population. It does have some things to teach us on that score.

Stability with integration was the explicit goal of the Midtown Medical Center Redevelopment Corporation. Indeed, its charter prohibited the displacement of established residents. Some of these persons were white, but most were black and not well-to-do. Ultimately, the charter was violated and a number of persons were compelled to leave the neighborhood. A good deal of conflict accompanied the redevelopment of this area; but the area does look better today and its resident population is more racially and economically mixed than at any time in its history.

Some Theoretical Reflections

Contemporary ecologists and Marxists would not have been surprised by much that occurred during the first phase of St. Louis' redevelopment. This was the period of urban renewal. Marginal businesses and even more marginal people were displaced from rundown neighborhoods in or near the central business district. Lots of land was cleared. Modern companies were invited to put tall buildings on the land. Efforts were made to attract relatively wealthy persons to live, work, and play in that part of town. Government promoted big projects and sometimes had to continue subsidizing those projects after the original investors pulled out. There was much talk about revitalizing the city, but most everyone's attention was on the central business district and the neighborhoods closest to it.

The inefficient manner in which much of this work was carried out would suggest to contemporary ecologists that government probably should not have been involved so heavily. One early and highly publicized project in St.

Louis, for example, consisted of three tall apartment buildings constructed along the riverfront. It was supposed to draw well-to-do persons back to the city, and many such people live in the buildings. On the other hand, the project remains over $50 million in debt after being in service for more than two decades. The fact that many of the early investors were very well-to-do themselves probably helps to account for the reluctance of the federal government to foreclose on the mortgage.[22] It also confirms what contemporary Marxists often say about the way urban redevelopment favors more wealthy and powerful parties.

No great public dialogue accompanied these early efforts to recast St. Louis as a postindustrial city. Pluralism was never entertained as a goal by the parties who did the rebuilding. Groups ordinarily excluded from public deliberations on such matters did not find their voice during this period. Local leaders did make some important decisions about what to build. Nevertheless, much of the initiative for suggesting when and how to build rested with agencies and individuals who were not easily constrained by local leaders. There was nothing democratic about what was done, or who benefitted from it.

Some things did not change during the most recent phase of St. Louis's redevelopment. Private investors and corporations still were attracted to projects that could save or make them money. Government programs and friendly tax laws helped to fuel interest in such work. Persons approached projects a bit more carefully when the subject of displacing minority people was raised. Yet there still was little serious public dialogue about what constituted good and bad redevelopment.

Some things did change, however. This was especially clear in the five areas described in detail here. There was the new emphasis on rehabilitating old buildings, of course. It allowed city leaders to preserve an important part of St. Louis's architectural history.

The manner in which redevelopment work was conceived and carried out also changed. Looked at from a distance, it conforms rather well to what political scientists call a *regime paradigm*. Central to this view is the idea that what happens or fails to happen when cities are rebuilt does not depend exclusively on changes in the national economy or the whim of corporate executives. Politics matters. Local public and private leaders create a coalition or "regime" capable of working within the limits set by prevailing economic conditions. They also can be responsive to the demands of groups often execluded from the redevelopment process. Plans are made and amended. Bargains are struck among parties interested in redeveloping one or another area.

There need be no single conception of how the public good is served by redevelopment. Like the targets and strategies of redevelopment, one's understanding of the public good is worked out over time; it is not fixed.[23] Even the idea that much redevelopment is better than little or no redevelopment is not taken for granted.[24] What we see here was a general but serious commitment to make the entire middle section of St. Louis the heart of a postindustrial city. Modern St. Louis would be a place dominated by tall office buildings and the professional, technical, and service companies they hold. Beyond that, most anything else was negotiable. Big corporations made their presence felt. They also made mistakes, often well-publicized mistakes, and they were not immune to public pressure. The types of redevelopment pursued in each area reflected a sensitivity to the constraints under which persons were working and no small amount of creativity.

Changes in national policy made it easier for local leaders to assert more control over redevelopment efforts. Much resistance to urban renewal types of projects already had been expressed in the city, however, and not all of it came from outraged liberals. Many persons realized that displacing large numbers of minority residents had created as many problems as it had solved. This is why an effort was made to strike a better balance between corporations whose directors wanted to make money and minority citizens who wanted decent housing and stable neighborhoods.

Pluralism became an important goal. Developers were encouraged to find ways to include low-income persons in their plans. Representatives of these same low-income people were much more involved in helping to fashion a place for themselves in the city. They did not always get everything they wanted, but their interests no longer were ignored. The way St. Louis was rebuilt and who benefitted from it became more democratic.

Although no serious public dialogue about urban redevelopment as such has occurred, much serious thought has been given to how one can build a city for everyone. Public attention is given to industrial development and improving schools inside the city. Both subjects go to the heart of discussions about the underclass. Sometimes an explicit connection is made among these varous topics. More often it is not. At this time, city leaders—including minority neighborhood leaders—generally prefer to work in more quiet ways.

That rarely seen private side of redevelopment discussions will be explored throughout the book, but especially in the last chapter. It will afford us a good opportunity to reconsider popular explanations of redevelopment and the prospects for rebuilding cities so that they accommodate a variety of groups. Before attempting such an analysis, however, it would be wise to consider each of the previously mentioned redevelopment areas in greater detail.

3

THE POLITICS OF COMPROMISE: DESOTO-CARR

Walling off the Underclass

People first discussed ways to improve downtown St. Louis during the 1920s. The philosophy adopted back then was straightforward. Redevelopment could proceed, if major commercial areas were walled off and protected from poor people. A generation later, the same reasoning was used to defend plans to renew a large strip of land that ran along the entire northern edge of the downtown area.[1] That part of the Near Northside came to be known as the DeSoto-Carr Urban Renewal Area.

The idea of walling off this part of town from the central buisness district had become attractive to many people by the late 1950s. Earlier in the decade, city leaders had launched a number of ill-considered projects to build housing for the poor.[2] More than 4,200 new units of low-income housing were built just north of downtown in the six years preceding DeSoto-Carr's formal

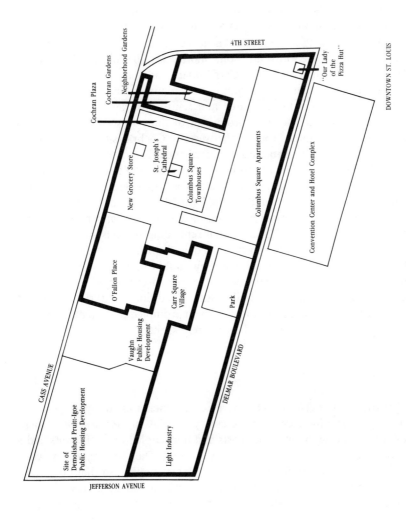

Figure 2. DeSoto-Carr Redevelopment Area

declaration as a blighted area in 1959. Spread among four different complexes with buildings between six and twelve stories tall, these units joined another 658 units built in the early 1940s on sites only two and three stories tall. These complexes were separated from the downtown area by only a thin, two-block wide buffer zone filled with rundown commercial, industrial, and residential properties. (see Figure 2). It was small wonder, then, that by 1959 the LCRA came up with a plan to renew this area by putting up brand-new buildings between the central business district and the public housing complexes.

Some new housing was to be built near the Cochran public housing site by the eastern edge of DeSoto-Carr. Some more was to be constructed near two other public housing complexes, Carr Square and Vaughn, by the western boundary of the urban renewal area. The remaining land, some twenty or more city blocks, was to be cleared and refitted for new commercial and institutional tenants. The most prominent of these was a new convention center and hotel complex to be built between the Cochran site and downtown.

Things did not work out quite as expected, though. Among the many things wrong with urban renewal projects was the length of time it took to mount and complete them. In the case of the DeSoto-Carr area eleven years separated these two events. It was declared blighted in 1959, but funds to begin work in the area were not released until 1970. During that eleven-year period, the entire area was allowed to rot. No individual rebuilding projects were mounted. Buildings were abandoned and gradually demolished. People displaced from other urban renewal areas were dumped into public housing units in DeSoto-Carr, allowing the sites to become rundown and crime-ridden less than a decade after they had been built. Such conditions and the calculated indifference of the housing authority to them prompted many tenants in 1969 to stage this nation's first public housing rent strike.

The 1969 Rent Strike

The strike was precipitated by a series of rent increases during the period of 1967-1968. These increases were necessary, officials argued, to erase deficits caused by growing maintenance costs and unoccupied units. Tenants had a different view of why the rents were being raised. They believed that it was a not-too-subtle move to force them out of "their homes" so that downtown redevelopment could proceed without their embarrassing presence.[3]

The fight was protracted and bitter. Strikers used all of the strategies adopted by civil rights groups of that period. They marched, picketed, made heated demands, and boycotted the SLHA by withholding their rents through the first ten months of 1969. They also had the assistance of a Legal Aid lawyer, Richard Baron, who gave them lots of advice. The SLHA and city officials responded by trying to break the strike, divide its leadership, and bully its supporters with eviction notices.

The tenants demanded that a Tenant Advisory Board (TAB) be created and that the TAB work with the SLHA on all matters affecting tenants. They also called for tenant participation on the Board of Commissioners that ostensibly ran the SLHA, and they demanded tenant management for all public housing complexes.[4] Finally, the housing and land clearance authorities were to be separated because, the strikers maintained, much more money and attention had been paid to urban renewal projects than to easing the public housing crisis.

The deadlock between the striking tenants and city officials was broken only after a local union leader convinced city business leaders to offer some money and oversee the rebuilding of the housing authority after the strike was over. In the face of such an effort and overwhelming evidence that the SLHA had performed incompetently, city officials finally relented and agreed to all of the strikers' demands. An agreement was signed in October 1969, and the many city leaders who had a hand in it believed that they had averted a disaster.

A great deal changed in the two years following the stike. A private group, calling itself the *Civic Alliance* and composed of notable city leaders, helped the SLHA find ways to cut its operating costs and improve its management of public housing sites. The union official who had been instrumental in ending the rent strike pressured other union officials to cut back on the number of expensive union laborers hired by the SLHA. Along with the new Tenant Advisory Board, the SLHA developed new ways to collect rents, increase security, process grievances, and prepare budgets, among other things. The SLHA also established a tenant management program that was to be implemented at different housing sites. In the meantime, tenant associations at each site "began to screen prospective tenants, participate fully in the development and expenditure of modernization funds, assist in contacting delinquent tenants, and deal with a variety of tenant problems."[5]

By 1971, there were any number of signs that the crisis in public housing was being resolved. The SLHA had reduced its monthly deficit from $125,000 to $35,000.[6] At this point the business leaders refused to continue subsidizing the TAB.[7] They had made it possible for poor people to stay in public housing; however, they balked at the idea of actually turning over permanent control of a building to its residents. As residents of the ill-fated Pruitt and Igoe sites were relocated into DeSoto-Carr over the next few years, business leaders did not complain loudly when control of the SLHA slowly reverted back to agency officials.[8]

The Jungle

Conditions in DeSoto-Carr made it easy for leaders to justify this reversal. The area became a place where anyone could live, and as such it attracted many predators: pimps, hookers, drug pushers, gamblers, burglars, muggers, con artists, and hustlers of every size, shape and age. DeSoto-Carr also had lots of victims: 11 year-old mothers, 27 year-old grandmothers, most everyone on a fixed income; children who were not allowed to play in the courtyards for fear of being hurt by broken glass or hit by a stray bullet and children who became apprentice thieves and drug pushers; elderly people afraid to leave their apartments; truck terminal operators who had their goods stolen; and anyone white who was foolish enough or unlucky enough to pass through the area. Crime was the only thriving industry left in DeSoto-Carr.

Cochran Gardens was a mess. Graffiti covered the walls. Garbage spilled from disposal units at the end of each hallway. Elevators, when they worked, and stairwells, when they were lit and you dared to use them, smelled of urine. Vandals destroyed the laundry equipment, and they kicked in mailboxes or set them on fire. Shootings were commonplace. Security was nonexistent; even the police were afraid to come into the buildings. The custodial staff set up penthouses in vacant apartments and, if they worked at all, only washed the first two floors of each building because they knew the building inspectors would go no higher. Carr Square fared just as poorly.

DeSoto-Carr was a jungle, and everyone knew it. The rent strike had not changed that fact, and everyone knew that, too. What the rent strike had done was to give many of these people the idea that they might be able to change these conditions. The rent strike settlement gave them a few short years to see if they were right.

Money to keep the TAB operating and to create Tenant Management Corporations (TMCs) finally was acquired from the Ford Foundation. Its support proved crucial. Two TMCs were organized, and former Legal Aid lawyer Richard Baron helped to train the TMC personnel. Though initially skeptical, the new director of the Housing Authority contracted out many of the SLHA's management functions to the TMCs to ensure that the agency could not again become inbred and unresponsive. There were signs that this situation was changing, however. John Poelker, mayor since 1973, had inherited a much calmer political situation and felt less need to reappoint commissioners who supported the tenants. The SLHA office staff began to grow, and one TMC lost its contract with the Housing Authority during the Poelker administration.

The early reviews of the TMCs' effectiveness were decidedly mixed. When it came to collecting rents and filling vacant apartments, the early TMCs did not do much better than the SLHA. On the other hand, tenant morale did improve; there was more community activity; and there were signs that security in the buildings was better and vandalism was declining.[9]

Critics harped on the failure of the early TMCs to run a public housing site smoothly and efficiently. Supporters of tenant management said that the tenants had inherited a mess and were doing their best to straighten out all of the problems created by the SLHA. There was a measure of truth in what each side said. Tenants did help to make the sites neater and safer, but the improved performance of the SLHA also helped to reduce the apparent level of disorganization at several of the housing sites. The problem was that the differences between the tenants and housing authority officials could not be reconciled ultimately without one or the other side losing some control over the public housing industry in St. Louis and all of the jobs and political leverage that the industry created.[10]

Reclaiming the Jungle

Five public housing sites had some degree of resident management during the late 1970s; only two still do. Both are in the DeSoto-Carr area. The people who run these TMCs today were instrumental in clearing the DeSoto-Carr area of its biggest and worst predators during the 1970s. They are black; most are women; and many still work as volunteers. Those who are employed by the TMCs do not earn large salaries. Back in the early 1970s, however, they were young mothers and grandmothers who decided to take on the big criminals when no one else seemed to care. The tenants put together an impressive system for gathering intelligence on those whose presence they objected to and for harassing such persons until they left the community or were taken from it. They did many things that developers are often accused of doing to rid an area of "bad" people. At times, however, they also engaged in activities more reminiscent of a vigilante committee. In either case, what they did worked.

Notwithstanding the competent and generous treatment of the community at the hands of some police officers, relations with the majority of police sent into DeSoto-Carr were awful and sometimes dangerous. It took a long time for concerned citizens to determine which officers were honest and which ones were not to be trusted. Once it was clear who could be worked with, however, the tenant groups passed a good deal of information along to those officers and cooperated in efforts to "set up" a number of criminals.

Slowly at first, more quickly later on, these officers and citizens went after the area's bigger and smaller drug dealers and violent residents. On occasion, citizens felt compelled to defend themselves against drug dealers who discharged guns in the area or they acquired the assistance of an outside gang to deal with local criminals. It took several years to make substantial progress. The criminals did not give up willingly. By the late 1970s, however, the "big crooks" were gone and many of the "little crooks" were on the run. DeSoto-Carr's major cottage industry, crime, was being dismantled.

Ridding the community of some of its nastier members was hard work, but no less so than the task of rehabilitating many of the young adults and children who had known little more than the violent, mean lives they had experienced up to this point. Breaking the bad habits of a lifetime proved more difficult, in fact, because there were so many more victims in DeSoto-Carr than predators. It seemed to some people that nearly everything important in the building of a healthy and stable community had to be learned again.

Those people willing to play by the new rules were encouraged to stay and have been given all of the social and moral support they need to make a success of themselves and their community. Those who could not be helped or refused to change their behavior have been kicked out whenever possible and otherwise harassed to the point that they left voluntarily. Tenant leaders in Cochran, for instance, put the number of families expelled from their buildings since the TMC came into existence in 1976 at somewhere between two and three dozen. A larger unknown number of other families and unrelated individuals who had been causing trouble in the area no doubt left on their own or were removed by the police since the tenants started to organize themselves in the early 1970s.

There are obvious costs attached to this kind of social control. Residents give up a measure of personal freedom to live in a community where people know about them, know what they do and with whom they do it. Whatever trade-offs the residents have made in the name of creating a more civil and orderly community do not seem to have been so severe as to discourage people from living there.

Carr Square has not fared as well as Cochran Gardens. It has not been substantially rehabilitated in over forty years, and the buildings have a rather worn and tired look about them. Nevertheless, the buildings are quite sturdy, having been constructed by WPA craftsmen. A number of families have lived in Carr Square for three and four generations. It is their home and their neighborhood. Some have moved to a new development across the street because of the generally rundown condition of Carr Square and the fact that some rents are cheaper. Yet they have not been lost to the neighborhood, and there is a good deal of foot traffic between the two developments.

The overall effect for the area is one of stability. People who begin to earn a bit more money no longer run as fast or as far as they can to escape the old neighborhood. They simply walk across the street. This ensures that the more prosperous individuals in the community are not lost to it. The alderwoman for this area, just to take one example, lives in the newer apartments. Children see their grandparents, and young men and women see that they have roots in the community and a stake in its welfare. The neighborhood is not torn up. Troublemakers are identified and are likely to be dealt with instead of being ignored or feared.

Rebuilding DeSoto-Carr

Creating an alternative set of incentives to keep converts on the right path and building new role models for these people to follow have not been easy chores. Cochran and Carr Square's residents worked hard to control their young men and women and to help the families of these youthful offenders. A downtown business group pressured City Hall to make some improvements in and around the Cochran buildings. Only one, however, was willing to support an ongoing job training and employment program for Cochran's young people.

About this time, 1976, the Cochran and Carr Square groups became a TMC. Richard Baron started to train the residents for the management program, but they already had some experience as volunteers in organizing and caring for their buildings. The leaders of these groups, Bertha Gilkey and Loretta Hall, along with a number of other residents participated in these sessions.

The Cochran tenant group volunteered to clean several of its buildings on a regular basis to learn how to establish a janitorial company. A bit later, the SLHA contracted with this group to clean a number of public housing buildings. The same arrangement was worked out for the provision of daycare services for the children of Carr Square and Cochran residents and meals for the elderly and young.

If most downtown businesses as yet were unwilling to hire persons from the neighborhood closest to them, then the people living in public housing were prepared to create their own businesses and train their own employees. Each business is a subsidiary of the TMCs or Tenant Affairs Board. The idea, back in the late 1970s, was that these subsidiaries would "eventually become self-sufficient through fee arrangements with the Housing Authority local and state agencies, and private companies...[thus] creating permanent job opportunties for residents of public housing."[11] Though still closely tied to the TMC or the Tenant Affairs Board, these little companies have grown. Today, the daycare centers serve several hundred children. The TMCs employ janitorial and maintenance crews, and the food catering service launched by the TAB in 1981 with $700 receives about $450,000 in contracts today. Much of the original funding for these enterprises came from the federal government's much maligned Model Cities program.

By far the biggest venture in economic development undertaken by the Cochran or Carr Square groups has been in the area of housing construction. "We became developers," Bertha Gilkey said, "so that we could make enough money to keep the TMC above water."[12] The early management fee paid by the housing authority (SLHA) to the TMC amounted to only $8 or so for every occupied unit. This was not enough money to run the buildings and provide some services to the tenants, so TMC leaders decided to acquire more money. Their strategy was straightforward. They would help sponsor projects that involve the financing, construction, and management of new housing units in their area. Both the Cochran and Carr Square TMCs have collaborated with a development firm founded by Richard Baron and a former Teamster, Terry McCormack, who was involved in the 1969 rent strike settlement. To date, there have been three major projects and about 800 new units of housing built in the area because of this partnership. A new cottage industry, this one built around efforts to redevelop the area, has repalced the old criminal enterprises that thrived on the area's destruction.

The resident management groups use the money they earn from the proceeds of housing development projects to offset their management expenses. Some of the money also has been used to support programs for residents: things like the daycare centers or meals for the elderly, scholarship aid, summer jobs for high school students, and job training programs. Some of the profits from the development projects, however, were used to subsidize the janitorial company and the catering operation or to sponsor additional housing construction projects. Several dozens of residents are employed in these various enterprises.

In the near future, the groups hope to sponsor the building of a shopping mall for the whole area and buy their apartment buildings from the SLHA. The Cochran group wants to rehabilitate an old apartment complex next door to its site, subcontract some work with a local cable company, and establish a daycare center at the downtown post office. The Carr Square TMC hopes to build some single-family homes that its more well-to-do residents could buy. The TMCs also acquired an abandoned school near Carr Square which they plan to turn into an apartment house. Both TMCs want to purchase their sites from the federal government, and recent administrations have been sympathetic to that desire.

It is important to note that the system devised by Baron and the TMCs is unique. There is nothing else quite like it in any other United States city. Yet, the custom of people contributing a portion of their income or wealth to a common fund so that they might multiply their buying power is well known. When businesses do this, we call it a *cartel*. When poor urban Mexican or Chicano people do it, anthropologists call it a *rotating credit association*. Nevertheless, the principle is the same.

People or businesses join together, ordinarily by pledging some measure of their wealth, so that they can limit competition among themselves and better control an unstable marketplace or achieve a common goal. In the case of rotating credit associations, most of the time one finds poorer families pooling their money. The money is reserved for a special purpose. The contributors to the rotating credit association take turns getting a portion or all of the money in the common fund. Usually, this money is used to buy something that the person could not afford or probably would not have the patience to save for on his own.

Rotating credit associations are not confined to the lower class of Mexican and Chicano communities, however. More wealthy people also use them. People employ this custom to build a safer and more stable community for themselves within their world. The absence of family-based mutual credit associations in the black community has been attributed to American slavery, which apparently stamped out this self-help system as it existed among African tribes. The TMCs might serve the purpose of an extended family in promoting such mutual credit associations today.[13]

The development projects sponsored in part by Baron's company and the two TMCs embody the best elements of a cartel and rotating credit association, but add a special twist to this custom. Like a good cartel, these groups have combined their forces to create a safer market for their services in an unsettled urban world. Like a good rotating credit association, these groups seek to help individual members of the community by pooling their limited resources in a common effort and then plowing the profit from that effort back into the community. They trust one another well enough to make that investment.

This special bond of mutual trust is unique in that it crosses several social classes and involves persons of substantial wealth who are far removed from St. Louis. The investors who contributed money to the housing construction projects and created a profit for Baron's firm and the TMCs knew little or nothing about the DeSoto-Carr area. They were interested in saving some money on their income taxes by investing in a "risky" enterprise.

Playing with the Big Boys

Business persons in downtown St. Louis had been dragged into the dispute over public housing quite against their will back in 1969. Once the immediate crisis was over and the threat of a riot had dissipated, they retreated to their stores and offices and waited for the LCRA to work on DeSoto-Carr. The plan was to have the whole middle section of the area become an industrial park serviced by a new highway running right through the center of it. On the southern end of DeSoto-Carr and flush against the busiest part of downtown St. Louis, the new convention center was going to be built with its backside thrust toward Cochran and a 12 foot tall chain link fence set around a parking lot to protect visitors from the public housing residents.

That plan was not to be realized. Business leaders wanted housing built close to the central business district, and there were plans to use UDAG funds (i.e., Urban Development Action Grants from the federal government) to construct new market-rate apartments just north of the convention center. The rebuilding of this part of the Near Northside was to complement efforts to build a new downtown shopping mall and entertainment center that had been talked about since the ealry 1970s.

The absence of any good neighborhood anchor around which to rally and build these new projects made it more difficult to build any of them. The Catholic Archdiocese had abandoned St. Joseph's Church, long the area's most prominent citizen, and spent more than $1 million to build a new church two blocks closer to downtown. (Public housing residents refer to the new church as "Our Lady of the Pizza Hut.") There was no natural sponsor for DeSoto-Carr's redevelopment, so Conway and his staff set out to create an unnatural one. During this period the Cochran TMC began to petition for funds that would be spent on the rehabilitation of its buildings.

The mayor's efforts complemented those of the TMC. Central to his scheme was a "forced marriage" among the downtown department stores whose caretakers wanted to build a fancy retail center to compete with suburban shopping malls, the backers of the convention center complex, and the Cochran TMC. Attendants at the wedding included the Department of Housing and Urban Development and St. Louis Redevelopment Authority, the Community Development Agency, which was the official matchmaker and allocated CDBG funds to the project area, and the Pantheon Corporation, whose owner had pledged to build a large number of market-rate apartments near Cochran as part of the deal. The TMC grafted its plan to rebuild Cochran onto the plans of business leaders to build new housing and a shopping mall for more well-to-do persons.

Money was allocated to the TMC for it to draw up plans for the renovation of Chochran Gardens. All the buildings were to be redesigned—reducing the number of residents, moving large families to lower floors, creating community space within each building—and their major utility systems overhauled. A small, 100-unit development, Cochran Plaza, would be built across the street from Cochran Gardens and serve as relocation housing for tenants while their apartments were being repaired. The TMCs along with Baron's firm would sponsor and help provide personnel to build the new units. (The construction of a community center at the north end of Cochran Gardens would come several years later and from another proposal.)

Federal officials reportedly were impressed by the comprehensiveness of the UDAG proposal and approved $18.5 million to begin the mall project. An additional $5 million from HUD's "major modification fund" was awarded to the Cochran TMC to initiate work on Cochran's rehabilitation. Two years later another $30 million would be approved to complete the "modernization" of Cochran Gardens and construct a multistory apartment building for the elderly. A good portion of these funds, unfortunately, would not be spent by the SLHA for several years. In the meantime, the cost of labor and materials would rise and ultimately force resident leaders to accept less work on their buildings than they had originally agreed to.

In any case, with the intial $23.5 million federal commitment in place, the other pieces in Conway's puzzle fell together. Additional federal money, some $4.6 million, was allocated for building Cochran Plaza. The city contributed other money from its CDBG fund to pay for the Cochran Plaza land. Conway also pledged 10 percent of the city's CDBG allocations for several years to maintenance projects at other public housing sites and an additional $1.6 million from other city accounts for additional work at Cochran.

Other funds became available to complete a parking garage for the convention center and to defray some of the costs for the $160 million dollar, four-block long St. Louis Centre mall. Conway acquired these funds in the form of tax-deferred bonds, to be publicly auctioned, from Charlie Farris's SLRA special fund and the Civic Center Corporation's accounts, held in effect by Anheuser Busch, which had sponsored the stadium project. Conway obtained Farris's reluctant cooperation by refusing to approve the construction of a park Farris had promised to build for a company that relocated in the convention center area. The company put pressure on Farris, and he relented.

The last pieces of the mayor's puzzle dealt with the construction of new housing in the area for people who could afford to pay whatever rents or mortgages the market would sustain. In many ways, this was the most questionable element in the plan to redevelop DeSoto-Carr. The big gamble was to see whether one could build apartments and homes that could attract more well-to-do white and minority citizens, especially when they would be so close to large public housing sites. The Columbus Square apartments were one response to this challenge. The building of O'Fallon Place several years later was another.

O'Fallon Place consists of 675 apartments and townhouses. It is bordered on the north and east by several blocks with little or nothing left on them except a spare truck depot, rundown tenement, or old warehouse. Carr Square Village is to its south, and the high-rise Vaughn public housing complex lies to its west. O'Fallon Place is separated from these complexes by no more than the width of a parking lot or city street.

Originally it was filled with both white and black families. Over time more black families moved into the complex. The precise reasons for this are not known.

The residents paid from $250 to $350 a month for a one or two-bedroom apartment, or paid up to 30 percent of their monthly income toward the $550 rent for a three-bedroom townhouse. Some 300 townhouses were set aside for families that received federal assistance to pay their rent.

The politics behind the construction of O'Fallon Place involved a genuine confrontation between several established black politicians and the two tenant management corporations. The politicians had acquired the rights to build a complex with both market-rate and subsidized apartments. Richard Baron filed a suit against this plan in behalf of the tenant mamagement corporations. The plan that he and the tenant leaders preferred had more of the subsidized housing being built first, and it had them building it. Constructing the subsidized housing first would have reduced their financial risk considerably. The politicians had expected to build the market-rate housing first or at the same time as the subsidized units, I was told. The compromise that was struck made Baron and the two tenant groups equal partners with another set of developers. The original black politicians were dropped from the project altogether. The successful completion of the apartments made the two tenant groups more credible actors in the area's future redevelopment.

The Columbus Square project was developed by the Pantheon Corporation which also rebuilt the Pershing-Waterman area. In many ways, it was the riskiest element to date in the revised scheme to redevelop DeSoto-Carr. It combined new homes and market-rate apartments, commodities that had been in short supply for many years in DeSoto-Carr. The 331 apartments were finished by 1982 and were built in two-story structures covering almost three city blocks. They filled the space between Cochran Gardens and the Convention Center complex that was to have been filled with nonresidential structures, had the original LCRA plan for the area been carried out.

The rents for these apartments range from $300 to $500 a month. The overwhelming majority of tenants are white and have been from the outset. Virtually all of them work in the cental business district.

Adjacent to the apartment complex, a set of forty-one townhouses was built. Some of the new townhouses have inner courtyards with fountains and cost more than $100,000. More than a dozen were sold before work on them was completed. These townhouses were built around St. Joseph's Church, the old cathedral abandoned by the St. Louis Archdiocese when the neighborhood became too dangerous. Today, the church was restored with private contributions and masses again are being held there.

Walking through the area today, one might question just how risky the venture had been. The apartments are as attractive as anything one would find in the suburbs. They are maintained fairly well and fill and important niche in the housing market for downtown St. Louis. Nevertheless, the vacancy rate tends to be higher than one would expect. Observers suggest that this may be due in part to the manager's interest in setting aside apartments for whites so that the area becomes more integrated.

The people who live there tend to be professionals who work and want to live downtown, but who had no desire to live in charming old flats. The Columbus Square townhouses cater to the same general clientele. So, too, does an even newer set of forty-four attached townhouses built by the same developer and selling for $75,000 to $100,000. Indeed, it is expected that some of the apartment dwellers will stay in the neighborhood and buy these homes once they can afford to do so or tire of paying rent to a landlord.

Despite the apparent appeal of the Columbus Square project today, there were few reasons to believe that it would succeed and many reasons why it might not. Yet, three things stood out in the project's favor. First, the developer was highly regarded. His firm was able to acquire good financing terms from a bank whose own construction efforts downtown would look much better or a lot worse depending upon what happened in DeSoto-Carr. Second, the city stood behind the project, having committed nearly $4 million to improve streets in the area, build a park and tennis courts, and to reduce the developer's costs in building the apartments. Third, and perhaps most important, the DeSoto-Carr area had become a safer place in which to live and invest because of the work done by the tenant groups.

Among people involved with the city's redevelopment efforts, there is nearly universal agreement with the first two points. One can have interesting arguments, however, when the question turns to how much credit for DeSoto-Carr's revival should be laid at the feet of the TMCs. Many people, in private and when pushed to offer an opinion, will grudgingly concede that the TMCs did make the area a safer investment site. At the same time, they may express a fair amount of distress, and sometimes anger over the running battle between the TMCs and the housing authority or mayor's office. Bertha Gilkey is the object of much of this verbal criticism for reasons that will be discussed later. The crucial point, in my opinion, is that without the TMCs it is unlikely that DeSoto-Carr's redevelopment would have proceeded as far and as fast as it has.

Who Will Benefit from DeSoto-Carr's Rebirth?

Whether DeSoto-Carr would be redeveloped never in doubt. It might take a long time, but the area was too close to downtown not to have something done to it. The question was what form the rebuilding effort would take.

The earliest plans to "revitalize" the area, plans that were acceptable to established black leaders, had it turning into a glorified industrial park. If public housing tenants were to remain in the area, they would have become "invisible" to downtown St. Louis. There was no expectation that a viable residential neighborhood could be built in the shadow of public housing, so none was planned. If Cochran Gardens had been destroyed, carrying out these early plans would have been easier. All the people, the good ones as well as the bad ones, would have been moved to some other rundown project. There would be no one left in the eastern section of DeSoto-Carr to hurt the area's redevelopment.

Fortunately, the people of Carr Square and Cochran refused to master the art of compliant clienthood. They were tired of being moved around the city. They resisted efforts to force them from "their homes," and they won the right to set down roots in DeSoto-Carr. This made the tenants, and later the TMCs, a political force with which to be reckoned. The tenant group in Cochran parlayed that political leverage into money, lots of money. There are nearly 900 new or renovated apartments spread among the dozen buildings that are part of the Cochran Gardens complex. The average cost of renovating and constructing those units ran between $45,000 and $75,000.

Today, the TMCs and Baron's firm are drawing plans to fill the empty blocks between O'Fallon Place and St. Joseph's Church with a small mall that will contain the kinds of stores and services that a viable neighborhood needs to feed, clothe, entertain, and employ its residents. Should it be constructed, the mall would be anchored by a large gorcery store that was built during the late 1980s.

The reintroduction of retail shops to DeSoto-Carr is considered crucial to its comeback as a residential neighborhood. Today, only one "convenience store" (selling a limited selection of grocery products, prepared foods, sandwiches, and beverages) and several "fast food" operations serve this purpose. A good deal more money can be made in DeSoto-Carr these days, but no one seems in much of a rush to help area residents spend theirs close to home. Part of the reason is the area's history. However, as one developer pointed out, some prospective shopkeepers could have difficulty choosing which of two races or social classes they wanted to attract.

The new St. Louis Centre undoubtedly attracts some of the area's wealthier residents. Its 150 shops and stores are geared to that clientele. Space already is leased to several fancy restaurants, any number of clothing boutiques and designer outlet stores, jewelry and other "accessory" shops, as well as a gourmet grocery.

The success of new residential projects in DeSoto-Carr has been mildly contagious. Baron's firm, along with the TMCs, has renovated a former school building and created thirty-five apartments in the neighborhood north of DeSoto-Carr. It also built townhouses and transformed an old brewery into apartments right by the school. The attitude of persons in and out of government is that the Near Northside can be recycled, albeit perhaps only for a predominately black clientele.

Whether the people who move into new or renovated housing in DeSoto-Carr build themselves a viable community remains to be seen. There is a strong sense of cooperation among the people who live in Cochran Gardens, Carr Square Village, and O'Fallon Place. It even extends to the Vaughn public housing complex that sits just outside the border of DeSoto-Carr. A number of these people have known and worked with one another for a long time. Some are related to each other through birth or marriage. Many have endured the frustration that comes from living in public housing but being unable to improve it.

These people have little in common with their new neighbors in Columbus Square. There is no hostility. They just do not know one another and have few occasions on which to strike up a relationship. Perhaps that is all that could be expected for now. Most persons still express mild shock that white people would even move into the area. In the long run, however, most careful observers expect that relations between the public housing "oldtimers" and the newer white residents will increase and grow friendly.

Notwithstanding all of the money that was spent on the Cochran Gardens complex, some of the renovation work was poor and did not conform to the plans agreed to by Cochran residents when Jim Conway was mayor. This was not his fault, according to many observers, but rather that of the public housing authority (SLHA) whose directors chose not to proceed with the rehabilitation work in a timely way. By the time the funds finally were released, the cost of labor and materials had risen to the point that the original funds no longer werre sufficient to pay for the renovation work that had been planned.

Corners were cut. Among other things, the plumbing and electrical systems in several buildings cannot meet the demands placed upon them, and the buildings are not insulated as well as they were supposed to be. None of this shows on the surface, but it will make the long-term costs of maintaining the buildings higher and it increases the expenses to the individual tenant who now must pay for his or her own electricity.

Other challenges await the TMCs. Cochran's leaders have tried to work through the manager of the Columbus Square apartments, but to no avail.

The management is not particularly interested in jointly sponsored softball teams or alley cleanups. As in any neighborhood, though, it is up to the oldtimers to introduce themselves to their new neighbors on a one-to-one basis and to strike up cordial relations.

The developers of Columbus Square have tried to bring their tenants together by throwing little parties and providing rooms where the tenants can come together on their own. That these efforts have not been especially successful in building a "community spirit" in Columbus Square is not a great surprise. These are people who are accustomed to moving around a great deal. The TMCs stand a much better chance of establishing good political relations with the people who will buy one of the eighty-five new townhouses in the neighborhood. As more permanent residents, they should be more interested in what the TMCs have to say.

In his 1985 State of the Union address, President Reagan proposed to sell selected public housing sites in about six cities to their tenants. The Cochran site was one possible site. The argument in behalf of tenant ownership was attractive. The poor could expect to practice self-reliance, enjoy the fruits of their own hard work, and participate in their city's future economic growth. There were other reasons why the Reagan administration would be interested in showing that public housing tenants could "go it on their own," local officials noted. Public housing is expensive and Republicans do not have a vested interest in keeping happy all the local Democratic politicians who had supported the institution.

There are stong feelings on both sides of this issue in St. Louis and elsewhere. Opponents of tenant ownership decry it as an attempt to divest the federal government of its responsibility to help secure decent housing for low-income people. Some also see privatization as part of a larger campaign to cut most federal domestic spending programs. Local officials in St. Louis objected to the proposal because it would remove the best maintained and "profitable" apartments from the SLHA's housing stock. They requested that the federal government replace the lost Cochran units with new public housing units.

The most potentially damaging and valid criticism of the privatization experiment is that the rents paid by the tenants simply will not be sufficient to maintain their buildings and pay the utility bills. Thoughtful critics do not believe that the present tenants can meet these expenses. The problem is that no one really is sure how much it would cost to renovate and maintain these buildings properly. Overruns in Cochran's rehabilitation were expected to be in excess of $1 million. No one inside the SLHA knows where the money went. They did know that funds for other sites will have to go to Cochran, though, if its rehabilitation was to be finished.[14] Beyond the question of money, it would appear that youth gangs and drug dealing are back in DeSoto-Carr. The TMCs may have begun to lose control over some of their residents.

For the time being, the future of homeownership in Cochran remains cloudy. The Department of Housing and Urban Development was unwilling to provide what SLHA officials demanded and did not move ahead with the sale of Cochran. This may have been in the residents' best interest. According to the author of an unpublished report on the ownership proposal, the subsidies set aside for Cochran's new owners would not have been sufficient to cover the difference between the cost of running the site and projected rent receipts.[15] No one is certain from where the extra money might come.

A comparable proposal by the Carr Square TMC would have tenants buying stock in a housing cooperative. There no longer would be rent subsidies for anyone except the elderly. Some of the units might be reserved for persons with good incomes, but the Carr Square group also is interested in building some for-sale housing in the neighborhood that its tenants could purchase. The ability of the TMC to attract and hold more well-to-do black tenants would increase once the site was rehabilitiated. To this end, the TMC would enter a joint venture with Baron's development firm. The improvements would be paid for with bonds, private investments, and foundation grants.[16]

There were good reasons not to sell the Cochran development to its residents. Until December 1986, the TMC had never had full control of its operating budget. The approximately $900,000 set aside each year for its maintenance and management was held by the housing authority. The TMC often found itself dipping into profits from one of its subsidiary operations just to repair something or to paint the walls in a building. Resident leaders claimed that their new budget provided less money than they needed to maintain the site. To the extent that this was true, it would be difficult to keep the site in good working order. Resident ownership probably would not have made that situation better. Ownership also could have retarded the TMC's efforts to create more jobs for Cochran residents. Money that otherwise could have been used as venture capital would have needed to be saved so that unforseen expenses could be met. As long as the Cochran TMC had full control of its budget and retained its status as a public housing site, it had much greater latitude to explore new ways to redevelop its neighborhood and create jobs for its people.

Some of the same arguments could be raised against the Carr Square proposal. It is entirely possible, of course, that the Carr Square group will raise sufficient funds to modernize and maintain its site. The proposed sale seems certain to be carried out. If it is, then public and private subsidies would have made tenant ownership possible. The rents provided by existing tenants would not be sufficient to cover the cost of repairing the buildings. The TMCs operate like many neighborhood-based community development corporations. These corporations tend to do well in real estate ventures, but they have a poorer record of success in other kinds of businesses.[17] Were the TMCs dependent on income from their subsidiary operations to keep the sites well-maintained and available to low-income renters, they might fail.

The groundwork for redeveloping the western part of DeSoto-Carr has been laid, just as the western edge of the central business district is being rehabilitated. An aldermanic committee endorsed a plan sponsored by Alderwoman Mary Ross, who lives in O'Fallon Place and once lived in Carr Square, to rebuild this part of the area and the blocks west of it. Proposed is the renovation of Carr Square and the demolition of the Vaughn high-rise complex just west of Carr Square and O'Fallon Place. In its place would be built low-rise public housing that would complement the Carr Square and O'Fallon Place developments. Another element of the plan calls for the creation of an industrial park just west of DeSoto-Carr.

The idea is to provide jobs for area residents where they live. Not only would this go a long way to rebuilding the economy of this part of the city, but it would reinforce or protect the work being done in the western portion of the central business district as well. Though not part of the current plan, the Carr Square TMC hopes to secure some land next to the Vaughn site on which it will sponsor the construction of single-family houses. These buildings would be sold to Carr Square residents who want their own home but also wish to live in the neighborhood.

DeSoto-Carr's Significance

The best data available show that DeSoto-Carr lost anywhere from 50 percent to 80 percent of its population between 1960 and 1980.[18] During that period, the area's population remained overwhelmingly black. The 1990 Census will show that the population of DeSoto-Carr has grown and that the percentage of residents who are black has declined a bit. Redevelopment has made the area less crowded than it once was, but it has not changed substantially the racial composition of the local population.

Signs that the area was "on the way back" appeared before many whites began moving into DeSoto-Carr. The black population became relatively older, as the percentage of minority youth in it declined. Crime in the area dropped even more dramatically. Other positive signs included decreases in housing vacancies and the average size of households. Something was working in DeSoto-Carr, and that something was the tenant management corporations. It will be important to recall later that these groups were not able to stop all the losses to the black population and did not really want to stop them. Indeed, we know that the TMCs helped to push a number of undesirable families out of the neighborhood.

The TMCs did complain bitterly about the loss of working families. They argued that conditions at the sites, particularly after the 1969 rent strike, grew worse and discouraged such families from staying. The declining number of working persons living in the area after 1970 certainly reinforces their argument. The losses were especially obvious among industrial and professional workers. Although the earning potential of area residents who worked decreased, the proportion of area residents who worked remained virtually unchanged between 1970 and 1980. This is consistent with TMC claims that they worked hard to keep working families in their public housing sites. Increases in the share of jobs going to clerical, sales, and service workers compensated for a drop in the share of professional, technical, and industrial jobs held by area residents.

These points are important in their own right. They take on added significance when one realizes that such changes were occurring before and during the early stages of DeSoto-Carr's redevelopment. What was happening in the minority community anticipated some of the changes that observers expect to find in an area being redeveloped.

To the extent that DeSoto-Carr's slow emergence as a viable area proceeds along the lines described here, it may provide some important lessons for pursuing redevelopment in other cities. It most certainly will be used as a yardstick against which the redevelopment of the remaining four areas described in this book can be measured. Four ideas seem particularly important.

First, it is feasible for central business districts to be rebuilt as postindustrial centers even when good-sized concentrations of public housing are contiguous to the downtown area. The presence of low-income minority residents need not retard the sponsors of professional, technical, or service industries from undertaking their redevelopment work or moving into an area. To be sure, the Cochran and Carr Square public housing sites are relatively well-organized. Yet the seeds of such organizations are present in many public housing sites.

Second, it is quite possible to rebuild an area for a racially and economically mixed residential population. Well-to-do white people would not be purchasing homes in DeSoto-Carr today, if the area were not safe. Real estate agents and developers with whom I have spoken are not reluctant to advertise the new houses and apartments as sites that would appeal to young professionals. Some even point with pride to what has been accomplished at Cochran and Carr Square.

Third, public housing residents can create a constituency for themselves that does not depend on government bureaucrats. They can learn how to coexist with business people and even cut deals with them. Over time, public housing residents can create the conditions for their own independence and build a neighborhood that better meets the varied needs of black citizens.[19]

Fourth, the independence they create is not only political but economic as well. They can profit from the redevelopment going on around them and not merely contribute to it as good neighbors. The equity interest both TMCs share in the O'Fallon Place development has brought then several hundred thousand dollars in fees. Should it be sold to new investors in the future, the TMCs would likely share several millions of dollars in the profits garnered from the sale. These funds have been and would continue to be reinvested in the community. Under some conditions, groups protesting poor housing conditions can move well beyond merely applying pressure and begin to participate in the rebuilding of cities.[20]

The people of Cochran and Carr Square refused to be displaced from their homes, first by criminals and later by bureaucrats. By organizing themselves and engaging in both legal and extralegal activities designed to build a power base in DeSoto-Carr, the people of Carr Square and Cochran were among the pioneers in efforts to bring tenant management to the United States. Ironically, they also were among those St. Louisans who called for a halt to the demolition of housing and for greater emphasis to be placed on housing rehabilitation. As such, they had much more in common with the middle-class rehabbers and real estate developers who came along in the 1970s than either they or more well-to-do people ever realized.

Popular expectations about urban redevelopment do not hold up very well in DeSoto-Carr. The original urban renewal plan as well as the coalition of business leaders, agency heads, and politicians that backed it fell before an effective grassroots organization and new mayoral administration. Changes in city politics made all the difference. The area was preserved as a residential site, and it accommodated prosperous white homeowners as well as black public housing residents.

Both contemporary ecologists and Marxists would be surprised by what happened in DeSoto-Carr. Marxists also would be pleased. Representatives of the underclass had managed to turn their small piece of the world on its head, as least in the short run. They lobbied and planned, executed and profitted from redevelopment. The process and results of redevelopment were "democratized." Social scientists do not expect this to happen.

If one accepts the idea that pluralism is in the best interest of a community, then what has happened in DeSoto-Carr so far is good. Persons from very different backgrounds are living in close proximity and behaving toward each other in a civil manner. Neither ecologists nor Marxists expect such outcomes from urban redevelopment.

Groups ordinarily excluded from deliberations about redevelopment were included in DeSoto-Carr. They gained a measure of political equality. If such groups become involved at all, theorists expect them to throw up some flashy but brief resistance to redevelopment plans and then be overrun or ignored. This did not happen in DeSoto-Carr.

Again, contrary to what established theories would have us expect, local politics did matter and grassroots groups have acquired support for their work. The TMCs have sustained their organization and its impact in matters of neighborhood and citywide interest. The TMCs can fight with City Hall even as they cut deals with one or another agency and business person. They have become serious "actors" in St. Louis politics.

It is possible that the way DeSoto-Carr has been rebuilt so far could change, and these short-term gains could be reversed. That does not seem likely, but it could happen. What seems more likely is that progress would slow or that lessons from DeSoto-Carr's redevelopment would not be used in other places.

There are signs that this is happening, at least for the time being. For instance, ingredients for good redevelopment that were discovered in this area are not being used widely in St. Louis. New tenant organizations are not springing up. Developers are not rushing forward to made neighborhood groups equity shareholders in new ventures.

Tenant leaders have tried to export their ideas and use their influence in other city neighborhoods. Thus far, however, they have not enjoyed much success. Bertha Gilkey has had better luck fashioning new tenant management groups in cities other than St. Louis. The lessons apparent from DeSoto-Carr's rebirth have not become part of a broader dialogue about good and bad redevelopment in the city of St. Louis.

More important, perhaps, is the slow pace at which plans to create employment opportunities for area residents are being implemented. The TMCs, some persons believed, would create businesses and employ their own people in those businesses. This has yet to happen to any great extent. A few dozen residents at each site may be employed by the TMC or one of its subsidiary operations. Others who could be employed either are not qualified for these jobs or would prefer to earn more money somewhere away from the site.

The industrial park being planned for the area west of DeSoto-Carr could help, but that help will be some time in coming. The public school system still is not educating youngsters very well, and thus not preparing minority children for college and more skilled jobs. In short, DeSoto-Carr may be a good refuge for the underclass, but it has yet to provide the mechanism for moving many persons out of it.

It is unfair to expect that the redevelopment of one area in itself could produce such a result. It is not unfair to expect that the area bring together parties that could make this happen. The redevelopment of DeSoto-Carr has brought such parties together. Now the hard work begins.

4

THE RELUCTANT GIANT: LASALLE PARK

The Area's Decline

Ralston Purina is an agribusiness giant, producing and selling food all over the world. The company was founded in St. Louis during the 1890s and remained a family-run operation until after World War II. Its corporate headquarters is located in the same area that grandfather William Danforth built his first animal feed plant. Grandson Jack is a U.S. senator. Grandson Bill is the chancellor of Washington University, another of the city's leading institutional citizens.

Ralston Purina is located today more or less where it always has been, just south of a railroad switching area that is set between the company and downtown St. Louis. From its inception Ralston also has been attached to LaSalle Park, a residential neighborhood of about 140 acres that stretches some ten city blocks south and a bit west of Ralston's corporate headquarters. LaSalle Park originally was connected to a second residential neighborhood, known as Soulard ("Soolard"), to its south (see Figure 3). Both neighborhoods were settled in the mid-1800s by working-class immigrants of French, German, Czechoslovakian, and Lebanese descent.

They lived in classic nineteenth century brick row houses, semidetached or detached two- and three-story structures built in Victorian and Federal styles. They worked in classic nineteenth century jobs, as skilled and unskilled

Figure 3. LaSalle Park Redevelopment Area

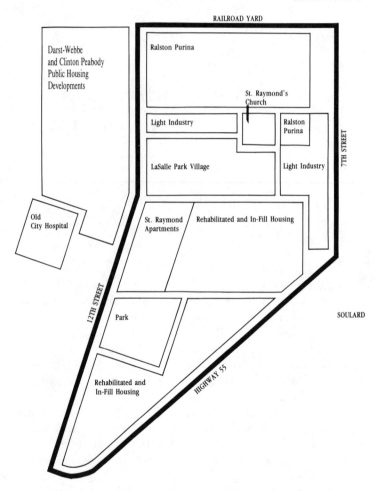

laborers in nearby breweries and manufacturing plants. They built their churches and raised several generations of children in the shadow of downtown St. Louis and these industrial sites.

After 1920, the area began to change. Fewer foreign immigrants settled in LaSalle Park, and many of the early settlers moved to newer neighborhoods farther from the sights and smells of the inner city. They were succeeded by rural Americans, virtually all of them white, who had migrated from the hill country of southern Missouri and northern Arkansas to find what work they could during the Great Depression. LaSalle Park, by this time already showing signs of its age, began to take on the character of a slum. Once a place where some middle-class families had chosen to live, LaSalle Park became one of those St. Louis neighborhoods where only the poor would live. The population of the neighborhood declined gradually, and the buildings deteriorated in like fashion.

Two decisions made after World War II contributed to the area's misery and ensured the decline of LaSalle Park. The first decision was to build a highway between LaSalle Park and Soulard that could carry suburbanites to their jobs in downtown St. Louis and back home again at night. Neighborhood leaders, especially its Lebanese politicians, were opposed to the highway and managed to block its construction for a few years. The highway was built, however, and long-time observers of LaSalle Park say that this was the major factor in the neighborhood's decline. Beyond being an eyesore, the highway split two companion neighborhoods and separated LaSalle Park residents from what traditionally had been their major grocery store, the large Soulard Farmers Market. Along most of LaSalle Park's western border is Darst-Webbe, the second bad decision. It consists of eight large apartment buildings with towers that originally were either nine or twelve stories tall. The complex was completed in two stages in 1956 and 1961, and it contained over 1,200 apartment units for public housing tenants.

Neighborhood leaders opposed the construction of these buildings just as successfully as they had the construction of the highway. "It was really awful," one person said. "Those big buildings had no security, stacked people like blocks, and the Housing Authority didn't do any screening of the tenants. It was no surprise that people wanted to get out of LaSalle Park."

The highway and public housing construction had a profound impact on the thinking of LaSalle Park's residents. In effect, people simply gave up. LaSalle Park would not formally be declared "blighted" until 1968, but that was done more as a legal nicety so that the area could become eligible for urban renewal funds.[1]

Ralston Purina, for all its importance, seems not to have had much if anything to do with the early decisions to build the highway or public housing complex. Like most other modern corporations, Ralston Purina had not taken a particularly keen interest in local politics. Its ties to the local ward organization consisted almost exclusively of yearly $5,000 contributions to the alderman's Christmas basket program for the poor. The politicians, for their part, apparently did little to encourage Ralston to take a more active interest in the neighborhood. They wanted only to keep the neighborhood pretty much like it always had been: stable, on the poor side, and predictable in its voting. Ralston Purina's caretakers had more important things about which to worry.

Foremost among the company's concerns back in the 1950s was where to build its new corporate headquarters. It had employees spread all over the city and no single place to set them. The company had an option on land in western St. Louis County near its research farm, and no one would have been particularly surprised if Ralston Purina had left the city for greener, cheaper, and safer pastures. The Danforth family rejected that proposal in 1955, deciding to cast its lot with the city that had been so much a part of the corporation's history and success. The decision to stay was crucial.

The project to redevelop LaSalle Park was undeniably self-serving. Central to it were the decisions in 1966 to build a new research building and corporate headquarters. In 1968, they started talking about the neighborhood. A quick survey of the area might have been enough to make them build out in the county, had not the decision to stay already been made. Officials knew that they would have to deal with the slum, "if they were to protect their investment." At the same time, they wanted to be a good corporate citizen. The redevelopment project, I was told, "was to be public relations of the highest order."

There is no question that LaSalle Park was a slum by 1968. It was "dirty, rundown," to quote one observer. "The streets and curbs were in terrible shape. Weeds were everywhere, waist-high in spots. Lots of homes were uncared for. Many had broken windows. A fair amount of demolition and abandonment already was underway. Whole blocks had been torn down. There were lots of bars and backyard car repair shops."

Urban Renewal's Last Gasp

The people in Ralston Purina who were most involved with this project, most notably former board chairman R. Hal Dean, had many questions and few answers. After all, they were in the business of manufacturing food not rebuilding neighborhoods. Ultimately, Ralston Purina turned for guidance to the LCRA and Mayor Alphonso Cervantes. These parties gave Ralston officials their first lessons in the politics and economics of redevelopment.

It is not that other people and groups had no interest in seeing that something be done with LaSalle Park. The urban planners from Team 4 had been invited by the local neighborhood association to help develop a renewal plan for the neighborhood. The poor whites who constituted the bulk of the association's membership understood that they could obtain relocation money from the city, if there were an urban renewal plan. Many left before the money could be given to them; some moved into Soulard. No one really wanted to stay in LaSalle Park.

Leaders from several churches in the neighborhood very much wanted to see something done. However, they also wanted to be sure that at least some of the area's old-time ethnic residents had a chance to move back into LaSalle Park. Some politicians were even more adamant on this point, I was told. They did not want the ward to turn into a place where the poor were not welcome and new well-to-do residents would vote for someone else. Ralston officials, on the other hand, talked about building new garden apartments for their employees. They expected that many professionals would like to live across the street from where they worked, but it would take some nice new housing to lure them into the neighborhood.

In the first plan drawn up by the LCRA in 1969, LaSalle Park was identified as "137 acres of broadly mixed land uses." Approximately half of this area, exclusive of streets, was devoted to homes. The other half was filled with industrial sites. Like the housing, these industrial sites were old. Though some remained in pretty good shape, the neighborhood generally was "beyond repair."[2] The decision was made to knock most of it down and to put new buildings on the land.

Talk in the plan of encouraging selective rehabilitation was no more than that. There were no incentives to recycle old buildings, and many incentives to tear them down. Besides, by 1961 virtually all of the buildings had been declared structurally deficient by the LCRA. The buildings probably deserved that label, but we know today that they could have been recycled. The LaSalle Park urban renewal plan was intended to be another "clearance program."[3]

What the LCRA, with Ralston Purina's tacit approval, proposed to do was interesting inasmuch as they had only 140 acres with which to work. Proposed was the creation of a "new town—in town." LaSalle Park would become "a self-contained area within walking distance of downtown St. Louis," providing its residents with "employment opportunities" as well as shopping and recreational facilities and a new school. Finally, at least half of the housing units proposed for LaSalle Park were to be "constructed especially for low and moderate income families."[4] This was an ambitious plan. Had all of the space allocated for industrial and nonresidential land uses been so filled, precious little real estate would have been left on which to build housing. That probably is why the LCRA planners envisioned the need for some high-rise apartment buildings inside LaSalle Park.[5] Yet high-rise apartment buildings had a bad reputation in LaSalle Park. They had brought large numbers of poor black people to the very edge of the neighborhood.

For all intents and purposes, one former public official told me, "there was no good plan to rebuild LaSalle Park." Ralston Purina "had the idea to help, but had no idea what to do." Corporate officials, in fact, had pledged up to $2 million of the company's assets to cover the money that the city would have had to contribute to the project to qualify for urban renewal funds. The LCRA planners had an idea of what they wanted to do with all of this money. The result of this union was a proposal that would have turned LaSalle Park into a more manageable version of DeSoto-Carr had it been carried out.

LaSalle Park eventually emptied. The 450 families and 200 single individuals living in the area in 1969 were gone by 1974. At least that many people, it was hoped, would move back into one of the 1,500 new and rehabilitated housing units planned for the area.

The LCRA proposal began running into trouble almost immediately in Washington, however. The Nixon administration had a real distaste for these kinds of renewal schemes. Many urban renewal plans were stalled. This is what happened to LaSalle Park's urban renewal plan.

Indeed, almost five years passed before any federal money for the project was made available. This meant that no relocation assistance could be provided to people who wanted to leave, and many buildings the LCRA wanted to buy to proceed with its plans remained untouched for the time being. According to the original schedule laid out in the 1969 proposal, the whole renewal project was to have been completed during this five-year delay.

All work in the project area did not stop during this period. The new corporate headquarters opened in 1969, of course. By mid-1972, the federal government had approved a revised plan that dealt with the 45 acres just west and south of the Ralston Purina complex. The city was awarded $4 million to start the project. Some unoccupied buildings in this section were demolished. A little more than half of the area, some 24 acres, was reserved for Ralston Purina's use. Almost 20 percent of the space, about 8 acres, was set aside for light industrial and commercial development. Another 20 percent, 9 acres of land, was to be used as a site for new residential buildings. The final 3 acres of land, all of which lies immediately across the street from the corporate headquarters, were reserved for the construction of a new church for the neighborhood's former Lebanese residents.

These were important decisions because they set the tone for what was to have been the general thrust of LaSalle Park's redevelopment: clearance, mixed land use, some new housing for an ill-defined resident population, and a passing nod to the old residents and institutions that had once given LaSalle Park its life and character. The delays had been discouraging and costly, if only in the sense that it finally seemed clear just how large, expensive, and drawn out this undertaking could become.

Sometime after 1969, one Ralston official said, "the notion of having garden apartments had sort of gone away." Ralston Purina still wanted to "get something going" in the neighborhood, though, and bringing people back into the neighborhood was one way to do it. The project would have to be big, too, if it were to have any impact.

At this point, Mayor Cervantes introduced company officials to a contractor who also happened to be a political supporter, and they were convinced to sponsor the construction of a good-sized apartment complex that Ralston Purina then could sell back to the public housing authority, which would rent units to poor people. Ralston would not lose a penny on the deal. An urban renewal regulation held developers responsible for replacing housing lost to low-income people. Besides, local officials still were feeling the effects of bitterness over the wholesale displacement of people from the Mill Creek area. Finally, "social scientist types" had been telling company officials that mixing residents from different levels "would be the best recipe for a successful neighborhood." Building 148 townhouse apartments for the poor at an approximate cost of $4.4 million seemed to be a pretty good idea at the time.

In retrospect, a number of people have had second thoughts about this deal. Each unit cost about $30,000 to build back in the mid-1970s, and no one has anything good to say about them today. They were poorly built, and with the exception of the first few years after they were finished, they have not been maintained well. Ralston Purina, for all of its satifaction at finally having work started in LaSalle Park, was sobered by this project.

The company's decision to build housing for low-income people in the first stage of its redevelopment program had other unanticipated results. During the early 1970s, Ralston executives discussed the possibility of scrapping the urban renewal plan. They were frustrated and considered transforming LaSalle Park into one large industrial complex. The decision to build low-rise public housing in the neighborhood spared LaSalle Park that indignity, but it also ensured that much of LaSalle Park would be saved for residential redevelopment.

Officials from the Department of Housing and Urban Development "eventually took the position that they did not want to approve subsidized housing in Phase I of the project unless they were assured that the remainder of the area would be redeveloped" for people. "The city would have to commit itself to residential development in the second and third phases of the project," one federal official told me. Just as federal officials had become sensitive to the charge that urban renewal projects displaced poor people and replaced them with wealthier folks, so, too, did officials not want to surround low-income people with industrial sites. Housing for poor people in LaSalle Park was approved. In the process, LaSalle Park was saved as a residential neighborhood.

This fact notwithstanding, the decision to build such housing was a very unpleasant surprise to the Lebanese backers of the Maronite Catholic Church and the few "pioneer rehabbers," who had begun buying the old brick homes. Some people wanted to ensure that nothing like this would happen again. "The Village really galvanized the rehabbers," one long-time observer told me. "They saw all those old buildings being leveled and what was thrown up to replace them, and they went nuts," another said.

Ralston director of community affairs Fred Perabo recalled that "preservationists made us aware that there were important architectural styles represented in the area."[6] "What happened," one rehabber said, "is that we invited Fred out to lunch . . . then went on a tour of a few neighborhoods where rehabbing was occurring so that he saw first hand the result of all this work." The house tour, Perabo reported, "gave us our first direct exposure to what could happen if we considered rehab."[7]

What made this eye-opening experience even more amazing was that the visited neighborhoods were no more than three blocks away from LaSalle Park. One of them was Soulard. This illustrates just how little consideration had been given to the possibility of rehabilitating any of the neighborhood's old houses, despite the support for rehabilitation stated in the renewal plan. It also was a reflection, however, of how modestly and informally word of this kind of residential redevelopment was spreading in St. Louis back in the mid-1970s.

LaSalle Park was the first place in the city where the new and old ways of rebuilding neighborhoods were to bump heads. "The CDA looked at things from a broader perspective," commented Ralston executive Fred Perabo, and with that the focus of LaSalle Park's redevelopment changed from clearance to rehabilitiation.[8]

Picking up the Pieces

This meant, among other things, that many of the old buildings left standing would be renovated. In a 1971 survey carried out by a local preservation organization, nearly 100 buildings were declared "architecturally significant;" 8 were out-and-out "treasures." Another 160 buildings were said to have "some architectural interest for the neighborhood." Nearly a third of these buildings, some 90 structures, were demolished by the time ground breaking had commenced for LaSalle Park Village in 1975. Most of the remaining buildings would be spared. An agreement between Ralston Purina and the CDA to bring $2 million in CDBG funds to LaSalle Park provided that "architecturally important buildings" standing in the southern two-thirds of LaSalle Park would be preserved and renovated.[9]

Similar buildings in the norther third of LaSalle Park were not forgotten. About 60 were designated for rehabilitation. Ralston Purina, through its subsidiary the LaSalle Park Redevelopment Corporation, bought and reconstructed the exterior of twelve of these buildings. It completed the interior renovations on a row of 4 townhouses in this group. New owners would finish the work on the other 8 houses. The company invested well over $500,000 in these buildings, and the work was good. The plan was to offer them for sale "at cost," but the company did not recapture all of its initial investment. Company officials were not too upset, though.[10] Among the new owners were attorneys, nurses, management consultants, city and Ralston Purina employees, builders, and the owners of a small news magazine.[11]

This was all very good news as far as many people were concerned, but there was still much unfinished business. LaSalle Park had many empty spaces in the early 1970s, and filling them would be a tough job. In general, holes in the northern end of LaSalle Park were filled with a combination of new apartments, for-sale housing, and buildings for industrial and institutional tenants. Those in the southern section were bigger and have proven harder to fill. Much of the federal money that went to the rebuilding effort came from the city's CDBG or block grant allocation.

The rebuilding of LaSalle Park continued into the 1980s, though not as quickly as area residents and Ralston Purina officials would have liked. By 1984, nearly 200 homes, townhouses, condominiums, and apartments had been rehabilitated. In excess of 300 similar structures had been built on vacant land. Another 65 townhouses were being rehabilitated, and there were plans to build almost 30 new townhouses. Fifteen commercial structures had been rehabilitated; and there were 6 new structures for light industries or commercial enterprises. Finally, Ralston Purina moved ahead with plans to complete its "corporate campus."

A brand-new building, five stories tall, was constructed on the northwest corner of the corporation's property to accommodate some 300 employees temporarily housed elsewhere in the city and moving to St. Louis from Rye, New York. This latter group consisted of people who worked for the Continental Baking Corporation, the company that makes Hostess Cupcakes and Twinkies among other things.

Much of the space between the CBC building and "the Tower" had been given over to parking spaces for Ralston employees. About half of that space, over 4 acres, was transformed into a wooded park for the pleasure of Ralston employees. The park has three small lakes, stocked with fish to keep them clean. Walkways and a jogging path surround and cross the lakes.[12]

All these changes, along with the creation of a new Garden Room dining area in the tower that looks out onto the park, are supposed to increase the employee's pleasure and sense of security while at work. Occasional car break-ins and robberies or assaults had frightened many employees and convinced company officials that they needed to do something to protect their people from "some of the residents in Darst-Webbe." If nothing much could be done about Darst-Webbe, somthing could be done to ensure the safety of Ralston employees and the integrity of the company's real estate investments.

'Succeeding Against the Rule'

There were many pieces to the LaSalle Park puzzle and increasingly more parties who wanted to push those pieces around as the neighborhood began to show new signs of life. The corporation had no hard or fast rule on what types of developers, industries, or residents it should invite into the neighborhood. After the creation of LaSalle Park Village, however, Ralston executives tried to maintain higher standards in the quality of the work that was done in "their" neighborhood. They did not always succeed. Nevertheless, given the constraints under which they were working, Ralston officials have done a good job in encouraging a mix of industrial, residential, and institutional land uses within LaSalle Park. The only major disappointment as of 1989, beyond the slow pace at which redevelopment has proceeded, is that not as many commercial tenants have taken up residence as officials would have liked.

This problem notwithstanding, one LaSalle Park resident observed that "the neighborhood has come a lot closer than most people realize to becoming the 'new town—in town' envisioned by the LCRA in 1969." The neighborhood has many full-time residents, even if they do not know one another all that well yet. The neighborhood does have a number of businesses, though few of the residents work in them. It has a large recreational area, but only the black youngsters from the projects play in it. It has one very healthy church, but most of its communicants no longer reside in LaSalle Park. The neighborhood also has new streets, curbs, street lights, sewers, and cul-de-sacs. LaSalle Park is a viable place in the sense that it has many of the building blocks of a community, but it is still a community in the abstract, a community waiting to happen. LaSalle Park, for all of its corporate sponsorship, has almost no corporate history.[13]

If LaSalle Park makes it as a community, then much of the responsibiity and credit will go the the leaders of St. Raymond's Church, the Maronite Catholic parish founded in 1912 by the neighborhood's Lebanese residents. St. Raymond was considered a small, dying parish in 1966. Only a dozen or so people would attend mass in the four-family flat that served as the parish church, and there was no parish life except for the few dedicated members of the Ladies Society. The original priest for St. Raymond died in 1944 and no one was appointed to take his place until 1967. That was when Monsignor Robert J. Shaheen came to St. Louis and bagan to revitalize the parish.

Father Shaheen turned to the dispersed members of his flock for support. Within two years, the parish was recovering nicely. Within four years, the parishoners began to collect funds to build a new church. It was decided to "stay in the old neighborhood and be an example of what could be done in the inner city." The new church, a handsome blend of Middle Eastern and modern architectural styles, was dedicated in 1975. The new rectory and parish center were dedicated in 1977 and 1979, respectively.

Church leaders are proud of their work, and they see St. Raymond as the neighborhood's anchor. Some people might take issue with such a bold claim, but it has merit. Many hundreds of people go to work in Ralston Purina every weekday. Most are gone by late afternoon, and only a few show up to work on the weekends.

The church brings a kind of stability to the neighborhood that Ralston cannot match. Its religious services and programs are capable of attracting up to 700 families at any time of day or night during the whole week. The cafeteria run out of the parish center by the Ladies Society brings in additional hundreds of people, many of them Ralston employees, for Lebanese- and Syrian-style luncheons. It also is a nice money-maker for the parish.

The contribution of St. Raymond's parish goes well beyond church services, bingo games, and ethnic foods, however. Church leaders wanted to help those who had been displaced from the neighborhood. They decided to sponsor the construction of an apartment complex that could house many of LaSalle Park's "oldtimers." Ralston Purina executives approved of the plan. They also helped the church acquire federal funds to build the apartments, 150 low-rise units, and to pay part of the elderly tenants' rents. Although the apartments themselves are attractive enough, they have not lured back many of the older folks who lived in LaSalle Park before it was "renewed."

LaSalle Park's revival also shows, even more than that of DeSoto-Carr's, that residential redevelopment can coexist nicely with light industrial development. Here again we find something generally considered out of place in a revitalizing neighborhood preceding and not discouraging the moving in of young and middle-aged urban professionals. More than 8 acres of land were set aside for new commerical and industrial buildings in the first phase of LaSalle Park's redevelopment. Most of this property was filled by new tenants: a printing company, an armored care and security service, a telegraph company, and a major distribution warehouse for Anheuser Busch products. In addition, Ralston Purina also offered space to a company that provides daycare services for children. Several other existing industrial companies remained and rehabilitated their buildings.

Protecting Its Corporate Investment

It is difficult to calculate just how much all of this work has cost Ralston Purina. By mid-1977, it was estimated that the corporation had laid out approximately $1.2 million for purchasing and clearing land, undertaking feasibility studies, and improving streets in the area. Another $500,000 had been spent on additional studies, reports, surveys, and salaries for corporate officials working on the project.[14] None of this money was expected to be recovered through the subsequent resale of properties acquired by Ralston.

Since mid-1977, $2 million more has been spent to acquire additional properties. Some of this property was reserved for the corporation's own use. Almost all of the rest was sold to others wishing to build new structures or renovate old ones in the neighborhood. Some portion of that $2 million would have constituted a "loss" to the corporation, at least in the strictest sense of that term.

Another $1 million or so has been spent on the operating budget of the LaSalle Park Redevelopment Corporation for things like staff salaries and promoting different projects. All of this money would be treated as a "loss" to Ralston Purina. The corporation has contributed considerably more than $3 million to the redevelopment efforts in LaSalle Park. This amount would not include the $40 million or more spent by the corporation in constructing its corporate campus since the mid-1960s.

Averaged over a period of fifteen years, Ralston Purina probably "donated" more than $200,000 a year between 1969 and 1984 to the redevelopment of LaSalle Park. That may seem a pretty modest sum for a corporation whose net income during LaSalle Park's most trying years in the mid-1970s was between $75 million and $100 million. Several things need to be kept in mind when assessing this contribution, however. First, no other party was willing to assume responsibility for overseeing LaSalle Park's redevelopment. Had it not been for Ralston's commitment and early financial support, LaSalle Park might still be a slum today. Second, Ralston's continuing presence in the neighborhood had an immense symbolic and psychological impatct on other potential investors. As one person told me, "You didn't have to be a genius to figure out that if Ralston was staying, the neighborhood was going to come back." It is estimated that by the time LaSalle Park's development is over somewhere between $30 million and $40 million will have been invested in the area by the city and other companies that were willing to take a chance in the neighborhood because of Ralston Purina's presence.

Estimates of Ralston Purina's "donation" to LaSalle Park have run as high as $4 million dollars.[15] Even if this higher sum were closer to the mark than the $3 million we have been discussing, that still is not a huge amount for such a big corporation. Ralston executives, ever mindful of the costs for redeveloping LaSalle Park, tried to be careful.

Some people had a less generous view of what Ralston Purina had done in LaSalle Park. They saw Ralston's adoption of the neighborhood as little more than a prudent investment by a corporation with good political connections. This argument was laid out in a series of articles in the *St. Louis Post-Dispatch* in March 1980. In that series, the reporters tried to build a case against Ralston Purina's conduct, noting just how much the corporation had spent and what it had received in return. Ralston executives could make such modest contributions, the reporters implied, because they were obtaining all of the property in LaSalle Park for a small fraction of what it really was worth.[16]

Some former LaSalle Park residents and business persons were less kind. "It was a land grab," said one.[17] That some of the replacement housing eventually built was done so by friends of the mayor did not help matters. Nor did the fact that several top Ralston executives were among the first persons to purchase and rehabilitate homes in the neighborhood. None of this probably would have caused much of a stir, however, had Ralston Purina and the LCRA not managed to increase the length of time for which Ralston would receive tax abatements on its new holdings without obtaining the approval of the Board of Aldermen. This was all quite legal, inasmuch as LaSalle Park was an urban renewal area under the control of the LCRA. The Board of Aldermen in effect could be bypassed because it already had "carefully scrutinized" plans to redevelop LaSalle Park and told the LCRA to proceed with its work. Its work, in this case, could include the appointment of the LaSalle Park Redevelopment Corporation as the official developer for the whole urban renewal area. This meant that the LCRA had something approximating the final word in determining who was to build what in LaSalle Park as well as how much, if any, tax abatement a project would receive.

What was novel about the application of such policies in places like LaSalle Park was not that some people suffered and others gained. Rather, it was that anyone would try to use these same policies in a place like LaSalle Park, a residential area outside of the central business district. That was the real risk Ralston Purina executives were taking.

Ralston executives tried to cut the best deals possible not simply because it was good business but because they were not quite sure how deeply they wanted to dive or could dive into the redevelopment game before being in over their heads. Some people came to criticize Ralston's adoption of LaSalle Park as nothing more than another smart investment by a big corporation. In retrospect only was the "smartness" of the investment apparent; moreover, much of the time they did not make choices that were guaranteed to bring them the best return on each dollar that they invested. Nor did they always make the wisest political decisions.

During the height of the controversy over Ralston Purina's conduct for example, one executive said that they probably should not have undertaken such a large project. "The way it works now, you have to buy the property, relocate the residents, do site improvements and demolish what you have to. You can't have any new development until those things happen." To make matters worse, the executive went on, the whole process takes much too long and you never can be certain of having the money you need to do something when you are ready to do it.[18]

These statements were made in 1980. Five years later, the attitude of at least some Ralston executives had changed. The worst signs of blight and abandonment were gone. People were moving into the neighborhood. New housing was being built. "Now I kind of wish we had claimed more of the industrial land east of LaSalle Park and redeveloped it too," one executive told me.

The point is that no one, least of all the executives at Ralston Purina, knew how LaSalle Park would turn out. If anything, the corporation probably had behaved too cautiously and depended too much on public money to initiate some projects in the neighborhood. The rehabilitation that the corporation sponsored was done very well and set an example for other rehabbers and homebuilders to follow. Some residents frankly wish that Ralston had done more rehabilitating on its own and pushed some people harder to fix their old houses once the buildings had been purchased. "Ralston had the power, they just didn't use it," one rehabber complained. "If they had, then all of the old homes would be repaired by now."

Equity and Community in LaSalle Park

Some of the people who live or work in LaSalle Park believe that all parts of the neighborhood need to work more closely together; some are content to leave matters much as they are. They either believe that the various pieces of LaSalle Park are coming together or they resist most efforts to think of "those other people" as part of the neighborhood.

Someone in LaSalle Park who talks about "those other people" usually is referring to the black people who live in LaSalle Park Village or anyone who lives in the southern half of the neighborhood. More generally, the phase *those other people* is used by homeowners in the northern half of the neighborhood to refer to anybody in LaSalle Park who lives in an apartment.

"Those other people" are not social outcasts. In fact, relations between individual homeowners and some of "those other people" can be quite cordial. For instance, youngsters from LaSalle Park Village are hired to run errands or cut lawns, and some have helped find the lost pets of homeowners from time to time. Politically, however, the adults who fall into that "other people" category are all but mute when questions come up about how to run the neighborhood. Some of the homeowners believe that they have a right "to call the shots" in the neighborhood. It was they, after all, who invested their own savings in houses that many people considered wrecked in a neighborhood that most everyone conceded was a slum.

The resale market in LaSalle Park has been less than what some persons though it ought to be, and they blame Ralston Purina and some of the developers Ralston allowed in for the problem. One person who bought a townhouse fixed up by Ralston tended to agree, up to a point. He said that he and his wife had liked the quality of the rehabilitation work undertaken by the corporation when they bought the townhouse back in 1979. They were less pleased by the developers Ralston let in to fill some of the empty lots left by the demolished buildings. Ralston "simply didn't pay enough attention," he said.

The lack of attention spilled over into the section with rehabilitated homes as well. Ralston "made a big deal" about incoming buyers signing covenant or rehab agreements so that everyone maintained the same high standards of work on their homes, another homeowner said. "Folks spent a lot of money to do things that were agreed to. Then a guy refused to build his garage according to the approved guidelines, and Ralston rolled over." Other people have bought houses and made no substantial effort to improve them.

"Corporate executives know about this," I was told. "They just choose to ignore it because they don't want to get sued again." "Maybe," he added, "this is because of the plastering they took in the newspaper." In any event, Ralston "has not been successful in upholding the agreements except when the owner voluntarily complied." Part of the problem here, I was told, was that Ralston was caught in the middle of an ongoing debate between persons who wanted to restore old structures to their original state and persons who were satisfied with merely improving the buldings. The corporation elected not to become involved in the argument between the restorationists and rehabbers, and it paid a price for that decision.

When Ralston Purina did try to push its residential redevelopment plans forward, on the other hand, sometimes the homeowners complained about that, too. A small playground constructed by Ralston Purina received much criticism, despite the fact that the corporation had paid $15,000 to have it designed and built. The homeowners never wanted it. After it was finished, they wanted it even less. As one person told me, "older kids from either Darst-Webbe or LaSalle Park Village would take it over after dark." One night, after eighteen months, it burned down. This happened, I was told, the day before bank examiners visited the area to certify it for home loans. The homeowners came together shortly thereafter and told Ralston that if it was rebuilt, "they'd take care of it and the corporation." It was not rebuilt.

Ironically, some of the homeowners also criticize one of the decisions for which Ralston Purina executives are quite proud. That decision was to give another relatively unknown developer named Mark Conner the rights to build on most of the empty lots scattered throughout LaSalle Park. Conner, unlike the developer who had started to build on these sites, really did intend to construct housing whose style fit into the neighborhood. Most observers believe that he has succeeded rather well. Driving through the neighborhood, it really is fascinating to see how much the facades of Conner's houses mimic those of the larger, older looking, three-story buildings renovated by individual homeowners. They look like new "old houses."[19]

What troubled many LaSalle Park homeowners, I was told, was that the infill houses were usually quite a bit smaller than their own and, thus, less expensive. The top price for one of Conner's houses in 1985 was about $80,000. Most have been sold in the $55,000 to $75,000 range. Owners of larger houses in the neighborhood believed that the value of their homes was reduced because people could afford to buy something in the neighborhood for substantially less money. They would have preferred Conner to build larger, more expensive houses so their home did not stand out quite so much. They also believe that Conner should have covered all four sides of his buildings with brick, rather than just the front and two side faces of the houses.

Needless to say, Ralston Purina executives are extremely pleased with Conner's work. Even his worst critics concede that the replica housing does fill an important niche in the city's housing market. A number of Conner's clients are buying their first home. They like the architectural style and the old neighborhood, but they also wanted a house that they could move into without having to spend lots of time and money on rehabilitation.

Within the past few years, the LaSalle Park Homeowners Association changed its name to the LaSalle Park Neighborhood Association in an attempt to make it look as if everyone could work together on a more permanent basis. Nothing much came of it, at least initially. The reasons for this are not hard to discern. The homeowners, I was told, "simply didn't understand that as long as they are separated politically from the renters, and especially the Village people, Ralston Purina has no reason to take us seriously." "To give you a sense of the suburban mentality of these folks," one homeowner said smiling, "they are going to pay someone to take notes at their meetings and to do their books." Recently, when a couple of youngsters from the Village started breaking into homes or stealing things from unlocked automobiles, "they decided to hire a private guard to patrol the neighborhood."

Conditions in LaSalle Park Village are becoming so bad that they really can no longer be ignored. In the last eight years, there has been only one "annual inspection," and nothing was done about the problems that were found. It is not just the physical condition of the buildings themselves that is so distressing, another tenant said, the people have become worse, too.

The homeowners reportedly were "shocked" when they finally met with the tenants and heard about these things. They have yet to take any steps to help their neighbors, though the discussions continue. "Ralston knows about our problems," one tenant stated, "but they've done nothing to help. We feel we're being neglected for a reason, that we'll be weeded out and that these places will be rehabilitated and sold as condos." "No one is willing to push the Housing Authority; and even if they did, nothin' would come of it."

Ralston executives and the ward's alderwoman have discussed these problems with the director of the Housing Authority. However, if the agency's record offers any insight into its future conduct, then there is no reason to believe that LaSalle Park Village will do any better in 1990 than it has in the previous fourteen years of its existence. In the absence of any substantial renovation work, conditions at the site can only grow worse.

A proposal was advanced before the Housing Authority in August 1984 to raze the top floors of several towers in Darst-Webbe. This would have removed nearly 400 apartments, or one-third of the units originally constructed in the complex. The buildings facing LaSalle Park are vacant. All are in various stages of disrepair. Removal of some upper floors began late in 1986. Funds to renovate the remaining units have not yet been made available. More recent discussions in City Hall have dealt with the possibility of dismantling most of the site.

LaSalle Park's Legacy

LaSalle Park and DeSoto-Carr were old residential areas attached to industrial and warehouse districts. Neither fit in a postindustrial city. But for the plodding of federal bureaucrats and the intervention of Ralston Purina, LaSalle Park might have looked more like DeSoto-Carr does today. There could have been much more new housing and empty space left to fill than is presently the case. Areas whose redevelopment began after the demise of the federal urban renewal program did not have nearly so much demolition with which to contend or empty spaces left to fill.

The population of LaSalle Park reflects the similarities and differences between it and DeSoto-Carr.[20] The neighborhood of LaSalle Park and its surrounding blocks lost much of their population in the period 1960-1980. Yet, the loss was less than that of DeSoto-Carr, and it was confined largely to whites. The number of blacks dropped slightly during this period. It probably continued to decline after 1980 as public housing units across the street from the neighborhood were emptied and razed.

LaSalle Park retained a larger white population than DeSoto-Carr. The 1990 Census probably will show that LaSalle Park's white population has made some gains, though not so large as those seen in DeSoto-Carr. The number of whites in the latter area was much smaller in 1980 and will show a more dramatic increase for that reason.

Such changes sometimes accompany efforts to redevelop an area. Other signs, in the case of LaSalle Park, were drops in the percentage of housing units remaining vacant and the number of crimes reported in the area. A more positive indicator of the area's revitalization was an increase in the percentage of area residents who were working. The increase was especially apparent in the case of professional and technical workers. It will be recalled that as of 1980 this had not happened in DeSoto-Carr.

Several things about LaSalle Park's population were not consistent with what often happens in a redeveloping area. Blacks remained the dominant population in the general area. The construction of public housing in LaSalle Park actually increased their presence inside the neighborhood. Minority populations in most redeveloping areas all but disappear.

The presence of so much rental housing also did not fit the profile of the typical redevelopment area. As late as 1980, most persons residing in and around LaSalle Park lived in rental housing. The same was true in DeSoto-Carr. Areas undergoing redevelopment work usually have detached houses that are owned, not rented. Most persons living in these two St. Louis neighborhoods resided in buildings with more than one household in them. Neither area was in any danger of becoming an inner-city preserve for white homeowners in 1980, and that is no less true today.

Yet, both were redeveloped. Their proximity to the central business district may have made redevelopemnt inevitable. Still, no consensus existed that they should be preserved as residential areas or that persons from quite different backgrounds would live there together.

The redevelopment of LaSalle Park has proceeded differently from that of DeSoto-Carr for several reasons. Foremost among them is the area's separation from the central business district . Prominent, too, is the timing of redevelopment efforts in LaSalle Park. By virtue of being redeveloped later, more of LaSalle Park's older houses were saved. Unlike DeSoto-Carr, which had no obvious institutional sponsor, LaSalle Park had one major corporation directing its comeback. Without Ralston Purina's sponsorship, it is unlikely that the neighborhood would have been preserved as a residential area. Several other lessons can be drawn from LaSalle Park's reclamation.

First, residential redevelopment can take place in an area with both "postindustrial" development and light industry. Ralston Purina's sponsorship of new industrial tenants did not discourage renters or buyers from moving into the area. This is an important point inasmuch as the next stage of development in DeSoto-Carr calls for a large industrial park along its border.

Second, the presence of a large housing complex in the area did not stop redevelopment. That this complex was not well-organized and even posed a threat to the surrounding area did not discourage redevelopment. It also must be recalled that the first major project initiated by Ralston Purina in the residential portion of LaSalle Park was the building of another public housing site. Even this did not stop redevelopment efforts, because many persons believed that Ralston Purina's presence would stabilize the area. These persons were correct.

Third, LaSalle Park has a more racially and economically mixed residential population than at any time in its history. There is nothing to suggest that LaSalle Park Village will be torn down or that its current residents, low-income black people, will be displaced. Despite the understandable anxiety of its residents, every sign points to the Village remaining a permanent feature in the neighborhood. There is no animosity expressed by people living in the Village toward the homeowners. Nor do the homeowners dislike the Villagers. Slowly, they are beginning to reach out to each other and discuss questions of mutual concern.

Fourth, the public housing residents of LaSalle Park Village are not well-organized and have made no serious attempt to take more control of their own lives or to carve out a more secure niche for themselves in the neighborhood. Nascent leadership has been frustrated. The site is too small to demand much respect and too close to Darst-Webbe's more substantial problems to generate much interest. However, its very size should make it easier for Ralston or some other organization to provide assistance should the tenants ever become organized.

Fifth, no serious effort has been made to secure employment for Village residents in any of LaSalle Park's small industries or Ralston Purina. Though individual residents have been employed at Ralston from time to time, many more people could find work in the neighborhood. A more permanent solution to conditions in LaSalle Park Village will include efforts to employ more of its residents in the area.

Sixth, and finally, the area is too small and isolated to support many commercial establishments. It is unlikely that LaSalle Park will ever become a full-service neighborhood with shops and retail establishments for area residents. However ugly the vacant parcels of land in DeSoto-Carr may look, there is every reason to believe that a healthy commercial district can be built there. There are many more people in the immediate and surrounding area who could shop in DeSoto-Carr. People in LaSalle Park will continue to do most of their shopping in Soulard.

These are important lessons in their own right, perhaps, but they also give clues to several broader theoretical points. In general, it would seem that popular explanations of urban redevelopment fare only slightly better in LaSalle Park than they did in DeSoto-Carr. The primary advantage enjoyed by these theories in the present case is that a major corporation was involved in the area's revitalization.

The presence of a large corporation whose directors wanted to expand its headquarters and clean up the slum next door would surprise neither ecologists nor Marxists. Also consistent with their arguments is the fact that the corporation was sold land cheaply and received any number of tax breaks for the money it invested in the area. Theorists also would point to the bureaucratic bungling that led to great delays in the urban renewal process and the destruction of many old buildings as being consistent with their arguments.

Ignored in such a critique are two points. First, part of the delay in LaSalle Park's redevelopment was due to the efforts of federal officials who wanted to end the wholesale destruction of urban neighborhoods. LaSalle Park was caught in the middle of a much larger national debate over the future of inner-city redevelopment, and it ultimately benefitted from that debate. Second, the value of the land in LaSalle Park had declined long before Ralston Purina ever considered adopting the neighborhood. One might argue that the corporation profitted from the earlier decisions of other "capitalists" to abandon the city; but that only would make the efforts of Ralston Purina all the more noteworthy.

Beyond these points, it is hard to find much that would support the explanations of redevelopment offered by contemporary ecologists and Marxists. It would have been easier and cheaper for Ralston Purina had it sponsored the creation of an industrial park in the area. However, the same odd mix of federal and local politics that led to a botched urban renewal plan also led to the preservation of LaSalle Park as a residential neighborhood. Ralston Purina executives really had no fixed plan and were open to suggestions. Some of the suggestions they received were better than others.

The fact remains that Ralston Purina did not behave in a rapacious or uncaring way toward the neighborhood. It tried to look out for its own best interests while taking the future of the neighborhood into consideration. Local officials, too, had an opportunity to exercise more control over the conduct of redevelopment efforts than they had in DeSoto-Carr, and their contribution is evident.

There was paternalism to be sure; it was not the paternalism of a Pullman, however. Ralston Purina set things in motion and then stepped back. It did not prohibit home ownership or insist on becoming the area's landlord. It created conditions that brought together persons from different backgrounds; but it did not tell them how to conduct their affairs. Corporate officials may be justifiably embarrassed over the condition of LaSalle Park Village, but they have been reluctant to impose their will on the tenants or public housing authority. Ralston Purina simply has not thrown its own corporate weight around as much as conventional theories would lead one to expect, and this was not an accident. Corporate officials did not want to attract any more attention to their work than was necessary.

If one accepts the idea that pluralism is good, then what has happened in LaSalle Park so far is good. Persons from different backgrounds live in close proximity and behave in a civil manner toward each other. Social contacts between whites and blacks or wealthier and poorer residents are more numerous in LaSalle Park than in DeSoto-Carr.

Groups ordinarily excluded from deliberations about urban redevelopment, for a short time, were included in LaSalle Park. Unfortunately, it was not in a way that most theorists would recognize. Low-income whites organized themselves to escape from the neighborhood. They did not like blacks and tried to develop an urban renewal plan so that they would qualify for relocation assistance. A plan eventually was approved, though it was not their plan. Most did not wait to collect relocation funds.

A neighborhood association has emerged since the area was redeveloped, but it has not done much to improve or change conditions in the area. Blacks from LaSalle Park Village have not yet organized themselves. One suspects that Ralston Purina would listen attentively to whatever its leaders had to say, if such a group were formed.

Ralston Purina's accomplishments in LaSalle Park were not ignored by other institutions stuck in shabby neighborhoods or developers eager to work in the city. Yet, what Ralston Purina did and why are matters that have not become part of a broader public dialogue about rebuilding the city. There were newspaper stories about the cheap land it acquired from the urban renewal agency and the persons it displaced. There also were stories about awards the corporation had received for its work. Otherwise, the public has not had an opportunity to think about what happened in LaSalle Park.

The most important, and as yet unexplored, possibility to emerge from Ralston Purina's work is the inclusion of area residents in the neighborhood's economy. The corporation has made no attempt to integrate the residents of LaSalle Park Village into area businesses, including its own. If the corporation is to make a louder statement about what can be done to improve the lot of the poor, this kind of effort will have to be made. Ralston Purina contributes to area social and church groups, and it encourages its employees to do the same. It could do something with more far-reaching consequences, if it experimented with job training and placement programs for area residents. LaSalle Park, like DeSoto-Carr, has become a refuge for a portion of the underclass. Ralston Purina is in a good positon to try to do things that might make the lives of those persons more secure.

BEDSIDE MANOR: THE WASHINGTON UNIVERSITY MEDICAL CENTER REDEVELOPMENT CORPORATION AREA

The WUMCRC Advantage

N eighborhoods near a revitalizing central business district are supposed to have greater survival value as residential areas than neighborhoods somewhat removed from downtown. One would have been hard pressed to prove this point by examining the experiences of DeSoto-Carr and LaSalle Park, however. The preservation of their residential character had nothing to do with the alleged natural advantage that they enjoyed by being so close to downtown St. Louis.

Both areas were a mess when local authorities began thinking about redeveloping them, and both areas only grew worse as the local and federal urban renewal machinery ground its way to a solution to their unique problems. It might have been obvious that both neighborhoods had to be salvaged; but it was not at all obvious that this had to be accomplished by preserving them as inner-city residential areas. On more than one occasion, people responsible for the redevelopment of DeSoto-Carr and LaSalle Park seriously considered plowing both neighborhoods under and turning them into the equivalent of a suburban industrial park. This changed in the late 1960s when the federal government began to reduce its support for massive demolition and clearance projects.

The time that the land laid fallow worked to the neighborhoods' advantage. In DeSoto-Carr, the Cochran and Carr Square Tenant Management Corporations managed to pull themselves together and make their influence felt. The results of their pushing and shoving have been good for downtown St. Louis and good for DeSoto-Carr as a residential area. In LaSalle Park, Ralston Purina came to exercise more control over redevelopment efforts and changed the focus from demolition to rehabilitation. The same mix of good politics and good business helped to save the residential character of the area discussed in this chapter, too. However, the territory for which the Washington University Medical Center Redevelopment Corporation (WUMCRC) is responsible had a good deal more going for it that that. Although it is far removed from the central business district, it nevertheless is set right in the middle of the region's "institutional, cultural, and employment spine." Its importance as an anchor for this part of the city has increased since the end of World War II.

When the area began to be redeveloped in the mid-1970s, in excess of 9,000 people at all skill and income levels worked in one of the six institutions formally affiliated with the redevelopment corporation. Moreover, the Medical Center had become "one of the foremost medical service, teaching and research complexes" in the nation.[1] Outside of the downtown area and the suburban municipality of Clayton to its west, the Medical Center has the largest concentration of institutions, people, and jobs in the metropolitan area. It is, in effect, its own little downtown.

To the west of the WUMCRC area, of course, is Forest Park. (See Figure 4.) The northern edge of the area is bounded by some major hotels, a lovely cathedral, and several blocks with large houses and limited public access. It also has a revitalized commercial strip with expensive shops and restaurants. The broad southern edge of the redevelopment area is bordered by a major highway. This highway serves as an important buffer between the Medical Center along with the blocks immediately surrounding it to the north and

Figure 4. Washington University Medical Center Redevelopment Area

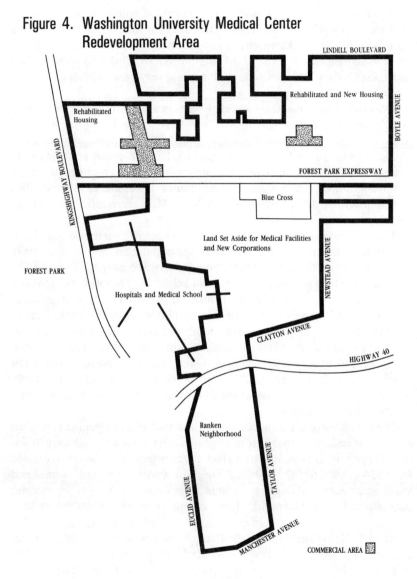

some less attractive residential blocks to the south. A small portion of this residential area, the Ranken neighborhood, also is part of WUMCRC's domain. Finally, to the east of the redevelopment area above the highway are some blocks filled with light industry, commercial buildings, and single- or multiple-family residences. It is not particularly attractive, but neither is it a wasteland. In short, the area surrounding most of WUMCRC's territory was never as threatening as some of the neighborhoods bordering DeSoto-Carr and LaSalle Park are even today. This was a very great advantage for the redevelopment corporation.

It enjoyed other advantages as well. Foremost among these was the absence of substantial abandonment in the WUMCRC area before the onset of redevelopment. A number of residences had been demolished since 1950. Unlike the situation in DeSoto-Carr and LaSalle Park, however, these empty spaces had been refilled almost immediately with highrise apartment buildings or nursing homes. The remaining older houses and small, multifamily flats were abused but never abandoned for long. Most were turned into cheap rooming houses.

The total number of housing units in the area actually increased from 3,100 in 1950 to 3,900 in 1970. Yet, the size of the population, at least after 1960, stayed around 7,400. A change in the population was occurring. The area, like many in the city, was losing its families and children. They were not replaced by black residents, as often the case in other neighborhoods. Indeed, as late as 1970, less that 5 percent of the area's resident population was black. Rather, there was a substantial increase in the number of older, "unattached" men and women moving into the blocks immediately surrounding the Medical Center. Many were alcoholics and in poor or failing health. There also were a fair number of people from certain "deviant" populations, such as homosexuals, prostitutes, and even a few transvestites. One business person characterized it as a "colorful" population.

The character of the population notwithstanding, these people kept filled most of the residences that were not demolished; the vacancy rate in 1970 was only 11 percent. They paid rents. In fact, the average rent in the area increased from $54 in 1950 to $139 in 1970.[2] They also saved the fine old houses and small apartment buildings in the area from becoming targets for massive vandalism. The buildings may have looked as shabby and tired as their tenants, but at least they were not completely trashed or demolished like so many in DeSoto-Carr and LaSalle Park. These people performed one other service along with the Medical Center staff: They shopped in the area. The section of the redevelopment area north of the highway never lost its commercial vitality, as had DeSoto-Carr and LaSalle Park. Most of the shops, retail stores, or service businesses were modest. They consisted of small markets and "convenience" stores, gas stations, bars and liquor shops, an occasional restaurant, and the traditional "five and dime" where one can buy anything from shoe polish and writing tablets to dishware and a pair of socks. A number of these businesses remained once the redevelopment effort began. Some of them, especially the numerous bars and liquor stores, were actively discouraged from staying. The gambling dens and houses of prostitution that fed off the bar trade also were invited to leave. However modest or undesirable these businesses may have been, the fact remains that the area never came close to losing its commercial base.

The location of the redevelopment area, its good institutional base, the strength of several of the areas bordering it, the absence of widespread property abandonment, and the relative vitality of its commercial base all worked to the advantage of the medical complex. Even the haphazard way in which some of the old houses had been demolished and the property refilled with different types and styles of buildings worked to its advantage. Nearly any kind of development project could be made to fit in the area.

Finally, an important institutional ally anchored the western edge of Forest Park: Washington University. As one of the larger landowners in the city, Washington University had a longstanding interest in helping the city. Many of the local people who helped to govern Washington University knew very well the people sitting on the boards of directors for the other institutions in the medical complex. The also had many friends in city politics or the city's business community. By all accounts, they were and still are among the most influential people in St. Louis. They had no particular interest in playing developer themselves, but they certainly encouraged the people who ran the Washington University Medical Center to exercise a good deal of discretion over who would be allowed to work in the area.

WUMCRC's Disadvantages

There was no Washington University Medical Center until 1962. Then, six institutions—Barnes Hospital, Jewish Hospital, Children's Hospital, Barnard Free Skin and Cancer Hospital, Central Institute for the Deaf, and the Washington University School of Medicine—created this corporate umbrella to provide a more effective way for them to identify and address their common problems. There was only one common problem, really. Their part of St. Louis was beginning to look rundown and to lose its most valuable possessions: paying patients and medical staff.[3]

Few buildings were considered by WUMCRC staff to have enough promise to warrant their being saved and restored. A small number of buildings were characterized as "having promise." Still, it was admittedly difficult to see that promise beneath the beer cans and trash piled on the floors, defaced walls, and rooms that smelled of urine and were occasionally spotted with abandoned drug paraphernalia. Most buildings in the neighborhood were dismissed as being unsalvageable and, hence, candidates for demolition.

A survey of buildings conducted by the redevelopment corporation was initiated in the early 1970s, even before a full-time director had been hired. Yet the characterizations of the buildings and their residents, I was told, would have been equally valid ten years earlier. That is why most of the institutions in the area considered the possibility of relocating in St. Louis County in the early 1960s. Two institutions—Shriners Hospital and St. John's Mercy Hospital—did relocate to west St. Louis County in 1963 and 1966 respectively.[4] "The remaining institutions determined that not only would relocation be extremely costly (the replacement value of the Center was estimated in the 1960s at nearly $300 million) but that the loss of almost 10,000 jobs could have a disastrous impact on the city, already weakened by a plummeting population. In addition, if the Center were scattered, this would imperil the region's quality of health care and its medical research capacity."[5] It also would have ended any hope of stabilizing the Central West End and probably crippled the entire city as well, hospital officials thought.[6]

Though the individual members of the Medical Center proceeded with their own expansion plans during the 1960s, the coalition itself was remarkably mute until the early 1970s. Only then were talks initiated with the university trustees to develop a plan to save the whole Medical Center area.[7] "The initial redevelopment proposal was a conventional urban renewal project to be undertaken by the city's redevelopment authority," the LCRA. "It recommended primarily luxury, high-rise housing. Little consideration was given to rehabilitation of the existing structures," many of which had been turned into rooming houses. "Existing street and utility patterns were ignored in the interest of design objectives. Neighborhood involvement in the preparation of the plan was minimal, and considerable relocation and demolition were proposed."[8]

There was an uprising, after the plan was leaked to the press. People were "just fed up with Charlie Farris's big schemes" by the early 1970s. Fortunately, I was told, the directors of the Medical Center and Washington University had the good sense to withdraw their initial plan. Another effort to develop a plan was initiated shortly thereafter.[9] In short, the focus of the plan shifted away from massive demolition and construction of more high-rises toward the rehabilitation of existing residential and commercial buildings. Some older houses still would be removed from time to time; but they would be replaced by and large with two-story apartment buildings and condominiums that were much more in keeping with the neighborhood's residential character.

In its own way, this turnabout in the plans to redevelop the Medical Center area mimicked the change in plans to rebuild LaSalle Park. The difference was that many more residential structures already had been leveled in LaSalle Park; there was less there to save. In both cases, however, a calculated decision was made to stop the LCRA from turning an old neighborhood into yet another "new town—in town." The hesitance or inability of a corporate sponsor to act swiftly and dramatically when the opportunity to redevelop became available once again had saved a neighborhood, or at least a much bigger portion than otherwise would have been preserved.

Just What Is a WUMCRC?

Before the two little words *redevelopment corporation* were added onto its title, the Washington University Medical Center, several observers noted, was merely a collection of institutions whose directors could sit around, complain about the state of the world, and deduct some of the expenses they incurred from their respective institution's budget while bemoaning their sorry situaiton. After the WUMC created the WUMCRC, its caretakers still could sit around, complain, and bill their respective institutions for the privilege; but it also could do somthing about the problems that had been identified. The difference was that this wholly-owned subsidiary of the WUMC had been given the rights to improve conditions within a given territory.

In this case, the territory in question was a 38-block, 280-acre piece of real estate around the Medical Center and on several blocks south of it and a major highway. The prospective developer, WUMCRC, became the party legally responsible for planning what would be done and seeing that the work actually was accomplished in good fashion. It would receive tax abatements for up to 25 years on all new development and on the value added to existing property through major rehabilitation.[10]

The politics and business of redevelopment were carried out similarly in LaSalle Park and the Medical Center area in some ways. Both redevelopment corporations are referred to as "umbrella developers." This means that under ordinary circumstances their directors would prefer not to undertake any redevelopment projects on their own. They will assemble property at discounted prices for someone else to improve. They will grant the developer tax abatements on the work done. They will work with the developer to secure private and public financing for the project. They will even see that the streets, sidewalks, sewers, and street lights around the property are improved. But they would prefer not to tie up the redevelopment corporation's limited capital and staff in a time-consuming property development scheme.[11]

WUMCRC also has a Citizens Advisory Committee. The twenty-two people sitting on it are residents and employees who meet five to ten times a year to review and comment on proposed development plans. WUMCRC's director, Gene Kilgen, and the ward's alderman select these people.

The WUMCRC itself, for all of its high-powered and well-connected backers, is a pretty modest operation. Today, it has but three full-time staff members: a director, an administrative secretary, and a "relocation specialist" who also is a real estate broker. When needed, WUMCRC also uses lawyers, appraisers, planning and architectural consultants, and an occasional student from Washington University's Department of Urban Affairs or School of Social Work. There were only five professional staff members in 1974 when the corporation began its work. These people had experience in different areas of real estate and business development.

At its height, WUMCRC had only ten staff members. Its operating budget, approximately $2 million for the initial ten years of the redevelopment corporation's existence, is provided by the WUMC. Staff salaries, consultants' fees, and the corporation's rent all are paid from an average annual budget of $200,000. The staff and its operating budget were kept small so that WUMCRC could not accidentally become a property developer. The idea was to avoid creating a coterie of development experts and related legal or technical professionals who could design, build, and manage residential and commercial properties—and who wanted to do so.

In addition to the basic $2 million operating subsidy, the WUMC provided WUMCRC with only $1 million with which to purchase property in the area. This sum represented an interest-free loan to the redevelopment corporation. The money was placed in a revolving fund that could be replenished as properties acquired by WUMCRC were sold off to approved developers at cost. This was fine as long as not much property was to be acquired at any one time, or if property could be picked up cheaply and sold quickly by the redevelopment corporation.

Much of the time, unfortunately, one or more of these conditions could not be met. On those occasions, the redevelopment corporation's leaders had difficult choices to make. They could lay out more money than they thought a piece of property was worth so that it could be recycled quickly or moved from the hands of an undesirable landowner. They could initiate the long and costly proceedings necessary to acquire a property through condemnation. They could let a building set there and deteriorate or increase in value as surrounding properties were improved. Or, they could harass and threaten an especially troublesome landowner to the point that the property was sold to WUMCRC for what it was really worth or for the amount that WUMCRC was willing to spend. At one or another time, WUMCRC's handlers used each of these devices to acquire properties or to stop the depletion of their account.

The redevelopment corporation's property acquisition fund shrank notice-ably after the first rush to buy property in 1975. The Medical Center's leaders were afraid that they had gone over their heads and refused to increase their contribution to the fund. Then, an additional $1.1 million was loaned to WUMCRC for this purpose by Civic Progress, a group of corporate and banking leaders whose businesses are based in St. Louis.

The situation confronted by the Medical Center was much different from that facing Ralston Purina. Although Ralston Purina is a major corporation, it is only *one* corporation. It was not necessary for it to fashion a series of nicely balanced committees to oversee one or another element in LaSalle Park's revitalization or to ensure that all interested parties were getting their share of attention or paying their fair share to get that attention.

Another problem faced in the WUMCRC area was that commercial and residential redevelopment had to be pursued simultaneously. It might strike one as odd to define this as a problem. None of the other redevelopment areas described in this book had much of a commercial or light industrial base left by the time reclamation had begun. If the area was going to become even more dependent on the "health care industry" for its well-being, some property near the Medical Center would have to be acquired so that the hospitals could expand or allied industries could be moved into the area.

This proved to be an expensive proposition for the redevelopment corporation, especially as its first major acquisition involved land on which a new medical insurance company building, Blue Cross/Blue Shield, was to be constructed and for which WUMCRC officials had to pay much more than they thought the old industrial site was worth. This had a chilling effect on all subsequent discussions of projects that would require WUMCRC to buy out the current owners of a property it wanted to pass on to someone else. It certainly impeded the plans of WUMCRC's backers to change the basic character of the area's commercial base by promoting shops and stores that would cater to people with elevated incomes and tastes. This, in retrospect, probably was a good thing because there already was such a commercial area only a few blocks north of the Medical Center's territory.

How WUMCRC Did It

In redeveloping anything as large as the Medical Center area, the interplay of local politics and something we call the *marketplace* really does shape how the entire process unfolds and what is produced. Neither the "will" of the institutions that pushed for change nor the rational calculus of those who hoped to profit from improvements in the area help us to understand very well what has been done. The Medical Center's caretakers did not always obtain what they wanted but what they eventually got tended to work out well enough. The lesson they learned was elemental. What was good for the Medical Center was not always good for the neighborhood or city, but what was good for the neighborhood and city could be made good for the Medical Center. The process of learning this lesson—stumbling and plodding toward and accommodation on matters of great and less-than-great significance—is the stuff of politics.

The directors of the Medical Center, for instance, wanted to make WUMCRC's first project a big one, something that would encourage other developers to work in the area. They decided to pressure Blue Cross/Blue Shield to relocate in the city rather than St. Louis County, as company officials already announced they were going to do, and build the new headquarters near the Medical Center. Blue Cross/Blue Shield officials were willing to consider relocating in the WUMCRC area, but they demanded an immediate and firm sale price for the site on which they wanted to construct their new headquarters.

WUMCRC accepted the company's $400,000 offer for the land in question. Unfortunately for WUMCRC, no one had secured a promise from the ice and fuel company that owned most of the site to sell it to WUMCRC for $400,000. Indeed, the current owners had an appraisal of $1 million for the property. WUMCRC was in trouble. It had to acquire and clear the desired property for Blue Cross/Blue Shield in six months or the insurance company would follow through on its original plan to move out to St. Louis County. As one observer told me, "WUMCRC didn't have time to use eminent domain to assemble property and had to lay out more money to buy people out."

WUMCRC bought them out, cleared the land, relocated sewer lines and alleys according to the plan agreed to with Blue Cross/Blue Shield, put all of the new utility lines underground—and did it all in six months. However, it cost WUMCRC $900,000 to do it, $500,000 more than Blue Cross/Blue Shield had agreed to pay for the improved site. WUMCRC had to swallow the $500,000 difference. WUMC officials saw their new $1.1 million property acquisition fund cut nearly in half after only six months and one big deal.

The Blue Cross/Blue Shield deal rattled everyone associated with WUMCRC, I was told. They could have come out of it in much better shape, people suggested, if the sponsoring institutions had only "kicked in enough money to build the property acquisition fund back up to its original level." Yet, they did not do that. Instead, "they tightened the budget and made it tougher to buy property."

It is impossible to say how much cheaper or faster the area around the Medical Center would have been redeveloped had WUMCRC not behaved so conservatively. In one sense, WUMCRC probably "saved" its sponsors some money. However, its "savings" were passed along as higher costs to developers and rehabbers who wanted to work in the area.

WUMCRC did not have to endorse more intensive, and hence more expensive, land-use projects on the blocks immediately surrounding the Medical Center to remain solvent. Nonetheless, its backers obviously supported this general approach to redeveloping the area at one time in the early 1970s. They never abandoned that approach entirely after the new "plan" to save as much of the old neighborhood as possible was agreed to, but they were compelled to pursue it much more selectively. As far as they were concerned, observers noted, it still made good sense to trade an old single-family house for three or four new well-to-do homeowners. The replacement housing built on property on which a single-family home once sat has often been pretty fancy. On one such site, a developer built 32 condominiums, each costing between $100,000 and $150,000.

These and other new residential developments notwithstanding, only 119 buildings (98 residential, 19 commercial, and 2 public) had been demolished in the whole WUMCRC area between 1975 and 1984. The tiny, six-block sliver of the area that is the Ranken neighborhood alone has twice that many buildings. So, the demolition that has taken place has been rather limited. Of the 119 buildings knocked down, 30 were located on the ground now occupied by the Blue Cross/Blue Shield headquarters. Another 38 buildings were demolished on property that either the Medical Center laid claim to or some commerical developer wanted to use. The remaining 51 demolished buildings made space for new residential structures. It was not expected that many more buildings on the blocks around the Medical Center would be demolished to accommodate new commerical or residential developments, and this has remained the case.

Those affected most adversely by all of WUMCRC's work have been the people displaced from the area's rooming houses. Approximately 634 households were displaced between 1975 and 1984; early in WUMCRC's career it was estimated that the number could go as high as 675 by 1985. The redevelopment corporation kept fairly detailed information on the 500 households displaced during the period 1975-1981. Among those 500, only 16 had included children. The rest were single-person households, consisting usually of students or elderly individuals. Most of the students were able to find other housing for themselves. The elderly tenants, many of whom were sick or alcoholic, were a much bigger problem. WUMCRC staff spent many hours trying to find suitable relocation housing for the elderly.

The expenses incurred by these people, students as well as elderly, during their relocation were paid by WUMCRC. It amounted to $200 on the average. By all accounts, the relocation effort was handled with considerable tact and compassion. Nearly half of the 500 households were relocated in the Central West End or in neighborhoods south of the WUMCRC area. Most of the other households were relocated throughout the city or suburban St. Louis County. Some people, probably the most derelict among those living in the Medical Center area, simply vanished into rundown tenements in other parts of the city. No record of what happened to them exists.

Approximately 2,800 people over the age of 62 lived in the Medical Center area in 1976. No one doubts that fewer than 2,800 live there today. Most of those 1976 residents were not considered desirable, and little effort was made to keep them in the area. Fewer than two dozen of those displaced in the first few years found new places to stay in the area. All of them moved into an apartment building that was first opened in 1977. The 242 units in this three-story structure were designed for elderly tenants, and every unit has part of its monthly rental fee paid for by the federal government under its old Section 8 program. The building itself is very nice, but even its biggest fans concede that its construction was only a modest gesture in behalf of the neighborhood's former residents.

In all, more than 800 subsidized units in the WUMCRC area are set aside for the elderly. An additional 450 are available in contiguous neighborhoods. According to WUMCRC staff, there also are other apartment buildings in or near WUMCRC's domain whose rents "are reasonable enough" to serve as a possible source of housing for elderly people who might yet be displaced by one or another project instigated by WUMCRC.

The decision not to press its legal right to acquire property through eminent domain except in a few cases, whether done for good business or good public relations, had important consequences for WUMCRC. It displaced people a bit more gradually and about as humanely as was possible under the circumstances. It thereby avoided the two biggest mistakes committed by agencies such as the LCRA: having huge tracts of property laying vacant until someone decided to do something with them and tossing large numbers of people from their "homes" in a dramatic and seemingly callous fashion.

They did one other thing in response to the Blue Cross/Blue Shield land deal that guaranteed them the aura of legitimacy and fiscal prudence they seemed eager to cultivate. They solicited just over $1 million from Civic Progress, a regional group of corporate leaders, to replenish WUMCRC's property acquisition fund. The money was raised through the sale of low-interest debentures to member corporations.

Individual members of the Medical Center could easily have contributed the $1 million loaned by Civic Progress. Within the past few years, for instance, Barnes Hospital announced plans to spend $2.7 million on an enclosed elevated walkway that would connect it to a parking garage across the street.[12] The Medical Center's representatives, instead, chose to "spread the risk" inherent in both the business and politics of redevelopment around to a broader segment of the St. Louis business community.

Directors of the Medical Center's several member institutions really were much more interested in seeing their own expansion programs accommodated and dedicating their resources to that end. The money involved has been substantial. In the first ten years of WUMCRC's existence, the Medical Center institutions spent $310 million on their own expansion efforts. This was almost four times greater than the $85.4 million invested during the same period on new residential construction ($31.6 million on 363 new units), residential rehabilitation ($17 million on 514 old units), and new or rehabilitated commercial structures ($36.8 million) in the whole WUMCRC area. When compared to this $310 million building spree, the Medical Center's original $1.1 million property acquisition fund really was modest.

The member institutions often fought each other in the pursuit of these plans. In the process, they sometimes came into conflict with outsiders who did not think that the Medical Center was behaving responsibly. There were two occasions when this was especially clear.[13] On one, a fight over where Children's Hospital could expand inside the Medical Center complex led to an expensive three-year legal dispute. Some area residents and the mayor did not want to allow the hospital to extend its building over a major thoroughfare. The hospital lost, and its officials had to find more expensive space inside the complex.

On the second occasion, Barnes and Jewish Hospitals were forced to build their own garages after it became obvious that reaching an agreement to build a single garage was not going to be easy. The redevelopment corporation's first director apparently refused to allow Jewish Hospital to tear down a lovely old commercial building on a corner of the area's commercial strip to build a garage. The garage eventually was built on property contiguous to the hospital.

Barnes Hospital built the first of two underground garages immediately to its south on a small piece of Forest Park left on its side of the major boulevard separating the park from the Medical Center. The hospital acquired the right to construct the garage in exchange for building a public tennis court and small recreational area on what would otherwise be the garage's roof or the ground's surface. It was a good deal, for the hospital.

Given its location, the hospital's staff gets the most use of these facilities. However, the hospital attempted to compensate the city a bit by donating the soil dug up for the garage for "victory gardens" on the empty lots in rundown neighborhoods across North St. Louis. The problem was that the "soil" was more like clay. Not to be stopped, the hospital contributed various chemicals and other additives that were mixed into the earth before it was dumped onto the selected lots. Silly as this gesture may have been, it nevertheless showed city officials that the Medical Center's leadership had some appreciation for politics. It was a trait that WUMCRC and its sponsors displayed on numerous occasions, even when they did not obtain what they wanted.

The ability to learn from its mistakes was apparent in WUMCRC's preference for certain types of development, home ownership over rental housing for instance, and even the developers who were allowed to work in the area. At first, WUMCRC's "umbrella" wasn't very open, observers noted. Its original director had grown frustrated with the Medical Center's leaders after a few years and began his own redevelopment firm. "It was hard for a while for other developers to get in. It was a closed shop. Gradually, WUMCRC started behaving more like an umbrella redeveloper, and good projects suggested by other firms were welcomed. That was when redevelopment really took off." WUMCRC and its sponsors learned to compromise, and the consequences were good as far as they were concerned.

Even the bigger compromises have had a way of working to the redevelopment corporation's advantage. Such was the case, for instance, when WUMCRC had to resolve a dispute over how many new housing units could be built on properties it had purchased and cleared down the block from its headquarters. People in the neighborhood association successfully resisted an effort by WUMCRC's former director-turned-developer to have 66 units built on that part of the site. They apparently saw the whole deal as something of a present to him. WUMCRC sold the land to its former director for $50,000 less than had been paid for it and agreed to build fewer units on it.

Perhaps the best illustration of WUMCRC's unwillingness to allow good principles to stand in the way of good politics came from that part of the redevelopment area in which no one had much interest: the Ranken neighborhood, a little six-block sliver of working-class residences that hangs from the bottom of the biggest portion of WUMCRC's area. The inclusion of this area was prompted by one of the neighborhood's residents and city's better-known power brokers, Joe Roddy. Roddy has served his constitutents and the Central Democratic Committee of St. Louis faithfully for the better part of his adult life. His price for assisting WUMCRC and seeing to it that WUMCRC's efforts met with no undue interference inside city hall was to have part of his neighborhood included in the redevelopment program.

There is nothing particularly exciting or even mildly interesting about the Ranken neighborhood. It has little that would lead one to think of it as a likely candidate for rehabilitation and certainly nothing that would inspire a medical center to embrace it as an investment site. Ranken had that tired, worn-out look common to many St. Louis neighborhoods. Some houses were abandoned; many were in need of substantial rehabilitation; a few people with professional pedigrees had moved into the area and begun the rough work of fixing up their own homes. Several would soon pool their money in order to purchase and rehabilitate a few houses so that other people with moderate or good incomes would move into the neighborhood.

In general, the neighborhood was pretty evenly split between its white and black oldtimers and relatively new black residents who had moved there after being displaced from one or another housing project or rehabilitated neighborhood. The only logical reason for the Medical Center to have adopted this neighborhood was that a number of people who worked as technicians or at less glamorous jobs in the hospitals lived in the neighborhood. Had it not been for Joe Roddy's gentle encouragement, the Medical Center would not have given the neighborhood a second thought, I was told.

The amount of money poured into the neighborhood has never been great. At first, WUMCRC refused to buy or sell any property there. Its contribution came in the form of special security patrols, preparing grant applications, closing a few residential streets, and building attractive brick entrance ways for these blocks. It was not until 1982 that WUMCRC established a fund that could be drawn from to acquire property from negligent owners. However, the $60,000 set aside for this purpose, $45,000 of which came from a neighborhood bank, was to be used to acquire a maximum of only twenty properties. By the summer of 1984, a total of fourteen properties had been improved or were in the process of being acquired through condemnation thanks to this modest investment; but the bank had been sold to people who withdrew their money. In 1985, WUMCRC was able to convince its confederates in Civic Progress to allow some of their $1.1 million loan to be used in the Ranken neighborhood. The additional $75,000 obtained in this way when combined with the $50,000 now contributed by WUMCRC brought the neighborhood's property acquisition fund up to $125,000. This is not a lot of money, but it had enabled WUMCRC to gain control of five more buildings by 1985 at a cost of approximately $70,000.

People who wanted WUMCRC to take a more active role in the neighborhood estimated that about fifteen to twenty additional buildings were waiting to be redeveloped on the blocks over which WUMCRC had authority in 1985. An equal number of similar buildings are on blocks that also are part of the neighborhood but not part of WUMCRC's territory. Many in the Ranken neighborhood's nascent middle-class population wanted to see WUMCRC extend its boundaries to include those blocks, so that the houses could be preserved under the redevelopment corporation's protective umbrella. Joe Roddy was interested in keeping a base of low-income residents to work with, people who had always been the backbone of his political operation.

These low-income black and white people were "his friends," and he tried to watch out for their interests as best he could. On the other hand, both he and WUMCRC's leaders saw a need for clearing out some of the "problem families" and improving the neighborhood. They quietly cooperated with local officials and police in an attempt to make life uncomfortable for these people in the hope that they would leave.

Until 1987, the result was something of a stalemate. The stalemate came to an end during the spring of 1987. Mayor Schoemehl announced a housing rehabilitation project that converted twenty row houses into ten townhouses in the Ranken neighborhood. The block on which this work took place is just outside WUMCRC's territory. However, WUMCRC played a major part in organizing the deal. City money helped to underwrite the cost of rehabilitating these buildings, whose sale price was under $65,000. As such, they benefitted low to moderate-income homebuyers.

The developer for this project also submitted a proposal to the CDA for assistance "in renovating eighteen more units in scattered-site two- and four-family buildings" in the Ranken neighborhood. These units were within WUMCRC's domain and were sold as condominiums for between $36,000 and $50,000. WUMCRC supported this proposal.[14]

Together, both projects will have an impact on the Ranken neighborhood. The housing produced will not be as fancy as some middle-class rehabbers would prefer. Yet it will go a long way in patching the holes in this predominately working-class neighborhood and preserving a workable racial and economic mix among its residents.

The problem is that neither Roddy nor the leaders of the Medical Center were prepared for everything they found once they struck their bargain. Yet, as they worked out some accommodation with the neighborhood's rehabbers, they addressed the biggest question that future redevelopers in St. Louis will have to address: How does one attract people with money to a neighborhood that needs them but does not need to be gutted or to lose its stable working-class population in order to be saved?

What WUMCRC Wrought

It is important to draw our attention to this question and, more generally, to how the great institutional investment represented in the Medical Center has been translated into more and better housing for people. It is important because one could easily lose sight of these matters in the crush of statistics that mark the area's passage from being rundown to becoming revitalized. Almost $396 million has been invested in and around the Medical Center since 1975.

The various projects undertaken with those funds were subsidized with $6.9 million from Civic Progress, the Medical Center, and the city of St. Louis. This $6.9 million represents a nonrecoverable investment, or loss if you prefer, by these parties. Most of it, some $4.2 million or 58 percent, has come from the Medical Center in the form of operating subsidies for WUMCRC and its property acquisition fund. The city spent $2.4 million on public improvements. Additional public funds went to individual housing developers and private homeowners who built or bought new housng in the area and to low-income renters.

With the expansion of the Medical Center and the attraction of new commercial firms, approximately 3,750 new jobs have been added to the area's employment base. In turn, the larger payroll has increased retail activity in the area, especially for the restaurants. Finally, $48.6 million has been spent on the new and rehabilitated housing.

All of this investing has and will produce new tax dollars for the city. WUMCRC officials estimate that between 1986 and 2020 the city will receive nearly $162 million from real estate and other taxes because of all this activity. Had redevelopment in and around the Medical Center not gone forward, that figure would be closer to $102 million. This assumes, of course, that property values and employment levels would have remained stable and not dropped. If WUMCRC's figures are correct, then the real estate taxes on abated properties coming back onto the tax rolls in 1986 and in succeeding years will be almost twice as great (i.e., $69.2 million) than they would have been otherwise; and other tax revenues (i.e., $92.4 million) would be 37 percent greater.

No matter how skeptically one chooses to treat these estimates, there is little doubt that redevelopment has brought more money into the area and will produce more taxes. Clearly, redevelopment activities do not have to be centered in the traditional central business district or the neighborhoods contiguous to it to work. Nor is it impossible to redevelop an area in which residential, commercial, and institutional tenants are thoroughly mixed, often on the same block and almost always around the corner from each other.

Frankly, the picture looks pretty bright for WUMCRC. It received permission from the Board of Aldermen in 1985 to continue its work for another decade; but it no longer will be able to grant twenty-five-year tax abatements, only ten-year abatements. Though the largest part of its work is completed, WUMCRC's leaders still see a lot of little things that can be done. They also would like to ensure that nothing happens to jeopardize the progress that already has been made.

A portion of WUMCRC's domain is now included in the city's large "enterprise zone" that occupies the better part of 7 square miles in midtown St.

Louis. A small shopping center opened in the area in May 1986; and several developers are now doing expensive customizing work on the remaining houses in WUMCRC's "$50,000-shell" portfolio. Several of these houses will be sold as office buildings.

The phrase *making the numbers work* often is used by developers when they describe the investments needed to make a project feasible. WUMCRC and the institutions supporting it have been able to make these numbers work very well indeed. They have brought in lots of money. They have made other numbers work as well, however. They have helped to change the area's population.

The population in and around the redevelopment area was changing before WUMCRC began its work. Some changes were consistent with what observers have come to expect in revitalizing areas; others were not.[15] In the future, WUMCRC will be seen as having contributed to both the expected and unexpected changes in the area's population.

Population losses preceded redevelopment here as they had in DeSoto-Carr and LaSalle Park. Again, the number of whites declined most noticeably; in the present case, the number of blacks in 1980 actually was rising or at least remaining fairly stable. The black share of the area's population had increased steadily after 1960. The 1990 Census probably will show some reversal of that trend because many whites have bought housing on the blocks contiguous to the Medical Center since the early 1980s.

Prior to 1980, the area had become less crowded. Housing vacancies actually increased between 1970 and 1980. Space was being made for the hospitals and development projects that eventually put more housing units in the area than had been there formerly. The surprising thing is that blacks were not pushed aside to make room for this new work. They never had been a large part of the population around the Medical Center and great pressure was exerted on WUMCRC so that blacks would not be displaced from the Ranken neighborhood.

This commitment was not taken lightly. The number of black families moving into Ranken increased dramatically during the 1970s. This kept stable the average household size and increased the number of young people in the area. When an area is being redeveloped heavily, as was the case around the Medical Center, one might expect those statistics to drop. No massive reclamation projects were undertken in Ranken, so the new black families stayed.

The presence of those persons also was revealed in occupational data. A greater portion of area residents were employed in clerical, sales, and service jobs after 1970. Most of the persons holding such jobs would have lived in or around Ranken. The persons who moved onto blocks closest to the Medical Center tended to have better jobs.

Too much should not be made of these statistics. It is not always the case that redeveloping areas experience substantial population losses or increases in the number of residents holding professional jobs. This happened in the WUMCRC area, and one can make sense of it in that context. Other things are harder to explain. The presence of a poor and relatively unskilled black population is one. A large number of renters as compared to homeowners is another. The Medical Center area, like DeSoto-Carr and LaSalle Park before it, had such anomalies. Yet, it also was redeveloped.

The presence of wealthy and well-connected sponsors, contemporary ecologists and Marxists would argue, certainly makes it easy to understand why the area was redeveloped. It does not explain why these institutions accepted an economically and racially mixed population in their territory. Let us assume, as most theorists do, that modern institutions have no interest in building such a community. The fact remains that the Medical Center did help to build one and did so as it pursued an ambitious and successful expansion program.

In truth, WUMCRC's contribution to racial integration was relatively passive. It did nothing to discourage lower-income blacks from staying in the Ranken neighborhood. WUMCRC was more aggressive in its efforts to attract expensive for-sale housing to the blocks contiguous to the Medical Center. Many more whites than blacks purchased this housing. Still, the overall effect of WUMCRC's work was to encourage the presence of a low-income white and black population in its territory and to bring in more well-to-do whites.

Most observers would have expected the hospitals to discourage any low-income persons from staying. Pluralism is not a predicted result of redevelopment. A community of relatively prosperous white homeowners is what theorists expect to find in an area once it has been rehabilitated.

Local politics helps to account for the unexpected result. The Medical Center's caretakers were more concerned about their expansion plans and losing money than they were about integration. Racial and economic integration could be accommodated, however, and it kept some important politicians happy. Sponsoring the construction of housing for the elderly made good political sense, too. It allowed WUMCRC to pursue more expensive projects with a clear conscience and no interference.

There has not been much grassroots organizing for or against WUMCRC's work since the early urban renewal plan was rejected by area leaders. Some homeowners near the hospitals wanted fewer houses built across the street from them. They managed to convince WUMCRC's officers that this was a good idea. Another group of white homeowners in the Ranken neighborhood, on the other hand, could not persuade WUMCRC to support a more ambitious rehabilitation program for their area. Grassroots groups representing low-income persons have not formed. One would have to conclude that less powerful groups have not been heard from in this area; but persons have organized successful campaigns against proposed redevelopment activities.

The Medical Center's accomplishments and mistakes were examined closely by would-be developers in other parts of St. Louis, just as WUMCRC watched what was going on in other areas. Information about builders, new city programs, and the latest political gossip was shared widely. Sometimes it was used poorly, but it never was ignored.

What WUMCRC did and how it worked, however, was not known by the general public. Its accomplishments and mistakes did not become part of a broader dialogue about rebuilding the city. If its work contributed to the public good in any substantial way, that message was not heard by many persons. Frankly, most everyone affiliated with redevelopment efforts in St. Louis prefers to keep it that way. Open discussions about such matters, in their view, can do them no good and some harm.

The Medical Center's officers accomplished what they set out to do. An important institutional anchor in the city's west end was stabilized and now is growing. The neighborhoods around it have had a similar experience. This is fine as far as it goes. Yet, it was as much in the Medical Center's interest to stabilize that part of St. Louis as it was in the city's interest to have it stabilized. The Medical Center has remained mute on the larger questions raised by its involvement in that part of town. In particular, it has tried not to become more involved in the Ranken area and issues related to its possible rehabilitation.

This is understandable, but too bad. It is not a question of money. The major institutions affiliated with the Medical Center have lots of money. It is more a matter of where they perceive their proprietary responsibilities end. The Medical Center took a fairly conservative position on that question and looked, at first, only to the area immediately contiguous to it.

Medical Center institutions had to be reminded on several occasions that they had assumed a larger role as public stewards when they began to rebuild the area around themselves. Their quick reversal on the urban renewal plan, reluctant inclusion of the Ranken neighborhood in the redevelopment area, ill-fated effort to expand over a major public thoroughfare, and campaign to donate clay for neighborhood gardens all speak to the Medical Center's acceptance of that fact. The Medical Center has been a fairly good proprietor and a reluctant steward. This would not surprise contemporary Marxists. Contemporary ecologists would shrug their shoulders and probably wonder why anyone cared.

The Medical Center's unwillingness to do more in the Ranken area reflects a tension in its roles as proprietor and steward. The irony is that the Medical Center did the right thing in Ranken by doing little. It stopped big changes from occurring in the neighborhood by refusing to contribute large sums of money to the area's rehabilitation. In effect, it forced those who wanted more done to reach an understanding with those who wanted less done. The result today is a neighborhood that is relatively stable and has a racially and economically mixed population. Neighborhood activists say that with very little effort the rundown blocks around them could be improved and stabilize Ranken further.

The significance of this missed opportunity cannot be overstated. There are many neighborhoods like Ranken throughout the city. Many have low-income black residents; and many have elderly, low-income white residents. Sooner or later, city leaders are going to be worrying about what to do with them. Some answers can be found in what was done in the Ranken neighborhood. Given the Medical Center's financial and political standing in the community, it is in a good position to show how these answers might be applied in a larger residential area.

PACKAGED REHABILITATION: THE PERSHING-WATERMAN AREA

What's in a Name?

The redevelopment area described in this chapter is known by two names. Most St. Louisans probably know it as DeBaliviere Place. The name is derived from the street on which the area's major commercial buildings were found (see Figure 5). In its heyday, the DeBaliviere Strip apparently was one of the more exciting entertainment districts in St. Louis. The other, less commonly used name for this part of town is the Pershing-Waterman area. The name is derived from the two major residential streets that run on an east-west axis through the neighborhood. The buildings on these streets, as well as several other blocks on the other side of DeBaliviere Avenue that also are part of the redevelopment area, were built during the late 1920s and early 1930s. They were apartment buildings. Some were only two or three stories tall and held six or eight dwelling units. Others were substantially taller and held as many as thirty to forty apartments.

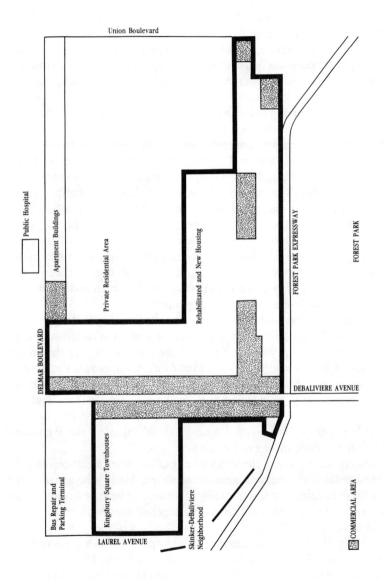

Figure 5. Pershing-Waterman Redevelopment Area

It was a predominantly middle-class neighborhood, built to accommodate smaller families whose senior members worked downtown. People rode to work on trolleys that ran from well beyond the city's western border, through this neighborhood and the rest of the city's midsection, and on into the central business district along the river's edge. There were few automobiles and little need for reserving parking spaces in the neighborhood. As a result, the neighborhood was densely populated. A few buildings along Pershing Avenue were reserved for businesses that catered to neighborhood residents. Virtually every other inch of space on better than twelve city blocks had housing built on it.

The reason for referring to this neighborhood as the Pershing-Waterman area is simple enough. It was along the residential blocks that this neighborhood's revitalization first took hold. People believe that the ultimate success or failure of this area will depend upon the redevelopment of the DeBaliviere strip. To this end a great deal of time and money has been spent, apparently successfully, to secure the reintroduction of light rail transportation on the tracks that run under and along the neighborhood's southern and western edges. Yet it will be several years before any updated trolley cars stop at the DeBaliviere station. Moreover, there is no guarantee that the new system will boost the neighborhood's commercial stock as much as is expected; though observers believe it will. If all of this does come to pass, however, it will only be because the area already had been reclaimed as a predominantly middle-class residential neighborhood.

The party most responsible for redeveloping the Pershing-Waterman area is the Pantheon Corporation, a local firm that specializes in commercial and residential rehabilitation work. It obtained the right to oversee the area's revitalization in 1976 when the city's Board of Aldermen approved Pantheon's redevelopment plan. When anyone is asked about redevelopment efforts in St. Louis, they are likely to mention the Pershing-Waterman area and its corporate benefactor. What they have to say usually is very positive or very negative. Few people have neutral feelings about the area, the Pantheon Corporation and its founder Leon Strauss.

Supporters point out that the area was all but lost when Pantheon took it over. Most buildings in the area were in bad shape. Many were abandoned. Some of those remaining at least partially occupied had become so dangerous that landlords refused to enter their own buildings to collect rents. In the words of one observer, it was a "war zone."

Opponents of Pantheon argue that the company displaced many low-income black people, some of whom had large families. The reason was simple, they believe. Pantheon's staff wanted to make huge profits by renting apartments or selling condominiums to high-income white people with few or no children. As far as Pantheon's critics are concerned, the "revitalization" of this area is part of a plan to clear blacks from the Central Cooridor, make it safe for investors and white residents, and protect the power base of the city's white political establishment. Pantheon has been so successful in its own territory, these people say, that now its directors also want to push low-income black people from the neighborhood just west of the redevelopment area.

The reasons why people express such strong feelings toward the Pantheon Corporation will be discussed in greater detail later. Whether one admires or despises the Pantheon Corporation, however, there is no denying that its work occupies a very special spot in the history of St. Louis' redevelopment. The rehabilitation industry, insofar as one can be said to exist in St. Louis, was conceived in the Pershing-Waterman area.

Pantheon's directors brought a wealth of experience to the Pershing-Waterman project. Some of it was their own. Some was borrowed from the experiences of other redevelopment areas. The lessons learned from these other areas proved especially useful, if only in terms of avoiding problems others had discovered first or been unable to avoid themselves. Foremost among these lessons, I was told, was the idea that one ought to control as much of a large area as possible. Great expense can be spared later on, if one holds title to many more buildings than can be worked on in the present.

The dilemma of being "victimized by your own success," it will be recalled, was something very much on the mind of people working in the WUMCRC area. In an odd way, it also affected the early rehabbers in LaSalle Park whose hard work inspired Mark Conner to build cheaper replicas of their grand old homes. This was not the only benefit coming to Pantheon by its ownership of most of the buildings in the redevelopment area. The ability to rehabilitate a series of buildings at a fairly brisk or consistent pace allowed them to reduce some costs. They could use the same window or plumbing features, appliances or carpeting in many apartment units, for instance, and this enabled them to purchase materials in large lots.

Much about the Pershing-Waterman area lent itself to being redeveloped. Many of the smaller apartment buildings and commercial structures were really quite lovely. Even the larger buildings had some handsome features that attracted the attention of persons interested in historic preservation work. The fact that so many pieces of property sharing these features were in the same small geographic area no doubt made the area difficult to ignore.

The neighborhood's location also was an important factor. Forest Park is just to its south, and DeBaliviere Avenue flows directly into a major entrance of the park anchored by a large memorial with a museum in it. Much of the neighborhood is bordered by the park, though separated from it by a four-lane street that sets atop ground that used to carry the old trolley line's tracks. A sunken rail spur emerges at DeBaliviere and moves north and west away from the neighborhood. The new trolley would run along this track and a station would be built to service both the neighborhood and Forest Park. This track does not really serve as the western boundary for the redevelopment area, because there are five good-sized blocks of residential properties between it and the formal western edge of the Pershing-Waterman redevelopment area. Also excluded from the redevelopment area are five blocks of large mansions set on deep lots.

The northern edge of the redevelopment area is bounded by a large street. On Pantheon's side of the road, it has two distinct sections. Its western section consists primarily of commercial buildings and a large facility for repairing and parking public buses. Its eastern section consists of more large apartment buildings, most of which the Pantheon Corporation has come to own. On the other side of the major boulevard that runs the whole length of this northern boundary is a large and predominantly black section of the city's Near Northside. There are a number of very nice blocks in this area. There also area many that are rundown.

Pantheon's work promises to redefine this situation by emphasizing the residential character of the Pershing-Waterman area. This is not likely to change once the empty commerical space along DeBaliviere is refilled. The types of businesses filling those buildings will be geared more for area residents than for a citywide clientele. There will be specialty food shops and a restaurant, among other things, and these businesses will attract the more well-to-do people who live in the area or are likely to move into it.

The Neighborhood's Decline

Those who know the area well say that it began to decline around the early 1940s. During this period, apartments in many buildings began to be cut into smaller units. In the absence of new housing construction, this was the only way to accommodate the city's growing population. It was something that happened across the city in single-family residences, including many larger houses in fancy neighborhoods, and buildings that had been designed for apartment living. Nevertheless, in a place such as Pershing-Waterman that already had many dwelling units, the effect of doubling or tripling the number of "apartments" was quite dramatic. A profound change began to occur in the Pershing-Waterman area's population. The number of families began to decline, and there was a corresponding increase in the number of unrelated adults living in these partitioned apartments.

Most of the property in the neighborhood came to be owned by people who no longer lived there or never had. These buildings tended to be among the first to fall into disrepair and, eventually, to be abandoned. Some buildings stayed in pretty good shape. These had resident owners who tried to maintain their buildings as best they could. This proved to be a very difficult chore in a neighborhood with a large transient and increasingly poorer population, especially for owners who, without exception, were growing quite old.

The residential blocks within the Pershing-Waterman area deteriorated a bit more during the 1960s, but their slide barely kept pace with that of DeBaliviere's strip. Indeed, by the late 1950s, more bars and striptease parlors had begun to make their way into the area. People were concerned. So much so that in the early 1960s a series of police raids was launched against many establishments along DeBaliviere Avenue. Other parts of the city acquired a reputation as being centers for nightlife entertainment, and the DeBaliviere strip became little more than a colorful piece of St. Louis' history.[1]

The last chapter of Pershing-Waterman's decline was written by the LCRA during the late 1960s and early 1970s. The LCRA had been relocating displaced black people in neighborhoods across the entire Near Northside for some time. These neighborhoods were not unlike Pershing-Waterman in the sense that they, too, had become rundown and showed signs of abandonment. Some of these people began to find their way into Pershing-Waterman. Just to the west, other federal housing programs were filling a number of residences in the Skinker-DeBaliviere neighborhood with low-income black persons.[2]

The situation was different on the private streets just east of the Pershing-Waterman area. There was little danger that low-income families would qualify for a mortgage to buy one of the mansions on these blocks. However, the value of those homes dropped precipitously during the 1960s and 1970s. It was possible to purchase most for less than $50,000. Those people who decided not to run took rather elaborate steps to ensure their safety. On either side of Pershing-Waterman, then, there was wholesale flight, property values were plummeting, and once stable neighborhoods were falling apart.

The decline of Pershing-Waterman was hastened and abetted by public policies and public agencies. The LCRA came to use the neighborhood as a relocation site for low-income black people displaced from public housing buildings closer to the downtown area. Many of these people came from the troubled Pruitt-Igoe complex just west of DeSoto-Carr as individual buildings at that site were closed.

By the early 1970s, the neighborhood's resident population was almost exclusively black. There were people in most of the buildings, I was told, but the vacancy rates also were high. "The average rents were $40 a month with the top being probably $75. This included the heating bill. There were drugs, pimps, prostitution, and sniping. Owners were afraid to go into buildings for fear of being shot. By the time Pantheon started buying buildings, maybe half of the residents were paying no rent, and there were at least ten buildings that even the police were afraid to enter."

Businesses and residents trying to carry on as normal an existence as possible under these circumstances found it tough. Robberies and assaults were routine. Attempts by a "civil rights group," known as the *Black Liberation Front,* to extort money from area business persons were quietly ignored by most everyone, and landlords found it difficult to resist the group's requests for them to rent apartments to blacks. No one really controlled Pershing-Waterman any longer, though.

"Take-back Time"

No one maintains that Pershing-Waterman was a safe or especially wholesome place to live and work after the mid-1960's. Yet, many people were upset when the Pantheon Corporation began to work in the area. Pershing-Waterman was unquestionably a low-income, black neighborhood by the time it was handed over to the Pantheon Corporation in 1976. That the neighborhood had not been so for very long and was a mess was, in the view of Pantheon's critics, quite irrelevant. White people had abandoned the area. Public agencies had encouraged, even compelled, black people to move into it.

I was told that a developer who controlled a number of buildings in the neighborhood had accepted Pruitt-Igoe's refugees, taken the relocation money his tenants were to have received because they were displaced, collected what rent money he could, and failed to maintain his buildings or pay for things like utility bills and property taxes. Then, when his tenants stopped paying their rents, he would turn off their power and gas and evict them. Some developers and public officials discretely concede these points and added, even more quietly, that this same developer had acquired the redevelopment rights for part of the Pershing-Waterman area.

Many people told me that it was Strauss's bad luck to have been tied up with "that other developer." Still, they quickly noted, "he might not have been there otherwise to pick up the pieces after the other guy failed." On the heels of that failure, Strauss "bought a few buildings...to see if the price was low enough that he could feasibly rehabilitate them, and...to see if the present landlords could make any money off them as they were, doing only the necessary maintenance." He discovered that the owners could not keep their buildings open, maintain them, and hope to make any money. He tried it in one building for eight months and lost $11,000. On the other hand, the buildings could be gutted and rebuilt from the inside out for a sum small enough to ensure that the developer could make a profit.[3] To do this, however, one would have to control the buildings in most of the area. To have worked on only a few sites, while most of the buildings in the 106-acre tract were rundown and owned by someone else, would have been a futile gesture.

This was all well and good, but Strauss was beginning to formulate his plan for the area at a bad time. Mayor John Poelker and his CDA director, John Roach, were being criticized harshly for "their plan" to redevelop parts of the Central Corridor while ignoring predominantly black North St. Louis. Roach already was disliked by many blacks who knew of his role in stopping the sale of homes to low-income blacks and engineering their repurchase by whites in the Skinker-DeBaliviere neighborhood. While Alderman for this part of the Central West End, Roach had helped to create the CDA, which many blacks distrusted. Now, it was alleged, Roach and the mayor wanted to allow the Pantheon Corporation to "toss out all the blacks" in Pershing-Waterman. When Poelker had Pantheon's redevelopment proposal approved in his last year as mayor, it was taken as the final proof that such a plan did exist and that "it was take-back time" in St. Louis. When Roach went to work for Pantheon after being replaced as head of the CDA, it only made the critics angrier.

It took a while, but Legal Aid attorneys managed to find some people displaced from Pershing-Waterman to file a suit. Among those named as defendants were the Department of Housing and Urban Development, the city, Pantheon, and a real estate firm. It was alleged that Pantheon eventually would displace over 800 households, many with several children, and had failed to compensate adequately those already moved for their moving expenses. Furthermore, it was argued, Pantheon had no intention of providing replacement housing for low-income blacks once its work was underway. Federal laws were available to protect such people and to see that they received quite healthy sums of money to aid them in their search for a new dwelling. These laws, they said, should have been enforced because CDBG funds had been used to support Pantheon's work. This public subsidization of a private venture had transformed Pantheon into a "quasi-public" entity and made it liable for paying higher relocation benefits.

Chief U.S. district judge James H. Meredith disagreed. He did not see how the displaced tenants had been irreparably harmed by Pantheon's activities or why they should qualify for higher relocation benefits. He had taken note of Pantheon's willingness to allow some families to stay in their apartments rent-free while they searched for new housing and Pantheon's policy not to force people out during the winter months or cut off their utilities. Meredith's decision in November 1978 was upheld by a three-judge panel of the 8th U.S. Circuit Court of Appeals in June 1979. That panel had seen no evidence of Pantheon using its eminent domain power to displace anyone.[4]

Pantheon's critics continued to insist that it played dirty: harassing tenants, boarding up their buildings, even tossing some out onto the street. Maybe Pantheon never did use its power of eminent domain to take over a building that still had tenants; but critics maintained that it used that power to threaten landlords to have them evict the tenants. Pantheon would have initiated court proceedings against any owner that had not complied and probably obtained the building for much less that it had agreed to pay.

There is no doubt that Pantheon played rough. People who know the area well, however, say that Pantheon only gave as good as it received. A number of owners tried to inflate the value of their buildings before entering into negotiations with Pantheon by filling it with tenants. Though these tenants paid little or no rent, the owner presented Pantheon with what appeared to be a full house and jacked up the price at which the owner was willing to sell the building. Pantheon's officers knew this was going on, so they did not fall for the ploy. Instead, they countered with what they considered to be a fair price and, as already mentioned, said that the owner could take it or leave it. Because the owners had no great sense of loyalty to their tenants, they usually took what Pantheon offered and evicted the people living in the building. Many tenants allegedly were aware of how they were being used and did not object. With any luck at all, "they could live in a place almost rent-free for six months or more before getting bounced. And some people did this several times," one Pantheon booster said. So, many people went along with the game. These people, I was told, were not treated especially well by Pantheon.

Other owners and tenants apparently were treated better. Pantheon left several owner-occupied buildings alone because they had been maintained. Pantheon's caretakers saw no need to weaken the neighborhood further by acquiring and emptying a building whose major defect was that it looked a little rundown. Some owners were quite anxious to sell their building. Tenants who were not troublemakers and cooperated with Pantheon were given some relocation assistance. Some were relocated on the periphery of the redevelopment area in a part of the Skinker-DeBaliviere neighborhood that is now being contested and where Pantheon as well as several other parties bought vacant or rundown buildings. Other tenants were relocated in areas far removed from Pershing-Waterman. One of these was the Ranken neighborhood that is part of WUMCRC's territory.

Estimates vary of just how many people Pantheon relocated or displaced. No good data are available to substantiate any of the estimates. Pantheon's lawyers contended during the trial that there had been 500 households in the area when the corporation was given its redevelopment charter in 1976. By 1978, they said about 150 households remained vulnerable to displacement. Legal Aid Society lawyers, citing numbers from Pantheon's own redevelopment plan, maintained that the 1976 figure should be closer to 850; and that figure did not cover all of the redevelopment area. What can be said with certainty is that the area was being abandoned rapidly. Pantheon's acquisition of property only accelerated this process and in doing so probably spared a few buildings from being ruined more than they already were.

An Inner-City Levittown?

The revival of Pershing-Waterman as a residential neighborhood depended upon Pantheon's success in rehabilitating apartment and condominium units. The key to Pantheon's success was organization. In Pantheon, Strauss created something that comes about as close to being the "complete development firm" as one can find. About the only thing that Pantheon did not have the capacity to do was provide long-term financing for its projects. Pantheon was a big developer, having rehabilitated over 1,300 housing units and a whole block of commercial buildings in the Pershing-Waterman area alone between 1976 and 1983. During this same period, it was working in other parts of the city, including DeSoto-Carr. Pantheon also was the largest development firm in the city until it was sold in the late 1980s. Prior to that, it established a rather complex corporate genealogy in only a few years.

There are many ways one might describe what Pantheon tried to do in the Pershing-Waterman area. Basically, it manufactured rehabilitated apartment units and condominums for middle-income people. In its own way, Pantheon's work complemented that of another housing manufacturer, Levitt and Sons, Inc., that did its most important work after World War II.[5]

Strauss obtained much financial assistance from the city and one local bank. This enabled him to manufacture rehabilitated apartments and condominiums in lovely old buildings more cheaply than his suburban competitors could construct firsthand in new buildings. Matters of price and attractiveness aside, Strauss still had to find people willing to rent or buy a place to live in a neighborhood whose reputation was anything but good. Hard work and a lot of "creative marketing" were the primary tools used to counter the bad feelings people still held about the neighborhood. Most of the hard work was put into creative marketing. Several of Pantheon's staff attended a lot of cocktail parties. There were free meals in popular Central West End restaurants and many informal chats with friends and people in the "artsy, socialite set," I was told.

Stocking rehabilitated buildings with "beautiful people" was as important to the neighborhood's apparent revival as packing rundown buildings with low-income blacks, who also paid little or no rent and had short-term leases, had been to the neighborhood's last descent. Both were part of an illusion that indicated something about the viability of Pershing-Waterman as a residential neighborhood. Both served a purpose, and both moved on. In so doing, they made room for many people who probably would have felt comfortable in the neighborhood fifty years earlier. There probably are more homosexuals and college students in it now. There certainly are more blacks and elderly white people living on fixed incomes. Nevertheless, the vast majority of people living in the area today are middle class and either live alone or have very small families. They are, in short, the kind of persons for whom the neighborhood had been constructed seventy years ago.

Strauss, like Levitt before him, had done his homework and thought he knew the kinds of people who eventually would buy or rent his housing. Pantheon's officers "saw that the private streets had sold out and that young professionals, especially women, were coming into the marketplace. Lenders had become more willing to give money to unmarried couples and singles. Yet there was no product to sell to those folks. Single-family houses were too large and too expensive to maintain, and there was a shortage of good apartments" in this part of town. No one in the city had done much with condominiums at this time either, so Strauss decided to mix buildings with condos among those with apartments.

Suburban developers such as Levitt had enjoyed a special partnership with the federal government, which offered builders "billions of dollars of credit and insured loans up to 95 percent of the value of the house." They also easily qualified for the FHA "production advances" that were paid to them even before homes were purchased and, in Levitt's case, commitments to finance thousands of houses before the land was even cleared.[6] When combined with their ability to buy large tracts of land cheaply, such federal incentives gave suburban developers a great competitive advantage over smaller building firms and anyone who would have dared to build in a central city. Cheap land and good financing were important elements in the suburban development game. They proved no less so for Pantheon and other St. Louis city developers. The great deterioration experienced in Pershing-Waterman and other St. Louis neighborhoods reduced the value of the land and buildings enough to make these places attractive for entrepreneurs such as Strauss to redevelop. Local governments helped developers by selling them land and buildings at greatly discounted prices.

The availability of money to finance these redevelopment projects was also something that made work in inner-city neighborhoods feasible. For a long time, many banks had refused to make any kind of loans in neighborhoods such as Pershing-Waterman. It would have been impossible to redevelop them, even if people like Strauss had wanted to do so. Now, long-term financing was available and suburban developers no longer enjoyed a privileged position with all lenders.

Federal dollars helped to improve the streets, curbs, and parks in the area. Such improvements doubtlessly save the redeveloper money and make the product easier to market. Suburban developments usually lacked such "public pretties" of an older city neighborhood. If they did not lack them, then the cost of improvements to the public spaces around new housing developments was reflected in the price of each house. The renters and condominium buyers in Pershing-Waterman did not have to absorb those costs. Nor did the people who bought the new single-family homes that Pantheon started building in the area. These latter people also took advantage of a property tax abatement scheme designed to encourage the construction and purchase of new housing in the city.

There was an understandable tendency on the part of some redevelopment critics in the city to dismiss all such tax savings and public improvements as sops to middle-class white people. The federal government, they pointed out, always subsidized middle-income housing more generously than housing for low-income and minority people. Nevertheless, in some city neighborhoods such as Pershing-Waterman the federal government's resources have been used to encourage racial and economic mixing to an extent unknown in most new suburban developments. This was not done by accident but as part of a plan to build more integrated neighborhoods.

In the case of Pershing-Waterman, over 25 percent of the housing units rehabilitated or built brand-new by Pantheon went to low-income people who had part of their monthly rent paid by the federal government. These subsidies will not last forever; and they help Pantheon by providing it a dependable source of rental income. Moreover, critics argued, one would be hard pressed to find any low-income blacks receiving this assistance. Much of it went to elderly Jewish people who emigrated from the Soviet Union.

Blacks live in Pershing-Waterman today, though they probably account for less than 25 percent of the resident populaton and definitely are not from the same social strata as those who helped to give the area a bad reputation. Just over 27 percent of Pantheon's renters are black. The renters in general seem to be young, single, childless, and in occupations that someday may earn them high salaries. For the time being, however, only about 20 percent of Pantheon's renters earn more than $25,000 a year. The condominium owners are more well-to-do. Over half earn more than $25,000 yearly.[7] The neighborhood today probably is more racially and economically mixed *and* stable than it has ever been. Few suburban communities can claim to be so balanced, Pantheon's supporters argued.

This did not satisfy many local critics of redevelopment. Some were opposed in principle to anything that weakened the political base of a black population. Blacks in St. Louis, they argued, have been weakened by being moved around almost continually since the late-1950s. Blacks also lose a measure of leverage when they become a numerical minority in a neighborhood dominated by whites. What happened in Pershing-Waterman led some critics to see its redevelopment as part of a bigger scheme intended to stop the flow of blacks into "white" parts of the city and, if possible, to reverse that process. Those critics not ideologically opposed to integregation complained that the kind of racial and economic mixing found in a place like Pershing-Waterman was not the right or best kind. They would have preferred to see more low-income black people in the area, and that those blacks be the same ones who were displaced when Pantheon took over.

In response to arguments such as these, Pantheon's defenders simply throw up their hands. The complaints are not taken seriously, and the complainers are dismissed as "leftist crackpots." "We have a major problem with race in this society," one developer told me, "but Pantheon or any other developer can't be expected to solve it. No way Pantheon could have kept those people in those buildings and made the project work. And there was no way Pantheon was going to bring them back after the damage they did. That would have been crazy." At the same time, it is apparent even to Pantheon's biggest boosters that its work did stop and reverse the spread of low-income blacks into this part of the Central Corridor. It also is clear to them that a succession of such neighborhood reversals would inhibit the growth of a black majority on the Board of Aldermen and reduce the chances of electing a black mayor.

"Building on Strength"

As long as Pantheon rehabilitated old buildings with assembly-line efficiency this worked well enough. When Pantheon tried to turn part of the area into a suburban oasis, however, the results were not nearly so good. At issue was what to do with a corner of the redevelopment area set apart by a block or two from the older apartment buildings along Pershing and Waterman Avenues. This section is tucked behind some of the commercial buildings on the old DeBaliviere strip, so it is easy enough to miss. The streets of this subdivision no longer reach into the Skinker-DeBaliviere neighborhood immediately to its west, they have been closed to traffic from that end. So the only way in or out of the subdivision is through a single well-marked, but otherwise inconspicuous, hole in DeBaliviere that announces you are at Kingsbury Square.

The name and everything about the place is new. It was the most bombed out part of Pershing-Waterman when Pantheon took over. Many of its two-and four-family houses already had been demolished, and those few left standing apparently were not worth saving even by Pantheon's generous standards. The decision was made to tear down the remaining structures and start over. The plan was to make Kingsbury Square into the city's first new subdivision in twenty years. It would have 100 units of for-sale housing built into 50 attached townhouses. Each two or two-and-one-half story house was to be outfitted with all the modern conveniences found in modern suburban dwellings, while being blessed with lower prices, abated property taxes, and the possibility of its owner qualifying for additional grant money from the Community Development Agency. Back in 1979 when the first houses became available they were sold for between $75,00 and $95,000. The same houses— each has three bedrooms and two and one-half bathrooms—were selling for $98,000 to $114,000 by early 1985. Plans to make some houses slightly larger and add more amenities promised to drive up the price.

All of this sounded very good at the outset, but Kingsbury Square has been plagued with at least three major problems. First, the development opened when interest rates for mortgages were beginning to rise dramatically. Whatever momentum housing sales might have received from being attached to an area "on its way back" was quickly dissipated when interest rates hit 18 percent. Pantheon stopped building houses in 1981 and offered another firm the rights to build in the area. Only twenty houses had been built by then, and those units looked mighty lonesome in the great expanse of vacant land that was to be Kingsbury Square. Second, the houses themselves have nothing in common with the buildings on surrounding blocks. Their unique appearance is more reminiscent of a modern Cape Cod beach house than something one would expect to find in a small midwestern town.[8] Third, the houses are relatively more expensive than the bigger, older, and more traditional looking brick homes in the Skinker-DeBaliviere neighborhood. Kingsbury Square's single-family homes, in effect, are overpriced for this part of the city and are likely to remain so. For all of these reasons, Kingsbury Square has developed more slowly than had been planned.

Kingsbury Square does provide a buffer between the bulk of the redevelopment area and the troubled blocks just west of it called *Nina Place*. The same penchant for building itself safe borders, combined with the idea of making money, drove Pantheon to acquire a whole block of large, rundown apartment buildings above its northern edge. These buildings back up against the private residential streets just east of the redevelopment area.

If, as one person suggested, Pantheon had toyed with the idea of leveling the buildings and leaving a big park in their place, it could not have been considered too long or too seriously. That just was not Pantheon's style. Besides, "there was talk" that something might be done with the privately run hospital across the street from this set of buildings. The city had been looking at alternative ways to provide health care for indigent people for some time, and officials had decided not to continue using an older city hospital near

LaSalle Park. They also had been searching for a way to combine the city's programs with those of St. Louis County. The private hospital seemed to be an ideal place to relocate everything. It was newer, more centrally located, and its owners were losing a great deal of money trying to keep it open. They seemed especially willing to sell out to the city after the mayor threatened to acquire the hospital by using the power of eminent domain.

Once the deal was cut, the hospital became the St. Louis Regional Medical Center and the apartment buildings across the street became more valuable pieces of real estate. Some people living in the large mansions behind these buildings feared that this kind of hospital might hurt their neighborhood. Their objections were politely noted and ignored. Its clientele notwithstanding, Pantheon's supporters maintained that the hospital will serve as an institutional anchor for the whole area.

One observer used the phrase "pecking on the fringes" to describe what Pantheon had done in Nina Place and on the block across from the hospital. Many of the buildings on these blocks had deteriorated badly. The effort to improve them was not crucial to the success of Pantheon's work in the Pershing-Waterman redevelopment area. It did provide a measure of protection for Pantheon's earlier efforts, however. It also pushed back a bit further the unredeveloped "frontier" of the city's Near Northside. Any further redevelopment projects in that predominantly black section of St. Louis would build on the strength of Pershing-Waterman's revival.

Pantheon's critics feared that the corporation, or some other redevelopment firm, would proceed to gobble up big chunks of the Near Northside and displace more black people. It is unlikely that any firm would be able to accomplish such a feat, much less try, because many strong residential blocks are in the area. People simply would not tolerate the kind of redevelopment blitz that occurred in Pershing-Waterman, even if it were necessary. Furthermore, the enthusiasm of local public officials for big residential rehabilitation projects has waned, and there is likely to be much less federal support for urban rebuilding programs in the future.

Pershing-Waterman's Significance

Pershing-Waterman's decline began a long time before low-income blacks were relocated there during the 1960's. Indeed, they were relocated there precisely because the area already was rundown and being abandoned. Their presence only made a bad situation worse.

In the fifteen years prior to Pershing-Waterman's reclamation, the area's population changed dramatically.[9] It went from being virtually all white to over 60 percent black. The percentage of young persons almost doubled. The number of residents who worked actually increased for a while. However, many more now were working in less skilled service, clerical, and sales jobs. The vacancy rate in housing more than doubled.

The population changed even more quickly in the mid-1970s, when efforts to redevelop the area began in earnest. The number of residents started to decline, as buildings were sold and tenants moved on to other places. Altogether, nearly 4,000 blacks left the area; but the losses were especially great among young blacks. Nevertheless, blacks in 1980 still constituted over 60 percent of the area's population. That figure could have dropped a good deal durig the 1980s, because property still was being assembled for redevelopment and the population was very mobile. Evidence to this effect was seen in an even higher rate of vacancies and the loss of nearly 2,000 apartment units.

The situation remained unsettled into the early 1980s. However, there were signs that early efforts to reclaim the area were having some effect. A dramatic decrease already was occurring in the number of reported crimes. The percent of renter-occupied housing dropped as well; but this probably had more to do with the destruction of some apartment buildings than any increase in homeownership. A real increase in homeownership came shortly afterward, as old apartments were turned into rehabilitated condominiums. Finally, the portion of the resident population employed in professional and technical jobs increased substantially during the 1970s. Here, too, the increase was only relative. The number of residents holding such jobs actually decreased during the 1970s, but the number holding less sophisticated jobs dropped quite a bit more. A change in the character of the area was real nonetheless. It was becoming more prosperous by losing its less prosperous residents. The first steps in Pershing-Waterman's revival were being taken.

The last steps in its revival will be filled with nearly as much uncertainty as were its first. The dangers and risks may be different, but there still are problems. The ultimate success of Pershing-Waterman as a good neighborhood *and* investment site is by no means guaranteed by the mere fact that the area looks healthy.

The long-term stability of a neighborhood like this one—a neighborhood whose population is still potentially very mobile—depends on its ability to generate capital to keep redevelopment efforts going and the neighborhood viable. If a lot of rich people were living in it, they would be property owners who had a stake in keeping the whole enterprise moving forward. Unfortunately, this neighborhood has comparatively few property owners (better than 80 percent of the units Pantheon rehabilitated are rented, not owned) and even fewer rich people.

Pantheon has had to subsidize each new stage in Pershing-Waterman's reclamation with some of the profits it earned from earlier projects. It has even sold off a number of buildings to maintain its earlier momentum and, quite frankly, to support its work in other parts of the city. The neighborhood is not yet able to sustain itself socially or economically. It has to depend upon Pantheon to see that enough new money comes into the area. Without such ongoing support the neighborhood will not be fully redeveloped. Nor is it likely to reach a point at which area residents and businesses will be able to generate the money needed to keep the whole enterprise running more or less on its own.

A number of small businesses that moved into the neighborhood have failed, despite receiving breaks on their rents from Pantheon. In several cases, it appears that the owners simply were not very good at business. Other businesses that could have done well, I was told, failed because neighborhood residents simply did not shop there in large enough numbers.

If a critical number and mix of shops is required to push this neighborhood's commercial life over some unknown threshold, Pantheon has yet to find it. This probably helps account for the great emphasis placed on rebuilding DeBaliviere's commercial strip by most neighborhood business owners with whom I spoke. It most certainly helps to explain Pantheon's eagerness to see that project move ahead even though the rights to the property were sold to another developer. Pantheon's attention to commercial redevelopment is not misplaced. A revitalized DeBaliviere strip filled with attractive specialty shops, restaurants, and people from the neighborhood and hospital would help to bring the area to the point of self-sufficiency.

In the meantime, Pantheon continues to subsidize its newer work in and around the area and indirectly the work of other developers, as well as the neighborhood as a whole. It has done this, as I noted, by selling its apartment buildings. A number of buildings that had not been rehabilitated were sold to developers beginning in the early 1980s. In fact, Pantheon no longer owns the apartment buildings it rehabilitated. Ownership was passed early on to a number of people all over the country who invested their money through a company known as the National Housing Partnership.

This is not the only way in which Pantheon has sought to subsidize the continuing redevelopment of Pershing-Waterman and, in the process, to protect its investments, and keep itself well fed. It also "tithes" approximately 10 percent of its profits each year to a variety of institutions and political campaigns. Several of the institutions in question are private schools that provide area parents with an alternative to the city's primary and secondary public schools.

The assistance provided politicians by developers such as Pantheon has always been received warmly. Not everyone would agree that this assistance yields good results, however. One of these skeptics was Bertha Gilkey who, because of her work in Cochran, became an advocate for low-income tenants throughout the city. She assisted the "civil rights group" Freedom of Residence in its fight to limit the displacement of blacks from Nina Place. Some neighborhood leaders, including the ward's political leaders, objected to Gilkey's intrusion in a part of town far removed from DeSoto-Carr. They noted her ongoing battle with the mayor at that time and her own unsuccessful efforts to gain a seat on the Board of Aldermen as reasons for her involvement.

The matter of personal grudges aside, it was clear that many people would have preferred to see the number of low-income blacks in Nina Place susbtantially reduced. Other neighborhood residents, with Gilkey's assistance, objected to this idea. There was nothing neat or clean about this argument, and the compromise worked out testifies to that fact. The most terribly neglected buildings would be rehabilitated, and their black residents would have have to move. Less rundown sites would be immune from the plan to improve Nina Place, at least for the time being.

The idea of redeveloping a neighborhood without moving its low-income minority residents was still novel. Most developers really do not have the luxury of working with well-organized groups of low-income, black entrepreneurs such as those in DeSoto-Carr. Pantheon's boosters talk a good deal about "building in the shadow of public housing" when discussing the Columbus Square apartments and townhouses sponsored by the firm in DeSoto-Carr. They also know, however, that the area had become a lot safer than most people believed.

Nevertheless, it has not been easy for Pantheon to make money off those apartments and integrate the neighborhood with white renters. "It would be a snap to fill the units with middle-income blacks," one person told me. "And, there are a number of them in the complex. But Pantheon wanted to show that white people would live downtown in a predominantly black neighborhood." So, the firm kept a good number of units "reserved" for whites.

This is an expensive gesture, especially for a firm alleged to be so consumed by the desire to make money that no one is allowed to resist it. "Most prospective black renters, if they question the practice at all, understand and even appreciate what Pantheon is trying to do," I was told. Some do not, though, and Pantheon has had to reach more than one quiet settlement with an angry black customer who wanted to live in Columbus Square. "Sooner or later," one observer noted, "Pantheon may be forced to rent those apartments to qualified blacks simply because of the expense involved. In the meantime, however, not even HUD is complaining loudly about this practice. Everyone wants to see if the experiment can work." The same thing was tried in the

O'Fallon Place apartment complex, and it worked for a while. Informed observers said, however, that the number of white families gradually declined.

Pantheon has tried to bring whites and blacks together in its projects, but they tend to be fairly well-to-do persons. It has not tried to bring many lower-income black and middle-income white persons together in its own projects. When Pantheon found an area with a well-disciplined group of low-income black people in it, the firm did not hesitate to work there or to encourage whites to move in. When Pantheon found a poorly organized and threatening collection of low-income blacks in or near one of its project areas, the firm did not hesitate to move against those people.

The residential mix in Pershing-Waterman increased a bit in the fall of 1987 whent Pantheon rented fifty-three apartments to upperclassmen from nearby Washington University. Campus dormitories were overcrowded, and the 100 or so students who moved into the neighborhood had a portion of their rent paid by the university. Perhaps because its population is so well mixed, the neighborhood no longer is a place where the question of bringing together people from varied backgrounds generates much excitement. This is a good thing in some ways, but not so good in other ways.

The only people seen walking through the neighborhood or sitting on park benches on anything approaching a routine basis, for instance, are younger black people and the retired people brought in by Pantheon. Everyone else living in the neighborhood, one long-time observer noted, "treats it like a large bedroom suburb." The only time one sees a good number of people milling about is during the summer months when people are playing tennis or swimming in one of several pools. Otherwise, "the yuppies don't come out."

Organized community activities are nonexistent. Organized complaints about rent increases are brief and polite. Pantheon has done almost too good a job at putting together a residential population that gets along well. There are no apparent issues likely to capture the attention of area residents any time soon; and this ambivalence is evident in the residents' reluctance to shop in the area. Life in Pershing-Waterman is quiet and safe.

This may be reason enough for celebration, given the stormy history of the neighborhood. Places like Pershing-Waterman may represent one way to build more racially and economically mixed residential areas inside cities. Pershing-Waterman has a great variety of people, but it is not the type of neighborhood where low-income minorities are likely to find a home.

If Pershing-Waterman is not as exciting or engaging as some people would prefer, it does provide a stable anchor for residential areas surrounding it. Yet, the very serenity of Pershing-Waterman has retarded its growth as a complete neighborhood. It had been hoped that the commercial space along Pershing Boulevard would be filled with shopkeepers catering to neighborhood residents. This has not happened. People simply do not treat the area like an inner-city neighborhood. They do not walk, dawdle, socialize, or shop in the neighborhood. They do treat it like a suburb, by and large. In the long run, the Pantheon Corporation may come to see that it created a place that was too quiet.

This possibility notwithstanding, many persons believe that Pantheon did a respectable job of preserving the neighborhood's integrity. It chose one way to deal with an area that was not yet gutted or abandoned. Pantheon's approach encountered stiff legal opposition, but the corporation did prevail.

Despite many apparent signs of success, Pershing-Waterman's reclamation violates several key assumptions that we tend to make when discussing what types of neighborhoods are redeveloped. The neighborhood had no ethnic identification or experience with home ownership. There was no institutional anchor or commercial area to breathe life into it. It had a well-earned reputation for being dangerous. By most conventional measures, therefore, Pershing-Waterman probably should not have been rehabilitated. Yet it was.

The irony is that this neighborhood's redevelopment in many ways is easier to explain than that of DeSoto-Carr, LaSalle Park, or the Washington University Medical Center area. Contemporary ecologists and Marxists would point to the collaboration of a developer and a big bank in planning and financing the reclamation project. They would have expected politicians to cooperate because the area was so near other valuable sections of town. Lots of public assistance was requested and granted, all but guaranteeing that the developer and bank would make money. Low-income blacks were pushed out. Middle-class persons, especially whites, were actively courted as new residents. In many ways, Pershing-Waterman's revival might be read as a typical urban renewal story.

Missing from this superficial summary, however, are the many problems and quirks in the neighborhood's redevelopment that made it anything but a typical case of urban renewal. The politics and economics of rebuilding this area were not as straightforward as portrayed in the last paragraph. Moreover, far from being an unqualified success, there still are many things not quite right in Pershing-Waterman.

The last steps of Pershing-Waterman's revival may be hurt by the very thing that prompted its comeback in the first place, and that is its quiet middle-class character. Early on, the Pantheon Corporation marketed the area as a "hot spot" and drew in renters on that basis. After a while, the true character of the new Pershing-Waterman began to sneak through and Pantheon had to compete with every other developer trying to rent or sell housing to the city's and county's new middle-class households. It is possible that in some instances Pantheon's projects in different parts of the city actually competed for the same customers. Pantheon also tends to charge fairly stiff rents in the Pershing-Waterman area or command high prices for the property it sells to other developers. Whatever the cause, the effect is the same. Units stand empty. Prospective renters or buyers demand substantial discounts. Businesses catering to more well-to-do persons do not have enough customers.

The revival has hit a plateau. Perhaps the introduction of a light rail train station in the neighborhood will help bring more customers and prosperous residents. Or, interest rates on mortgages could rise again and keep more persons in rental housing. One or both things could help the Pershing-Waterman area.

The problem is not that Pershing-Waterman is segregated on the basis of race or income, far from it. Pershing-Waterman today has a more stable mix of persons from different ages, races, income levels, and life-styles than at any other time in its history. A degree of pluralism has been achieved in the neighborhood's population, but it is pluralism with a distinctly middle-class edge to it.

Pershing-Waterman is a fairly viable neighborhood; but not a particularly vital place. It shows that a redeveloped neighborhood can bring persons from different backgrounds together and that these persons can live in relative peace and harmony. This is no mean accomplishment. At the same time, Pershing-Waterman is not a place where groups unaccustomed to being part of the political process had much voice or impact. Extending equality and efficacy to such groups was definitely not part of the plan to redevelop Pershing-Waterman. Given the population of low-income persons left in the neighborhood when Pantheon took over, it probably was unrealistic to think that they could have had such a role. Nonetheless, these qualities of "good" redevelopment are missing in Pershing-Waterman.

It is precisely for this reason that what happened in Pershing-Waterman provoked a broader discussion about "good" and "bad" redevelopment in St. Louis. There was sensitivity to the plight of low-income minority residents in redevelopment areas, even when it was difficult to have much sympathy for the specific individuals involved. Whether one agreed with the solution worked out in Pershing-Waterman really did not matter. The persons at risk already were gone, and the outline for the area's reclamation already was set. What mattered was that Pershing-Waterman's reclamation forced St. Louisans to consider the social costs and benefits of redeveloping an area in a particular way.

In this sense, the redevelopment of Pershing-Waterman made an important contribution to future rebuilding efforts in St. Louis. It brought together property owners and renters, young and old persons, white-collar and working-class people, whites and blacks, straights and gays in an area with rehabilitated and new housing. It may have provided no good lessons on how to integrate low-income minority groups into the postindustrial city. On the other hand, it did show that persons worried about this problem and that the Pershing-Waterman solution was not popular in some quarters. This problem received more serious attention in the last of our five redevelopment areas.

BROKEN PROMISES:
THE MIDTOWN MEDICAL CENTER
REDEVELOPMENT AREA

Some people involved in the city's redevelopment saw a connection between the kinds of businesses and institutions that would become the backbone of a new St. Louis and the kind of community that could grow around them. Mayor Conway made the connection explicit during his term in office. He subsidized the creation of mixed neighborhoods in a self-conscious way. Others, such as Ralston Purina, did it because they had been told it was a good idea. Developers might have done it because it was the only way to shake money loose from the city government to keep the rebuilding boom going and themselves fed. Whatever the reasons involved, the redevelopment of the city's midsection carried with it a serious commitment to build more integrated neighborhoods.

Many persons, including those affiliated with the companies and institutions sponsoring redevelopment areas, are well-pleased and at times even surprised by the outcome of their work so far. Other persons, including those who object to any further disruptions of segregated neighborhoods, are neither surprised nor pleased with this work. Local people on either side of this issue see redevelopment as a good or bad thing. The claim that redevelopment benefits the whole city is tough to believe when neighborhoods are being reduced to rubble. It also is tough to believe that your neighborhood benefits from tax breaks and federal funds given to a developer working on the other side of town.

People became very upset with large urban renewal programs, not only in St. Louis but in many cities. Gradually, the tearing down became more selective and fewer people were being moved around in the name of progress. The questioning did not stop. People were tired. It became easy to condemn any rebuilding and relocation effort because everyone could see that progress might end up hurting them. It became harder to convince people that the long-term effects of redevelopment could be good, if any of its short-term effects were bad.

Reflected in the Midtown Medical Center area were all the problems and possibilities associated with thirty years of redevelopment activity in St. Louis. It is big: At 270 acres, it is as large as the WUMCRC area and twice as large as LaSalle Park. It is diverse: Only LaSalle Park can match its mix of residential, commercial, institutional, and industrial land uses in such close proximity, but nowhere are the telltale signs of "older" industrial land uses more obvious. There are large, gaping holes on many blocks that can support new housing construction. There are some spots inside the redevelopment area where rehabilitation would be preferred.

For all these reasons, the long-simmering argument over "good" and "bad" redevelopment finally boiled over in the Midtown Medical Center area. How the argument has been addressed in this spot will tell us much about the city's future. We will see whether a neighborhood can be rehabilitated without first being completely ruined or emptied. We also will see if people from different backgrounds who learned to dislike each other can now learn to work together for their common good. In the long run, what happens in the Midtown Medical Center area may prove more important to the eventual reclamation of neighborhoods outside the Central Corridor than anything that has happened in the four previous redevelopment areas. This is why the area and its redevelopment history are well worth considering in detail.

The Redevelopment Area

The Midtown Medical Center Redevelopment Area (MMCRC) (see Figure 6) looks like a big square. Within this big "square" are four smaller

Figure 6. Midtown Medical Center Redevelopment Area

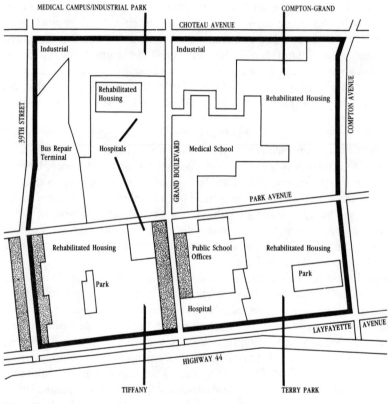

Commercial Area

"squares" of nearly equal size. These smaller parts are formed by the intersection of two streets: Park Avenue and Grand Boulevard. Park Avenue, like Chouteau Avenue some four blocks to the north, eventually runs into LaSalle Park. Grand Boulevard is one of the city's major north-south thoroughfares and cuts the redevelopment area in half. Four of the five medical institutions affiliated with MMCRC are located on either side of Grand Boulevard. It is the area's institutional and commercial hub.

Each of these four parts or neighborhoods has its own name and distinct character. On the east side of Grand Boulevard, there are the Compton-Grand and Terry Park neighborhoods. On the west side, there are the "Medical Campus/Industrial Park" and Tiffany neighborhoods. By its name alone, one gathers that the Medical Campus/Industrial Park "neighborhood" could not resemble a residential area very much; and it does not. Among the three neighborhoods that were once residential enclaves, only Tiffany has received much attention; and much of this attention has not been well received.

Some of the discord over Tiffany's rehabilitation can be accounted for by what was promised but not delivered to the Compton-Grand and Terry Park neighborhoods. Today, these latter neighborhoods are residential wastelands. Even at their best, they were unimpressive working-class neighborhoods; and they had seen their best days long before MMCRC came onto the scene. By 1978, only about 200 occupied housing units were left in both neighborhoods. Many buildings in Terry Park already had been demolished. Little of the housing remaining in the two neighborhoods—a mixed bag of single-family bungalows, two- and some four-family dwellings—was not in good condition. Indeed, they would have required a "major reinvestment to achieve modern residential standards for safe and sound habitation."[1]

The decision, as evidenced in the 1977 redevelopment plan, to call these neighborhoods candidates for rehabilitation was not well-informed. It probably had more to do with securing the consent of area residents and politicians for MMCRC's plans, observers suggested. In any event, it was a decision that no one has shown any interest in pursuing. The remaining residential blocks have continued to deteriorate in the absence of any substantial redevelopment activity on this side of Grand Boulevard.

Some of MMCRC's critics take this as evidence of the hospitals' "real plan" for the area. The "real plan," they maintain, has always been to clear out this part of the redevelopment area, displace all the low-income blacks, and give the property to the big institutions on this side of Grand Boulevard. The big landholders in this case are the St. Louis University Medical School, Incarnate Word Hospital, and St. Louis Public Schools, which has several large administrative buildings in Terry Park.

Allowance had been made in the original 1977 plan for these institutions to expand their holdings and construct new buildings or parking facilities, some of which has been done. However, the new housing that was to be built for people who lost their homes has not been constructed, and an amended redevelopment plan called for even more land to be offered to these institutions. No matter what the original intention was, one politician's "guess" was that Compton-Grand and Terry Park now "will be allowed to slide and the hospitals will gobble them up." This side of Grand Boulevard looks like an old urban renewal area: bombed out and waiting for its new institutional tenants to move in.

On the other side of Grand Boulevard, virtually all of the institutional expansion has been confined to one corner of the redevelopment area. The so-called Medical Campus/Industrial Park "neighborhood" has one and one-half blocks of housing, consisting exclusively of one story, single-family bungalows. The housing, by most accounts, was in pretty good shape. Much of it was already owned by Bethesda Hospital. The rest of the area belongs to three medical facilites, a few viable industrial tenants, and the metropolitan area's bus service. The big fights in this part of the redevelopment area have been among Bethesda Hospital, St. Louis University Hospital, and Cardinal Glennon Hospital. Each has acquired some property and done some work on it. Nothing substantial has been done yet with the industrial properties.

Just below the Medical Campus/Industrial Park neighborhood, in the southwestern corner of the redevelopment area, is the Tiffany neighborhood. This neighborhood is four blocks long and two blocks wide. With the exception of the 39th Street and Grand Boulevard commercial areas on either side of it, it is a residential neighborhood whose blocks are dominated by one-and two-family residences. There are a few apartment buildings with as many as twenty-four units in them. These are clustered in several spots throughout the neighborhood. Altogether there were 694 housing units in this eight-block area in 1977. Though terribly rundown in many spots and deteriorating quickly, none of the housing had yet been demolished. This gave Tiffany the largest and most substantial housing stock in the whole redevelopment area.

The homes in Tiffany will never be mistaken for the Victorian townhouses that are supposed to appeal to rehabbers. They are solid, unpretentious brick buildings, usually two or two-and-one-half stories tall. They were built around 1900 for equally solid and unpretentious working-class families who could afford to buy a home, but who were not wealthy enough to live farther from busy city streets and industrial properties. Tiffany's housing stock was apparently classic enough, in its own democratic way, to qualify the neighborhood for inclusion in the U.S. registry for historic places. The only reason to care about this in a place such as Tiffany, of course, was that the designation also made many of the "classic" working-class houses eligible for special tax credits, if they were rehabilitated in a way that captured their outward charm. The really important point to be made here is that Tiffany's housing could be rehabilitated. In a redevelopment area that seemed to have relatively little else in its favor, this mattered a lot.

Tiffany had been a pretty good neighborhood, long-time residents say. Tiffany's problems really began, one resident said, "when the kids moved out of the neighborhood and never came back. This was in the 1960s. Our parents were left, and they were getting older." The neighborhood was ready to be pushed over the edge, and "city officials did the pushing."

In truth, these long-time residents really were talking about officials from LCRA and SLHA, the city's urban renewal and public housing agenicies. These officials used Tiffany's homes and apartments as relocation housing for people with nowhere else to live. In this case, the people were low-income blacks from the area just east of Compton Avenue and the infamous Pruitt-Igoe public housing site. Much of the area east of Compton Avenue had been cleared in the late 1960s, and Pruitt-Igoe was being emptied about the same time.

By all accounts, Tiffany changed dramatically during the 1970s. Approximately 1,800 people lived in Tiffany in 1970, and they were spread among almost 1,100 households. By 1980, the number of households had dropped by at least one-third, approximately 400 housing units were vacant, but the population dropped by only 100 or 200. The type of people who lived in Tiffany had changed. Less than 10 percent of the residents were black in 1970; by 1980, almost 80 percent were black. The neighborhood lost many of its long-term residents during the 1970s and gained many larger and poorer families.[2]

The impact of these new residents was equally dramatic. "They tore up the neighborhood, made it into a drug center, and scared the oldtimers to death," one person told me. "You couldn't let your kids out to play. It was too dangerous. I'm not making this up. Some guy got shot right in front of my house. My neighbor was chased into her car and taunted."

Even the people who later complained about MMCRC's redevelopment program concede that Tiffany had become a mean and dirty place by the late 1970s. People draw parallels between the condition of Tiffany just before MMCRC took over and Pershing-Waterman before Pantheon took it over. They apparently were very similar. The important differences were that Tiffany had more owner-occupied housing and more people left in the neighborhood. These would prove to be big obstacles to the neighborhood's redevelopment.

The Redevelopment Corporation

MMCRC was modeled after the redevelopment corporation established by the Washington University Medical Center. Both were organized under Missouri's Chapter 353 Urban Redevelopment Corporation Law. Thus, both could grant liberal tax abatements for development projects in their area. They also could exercise the power of eminent domain and initiate condemnation proceedings against uncooperative property owners.

Even the ostensible reasons for creating MMCRC sound familiar. As one Midtown Medical Center official put it, "there was the loftier motivation. . . of wanting to be good citizens" and help the city. "We had a chance to move out in the late 1960s," he said, "and it was a good offer. But we turned it down." "We had a real commitment to the city," just like Washingtong University, "but we also had a cetain religious mission to the area." On the other hand, "there was a less lofty motive for setting up MMCRC. If we were to stay and survive as institutions, we were going to have to attract patients, students, and employees." He conceded that this had become increasingly harder to do.

There was more to the decision to stay than this, of course. The more important institutional members of MMCRC are closely tied to St. Louis University, which is only a few blocks away, and the St. Louis Archidiocese. It was much the same way between the Washington University Medical Center and Washington University. Only in the case of MMCRC, several observers noted, St. Louis University was very dependent upon St. Louis University Hospital for financial support. Hence, it was less a question of whether they would stay than what they would do with the area once it was ceded to them.

In answering the latter question, important differences between MMCRC and WUMCRC begin to emerge. WUMCRC's directors and supporters were well-placed in city politics and business circles, far better-placed than those for MMCRC. They also had access to more money. Although both were profit-making entities in the strict legal sense, WUMCRC never has made any money and never was intended to show a profit. The institutions sponsoring WUMCRC wrote off their yearly contribution as a deductible loss. It was a cost they were willing to absorb to promote their area's reclamation. WUMCRC is an "umbrella developer" for the area. It is a clearinghouse for all redevelopment projects.

MMCRC also has never made any money, but it has not been for lack of trying. Its original director, John Abramson, and board intended that MMCRC should take a more active role in their area's redevelopment than WUMCRC had taken in its own. MMCRC was not going to wait around for something to happen. It was going to make things happen. It was going to involve itself as both an investor and an administrator of redevelopment projects in its area.

There is some disagreement over whether MMCRC assumed a more entrepreneurial role in redevelopment activities because no one wanted to work in such a troubled area or because MMCRC's officers simply wanted to become developers. Local observers suggested that there was some truth in the first position and a lot of truth in the second. It should be recalled, however, that at this time Pantheon was the only large residential developer in the city. This made it more likely that smaller, less experienced developers would have to be invited to work in the area.

Developers were reluctant to work in the area at first; at least this was true of the Pantheon Corporation. There was not even a long line of applicants for the job of director for MMCRC, several people recalled. Furthermore, the man who took it was advised not to take it because of the area's problems. "It was obvious that MMCRC was going to have to do something to help itself," said one person. "It had to create interest in the area. It had to show that there could be a market for housing, at least in Tiffany. Otherwise, nothing was going to get done."

Other developers took exception to the obvious desire on the part of MMCRC's leaders to be involved in *all* of the area's major redevelopment projects. Its directors decided early on to "assume an entrepreneurial role" in area redevelopment projects, I was told. They would accomplish this through "joint ventures or partnerships with other investors who [would] provide equity or specialized development expertise." MMCRC would act as the general partner in these deals; it would sell shares in projects to private parties. These limited partners would receive short-term losses on their income taxes and long-term capital gains once the project was successful and sold. This, it was argued back in 1979, would enable MMCRC "to become self-sufficient within about five years."[3] All of its operating expenses, which were expected to be about $250,000 per year, would be paid for by investors and renters after that.

The institutions sponsoring MMCRC were promised more than this, apparently. They were going to be paid back all the money they had invested in MMCRC's various projects. To this end, the "original interest-free notes" provided by Medical Center institutions were "converted to preferred stock" in MMCRC. This included $650,000 from St. Louis University and just over $200,000 more from Cardinal Glennon, Bethesda, and Incarnate Word Hospitals. Another $30,000 in common stock was held by St. Louis University and two banks. As projects were refinanced by being sold to new investors, it was expected that the stock holders would be reimbursed "for their critical front-end involvement."[4] The idea was that all of the redevelopment going on around the hospitals would end up costing the hospitals nothing..

Some persons believe that MMCRC's board was manipulated by the corporation's director. Others say that the board wanted him to be aggressive.

The effect, in either case, was the same. MMCRC was going to be the primary developer in its own area, even if no one in the organization really knew how to do that kind of work.

It may be that this apparent problem was not nearly so clear back in the mid-1970s when these different redevelopment areas were beginning to be reclaimed. Several important things were obvious by the time MMCRC began its work, however, and these should have warned people that this plan would be hard to implement successfully. Foremost among the factors were the condition of the area and the substantial amount of money needed just to begin the reclamation campaign. This was not the Washington University Medical Center area.

MMCRC was paying out nearly $200,000 more each year for salaries and professional services by the early 1980s than it was taking in; and it had paid out another $1 million for land in the area that no one was willing to buy or develop. Some of this might have been avoided, if MMCRC's benefactors had made more substantial contributions in the beginning. When they did not and became frightened by the prospect of getting in over their institutional heads, they behaved just as the WUMC institutions had. They went to the same group of St. Louis leaders the WUMC had solicited and asked for over $1 million in assistance. They received a bit more than $750,000.

MMCRC never received anything near the amount of money it was going to need to sponsor the whole area's redevelopment. By 1978, people had a much better sense of the money needed to undertake these kinds of projects. The money being set aside for MMCRC's work clearly was insufficient.

It may have been necessary at first for MMCRC to do some things that "got its own ball rolling." That accomplished, it could have done exactly what Ralston Purina wisely did. It could have welcomed other developers to move in and assume the financial risks entailed in redeveloping the Midtown Medical Center area, or at least that part of it in the Tiffany neighborhood. For whatever reasons, though, this transition did not take place. MMCRC remained the area's primary developer until well into 1986.

MMCRC's insistence on taking both the financial and political risks had understandable results. It could not muster the resources to initiate many projects in all four parts of the redevelopment area. Nor could it smooth the way for other developers to come in by establishing itself as an honest broker between them and the community. Rather than making the situation better, MMCRC only made it worse. Established developers saw MMCRC as either its chief competitor or a potentially troublesome partner.

People in the community, even some who agreed with what MMCRC was trying to do, saw MMCRC as an overbearing and often unreasonable patron. Thus, the city's major developers were not keen on the idea of working in this area, even after it was shown that Tiffany's houses could be restored nicely. MMCRC also failed to secure community support for its work. "It was a terrible situation," one developer told me. "The politics and economics of the place stunk."

MMCRC had its defenders, of course. These people maintained that what MMCRC did in its area was not much different from what Pantheon had done in Pershing-Waterman. Pantheon, they pointed out, had controlled both the politics and economics of redevelopment in the Pershing-Waterman area. "It also played a much tougher game than they did in Midtown," I was told.

There is some truth to this. Ignored in this argument, however, are several other facts that reveal equally important differences in their respective situation: Pantheon's leaders really were developers. They knew the law. They knew the construction trades. They knew how to set up and execute the complex deals that are written into so-called syndication agreements with outside investors. Moreover, they really did have complete political control of the area in which they worked.

MMCRC had none of these things in its favor, and it made two mistakes that Pantheon avoided making. First, MMCRC did not leave alone all the resident homeowners whose houses could use some exterior improvements but otherwise were in acceptable, if not great, shape. Second, MMCRC tried to change the neighborhood more than was necessary to achieve its ostensible goal of having a racially and economically mixed residential population.

Changing the Area to Fit the Plan

Even if MMCRC had been a less greedy and more sophisticated developer, it faced two rather novel problems that might have subdued anyone's desire to work in this redevelopment area. Both problems involved the area's residents and housing. The 2,000 or so people who still lived in it by 1978 were supposed to be allowed to stay in the area. If their residence needed to be rehabilitated, another place for them to live was to be found within MMCRC's boundaries. This restriction was placed on MMCRC by the Board of Aldermen in 1978 when the redevelopment corporation was formally approved. People had grown weary of redevelopment projects that displaced large numbers of residents. MMCRC was going to be held accountable for those people who had to be moved from their homes.

MMCRC's leaders agreed to this in 1978 and, according to several observers, seemed to think it was feasible. Upon closer inspection, however, the housing into which these people would have been moved turned out to be in much worse shape than was originally thought. Perhaps more importantly, MMCRC's leaders decided, upon closer inspection, that many of the people themselves looked a whole lot less desirable than was originally supposed. The housing in which these people lived might prove salvageable, but many of the inhabitants probably would not.

It is impossible to say which of the two, the poor housing or "undesirable" people, actually made unworkable MMCRC's original plan to rehabilitate the neighborhood around its current residents. Each made a contribution. "The real problem," one former city official told me, "was that MMCRC didn't know when to stop. They went after folks they could have left alone."

Given the redevelopment area's population, most of the people MMCRC pushed out were low-income blacks. This only made matters worse and, in the words of one MMCRC supporter, "gave every left-wing kook in the city an excuse to jump on MMCRC." Some of those who sought to speak in behalf of area residents were content to wag their fingers and try to stop any redevelopment. Others maintained that MMCRC should have worked with the families that clearly were not "bad" but did have some financial or social problems, "just like Bertha Gilkey did up in Cochran."

"That sounds real good," said one person, "but MMCRC was not a social service agency. It was a development firm." It did not have the personnel, money, or time to deal with these people. (It did try to provide some social services, but those were dropped pretty quickly.) "Besides, the hospitals didn't really want all those poor blacks hanging around," I was told. "It was bad for their business, and it sure didn't help sell the area to new renters and homeowners." Variations of this statement were made by a number of persons who supported MMCRC's redevelopment efforts.

"The ostensible goal of MMCRC," one critic stated, "was to make Tiffany more racially and economically mixed." That may have been a "nice idea," she said. "But how could that be achieved when rehabbed houses being sold for more than $90,000" stood next to homes whose market value was less than half that and whose owners had only modest incomes?" The only way to achieve that goal, critics argued, was to change the neighborhood. To change the neighborhood, MMCRC had to broaden its definition of what constituted an "undesireable family" so that more houses could become available for rehabilitation and sold to "desireable families."

The charge that MMCRC was willing to change the Tiffany neighborhood to save it tainted nearly everything the corporation accomplished or even mildly thought about accomplishing. This particular charge provoked such a strong reaction on the part of many people because it was rooted in the much bigger and lingering dispute over the use of eminent domain powers by private developers.

More recent attempts to invoke this power against resident homeowners had failed. The Washington University Medical Center Redevelopment

Corporation had threatened to use it, but backed away from legal confrontations. Ralston Purina had sued one of LaSalle Park's new homeowners because he had failed to live up to the provisions of the "rehab agreement" with Ralston Purina. The corporation lost that suit. This probably helps to explain why WUMCRC took the tack of denying tax abatements to homeowners who did not fulfill their rehab agreements. Stronger sanctions for not fulfilling such agreements, including the loss of one's home, were not likely to be called for by a court. Furthermore, WUMCRC did not have enough money available to buy much of the property that it might have wanted the courts to condemn.

All of this was known by people in the city's nascent "redevelopment community." Nevertheless, it did not stop MMCRC's director and board from trying to use rather elaborate rehab agreements as a means to impose their will over the kind of redevelopment and homeowners that would be welcome in the "new Tiffany." The results of this practice would have been bad enough, but they made worse the problems MMCRC already had experienced in relocating people who had been renting apartments. The consequences were predictable and sorry.

Broken Promises and Bad Politics

The promise that MMCRC's leaders and sponsors had made to the people living in the area and city leaders was broken. More people lost their housing than could be accommodated in rehabilitated units; they had to leave the area. Precisely how many households were moved out or "chose" to leave on their own is hard to say. Households had been moving in and out of the area at a brisk pace since the late 1960s. In 1970, for instance, nearly 43 percent of Tiffany's residents reported that they had lived in the neighborhood for less than two years. That figure did not change when a comparable survey was made in 1978. However, the percentage of residents that had lived in the neighborhood over ten years had dropped from 27 to 12. Long-term residents were being replaced by a steady stream of transient households and people who had lived there only a few years. There was little stability in the neighborhood's resident population.[5]

Tiffany really was on the verge of becoming another Pershing-Waterman. MMCRC tried to stabilize the situation as best it could; but it would have been difficult to achieve stability with such a transient and increasingly poor population without someone being inconvenienced. Its promise to keep all of the area's residents notwithstanding, MMCRC sped up the process of abandonment by the most transient and poor to preserve as many of the neighborhood's buildings as was possible. It may have been the best that

MMCRC could have done under the circumstances, but many people did not see it that way. Part of the explanation may be that people had grown especially sensitive to the displacement issue. Moreover, MMCRC had promised not to displace anyone. Yet these partial answers ignore the enormous energy and personnel that Freedom of Residence, a civil rights group, put into its campaign against MMCRC. "FOR really pulled out all the stops on this one," I was told. "Sure, they may have had a commitment to Tiffany's poor; but they also exploited the controversy so they could drum up contributions." The politics in Tiffany were as unstable as its population. This helps to account for the haphazard way in which redevelopment activities were carried out. However, it also provides a clue to why MMCRC could be harassed so effectively by a tiny band of activists who sponsored marches and demonstrations against MMCRC.

No one came rushing to MMCRC's defense. Those who might long since had become disenchanted with MMCRC or figured out that there was little to gain politically by protecting MMCRC from itself. The redevelopment corporation was allowed to stand alone until its position became untenable. Only then did private and public leaders quietly come to MMCRC's rescue.

The challenges to MMCRC started almost immediately. One alderman wanted relocation housing for the poor to be prepared first, so that they could not be forgotten once the area was a success. This was a nice idea, but experienced developers and city officials knew that it was an ineffective way to rebuild such a neighborhood. No effort was made to award subsidized units— with their guaranteed income—to a developer willing to build or repair even more market-rate units in the same area. In other places, such as Pershing-Waterman, the city offered subsidized units as presents to developers who were willing to take some financial risk by creating market-rate units. Usually, the developer was expected to provide at least three or four market-rate units for every subsidized one it was awarded. This never happened in MMCRC's area.

Nearly two-thirds of the 102 apartments that MMCRC rehabilitated between 1979 and 1981 were set aside for low- and moderate-income households. The ratio of market-rate to subsidized units improved in subsequent projects. Only 40 percent of the 179 apartments rehabilitated between 1982 and 1985 were subsidized. Nonetheless, as of 1986, there still were about as many subsidized units in Tiffany as there were market-rate ones (i.e., 138 subsidized versus 143 market-rate). No one with whom I spoke considered this a good return on the city's investment, at least not in comparison to what developers did in other areas with the subsidized units they were awarded.

Observers were quick to add, however, that this was not a major concern to MMCRC's leaders. "They wanted to take care of their 'political problem,' so [the director] put in all of that subsidized stuff first to get the area's [politicians] off his back." This may have been a bad business decision, but MMCRC's leaders were not worried about the future. They worried about what was happening to them right then, and right then they were being pushed to "do something for the poor." Setting aside apartments for the poor was the easiest and quickest thing to do, I was told.

At least one bad political consequence came from having MMCRC produce relatively few market-rate apartment units, especially during the early years of its existence. More single-family residences would have to be made available to middle- and upper-middle class households, if the goal of creating an economically mixed neighborhood were to be reached. Many houses were abandoned by 1978 and made available to the public; more have been added since then. Some of these were relatively large and potentially attractive enough to have drawn more well-to-do homebuyers. Other houses like this were in the neighborhood, too. The problem was that they still had people living in them.

A number of homeowners knew their houses needed to be worked on. A few owners had done some work, but more said that they had not begun their "fix-up" projects because they did not know what was going to happen in the neighborhood. It was not only MMCRC's critics who said this. Long-time residents who liked the way Tiffany was being cleaned up said this, too. Many people feared that their homes might be condemned and taken from them, so they did not work on their houses.

This was not an unrealistic fear. A number of their neighbors, some of whom they did not like, already had lost their home to MMCRC or were being threatened with the loss of their home. Many people believed that MMCRC was going to increase the pool of houses that it could rehabilitate and sell to more well-to-do homebuyers in this way. This issue, and not the question of finding relocation housing for low-income renters, brought Tiffany to the edge of political chaos.

The argument over relocating displaced renters had been resolved, at least in the legal sense, by 1981. At that time, the Legal Aid Society helped several Tiffany residents file a suit against MMCRC regarding this matter. The plaintiffs alledged that MMCRC had forced them out of their apartments and failed to help them find alternative housing.

The case was never tried because an out-of-court settlement was reached. Something should be noted in MMCRC's defense at this time. Even if MMCRC had wanted to keep all of the low-income tenants it had inherited, it could not have done so. One former alderman for the area said "that compared with other developers, Midtown had done well—especially considering its 'impossible' relocation requirements." Moreover, MMCRC's ordinance "had been made at a time when the city appeared to have almost unlimited access to federal housing money." After Reagan was elected, "it all dried up." Midtown "lost the federal funds necessary to fulfill its requirement of building enough low-income housing." It "had no choice but to move poor people outside Tiffany to find them decent new housing."[6]

Knowledgeable outsiders had expected all along that many of the area's current residents would have to move. Federal cutbacks only meant that more would have to go. They do not fault MMCRC for displacing many people, and they echo the opinion that MMCRC did a pretty good job just to keep as many of its low-income renters as it has. There also is near unanimity on the question of how the relocation process was handled, however: They think it was done poorly. The fact that MMCRC stood to profit financially from any improvement in a building's rent receipts only made protesters angrier and MMCRC's need to push people out quickly look more desperate.

Had this been its most serious political misjudgement, MMCRC might have avoided the maelstrom that eventually helped to topple its original director and board. Unfortunately, MMCRC's leaders recalled the history of Pantheon and WUMCRC too selectively. Decent homeowners and resident apartment owners had been left alone. Even though their buildings could use a tidying up, no great pressure was placed on the owners to make big improvements.

Pantheon's and WUMCRC's directors knew that no good purpose would be served by creating yet another empty building in neighborhoods that already looked ripe for disinvestment. If anything, the presence of a relatively well-kept house or apartment building and decent people in a neighborhood helped these corporations make the point that there was much worth saving in their redevelopment area.

It must be noted, in all fairness, that MMCRC was not the first party to propose that homeowner displacement in Tiffany be carried out in a relatively aggressive fashion. This honor apparently belonged to area politicians who, back in 1979 and 1980, tried to save an old church in the middle of Tiffany that was scheduled to be razed along with one house next to it. A park was to be built on the cleared land. The church, by universal consensus, "was nothing special to look at" and had a small congregation.

A walk through the neighborhood today quickly reveals which side won the opening round. The church is gone. A $360,000 park—complete with a permanent gazebo, a court once used for basketball, childrens' playground equipment, and benches—rests in its place. It is really a lovely little park, and many people use it. Its real significance, however, is as a symbol. Opponents of redevelopment saw the proposed park as a challenge to their sovereignty.

Proponents of redevelopment considered the charge of racism to be trumped up. Mayor Conway, who pushed for the park, "played hard ball," said one disgruntled politician. "We had made a promise to those low-income people," said another. "They were our friends."

What is important here is not that Conway approved the park over the objections of local political leaders or area residents, though it came back to haunt him when one of those leaders, who aleady disliked Conway, began the push to have alderman Vincent Schoemehl elected mayor. It is what those local leaders allegedly proposed to do with the park. I was told by local observers that some wanted to build it on a hill across the street from MMCRC's headquarters. The major problem with that site, aside from some obvious landscaping difficulties, was that some of the neighborhood's nicer single-family resiences were located on it.

"We would have had to take out the better part of a block of houses just to save that church," one MMCRC supporter told me. That was unacceptable. MMCRC was dedicated to saving those buildings, if not necessarily the people in them. No matter who was in them, though, those houses were part of a small supply of buildings that could have appealed to middle-class residents. Area politicians seemed willing to lose that potentially middle-class housing to keep the neighborhood poor. They did not seem to care about displacement, or even more demolition and clearance, MMCRC supporters argued.

In such an atmosphere, tempers were easily frayed and few believed that an accommodation could be reached between many existing homeowners and MMCRC. Both sides actively avoided compromise. Signs protesting MMCRC's actions or warning prospective homeowners not to buy in Tiffany appeared on dozens of porches. Suits were filed. Candlelight marches were held.

MMCRC responded with alley cleanups and flower shows. FOR organized a community group composed of MMCRC opponents because MMCRC had "stolen" the original neighborhood organization. MMCRC denied this, adding that it was not unreasonable for voting privileges to be apportioned according to how much property someone owned. Because MMCRC owned more property, it was only natural that it should help to shape neighborhood policy. FOR charged that MMCRC had vandalized the park's new basketball backboard ("It came down with the first 'slam dunk'") so that fewer black teenagers would be seen hanging around. MMCRC countered with volleyball nets and outdoor festivals.

The house of one MMCRC opponent caught on fire. Someone tried to start a fire through the mail slot in the front door of MMCRC's rehabilitated headquarters. It was big-city trench warfare, with each side beating its opponent and itself into a state of exhaustion. Rehabilitated apartments remained unoccupied. Houses were left vacant. Competing elements within the St. Louis Archdiocese fought behind the scenes.

Through it all, MMCRC's director pushed on. Despite all the bad publicity, his request to allow tax abatement for commercial property along 39th Street and to authorize construction of subsidized housing for elderly people was approved by the Board of Aldermen in October 1983.[7] These issues had galvanized MMCRC's opponents. The public forum that had been provided to MMCRC's opponents was removed; but the conflict, protests, suits, and bad feelings persisted. The only thing that gave anyone hope that these issues might be resolved was the dismissal of MMCRC's director and board late in 1985.

Broken Plans and Bad Business

Many outsiders assumed that all the bad publicity and politics finally forced the St. Louis Archdiocese and other concerned parties to dismiss MMCRC's leadership. The protesters believed they had won by making a strong case against MMCRC's displacement and relocation practices, which probably was not the case. As embarrassing as disclosures about these matters had been, they were not the real cause of MMCRC's political fall from grace. The protests and legal suits against MMCRC had cost it time and money, to be sure, and rattled a good number of people in the process. However, MMCRC had weathered the political challenges mounted against it. Even a legal decision against its use of rehab agreements could have been handled. After all, both Ralston Purina and WUMCRC had survived the rejection of their attempts to enforce similar arrangements; and a political compromise allowing rundown but occupied buildings to remain untouched in Nina Place had been reached.

City leaders "temporarily resolved" the 1983 controversy over displacement and relocation problems in the MMCRC area in much the same way. It "was done through the simple expedient of promising...[MMCRC], 31 units of government-subsidized housing for families dislodged by the redevelopment project. In return, Midtown would continue to operate under the requirement that it relocate families within...the 37-block area surrounding the St. Louis University Medical Center."[8]

This, of course, was nothing more than MMCRC had promised but failed to do all along. The public laborings over the sensitive issues raised, once again, in Tiffany provided St. Louisans with a political solution that worked well enough. The fact that thirty-one units had not been constructed or rehabilitated by 1986—plans to do so were temporarily suspended by MMCRC's new board—simply reinforced the point that the original MMCRC board was not dismissed because of its poor political performance.

The bad business decisions made by MMCRC's director and blindly acceded to by the board of directors led to its dismissal. MMCRC was losing a great deal of money by the early 1980s. The political agitation of FOR and other parties made it impossible to overlook the fundamentally unsound business practices engaged in by MMCRC. There is no way of knowing how much longer people would have been willing to invest more money in MMCRC had they not been forced to look at what the corporation was doing.

Officials in the Conway administration had made their displeasure with MMCRC's director very clear to his board, but nothing was done to remove him. The consensus of opinion was that the board was not displeased with what he was doing, so, it did not fire him. Once it became clear just how much financial trouble MMCRC was in, both the board and its director were removed. Had MMCRC been able to cover its losses, the original director and board might still be there.

The basic mistakes MMCRC made have been noted in one place or another throughout this chapter. Foremost among these was its insistence on acting as the area's chief developer. Other developers may not have wanted to share their profits with the redevelopment corporation or preferred to work on larger numbers of buildings at the same time. However, apartment buildings that MMCRC could have used to entice developers to do some of the more speculative scattered site rehabilitation work in Tiffany were reserved for MMCRC's own redevelopment portfolio. These were the same buildings into which MMCRC poured so much of the subsidized housing allowance it received from the city. In effect, MMCRC did the safest buildings in the neighborhood, guaranteed itself healthy rent receipts, and expected other developers to rehabilitate the scattered single-family residences and duplexes. MMCRC quickly acquired a reputation as a difficult and untrustworthy organization with which to deal. This, in turn, cost MMCRC more money. One developer told me that he added a 10 percent surcharge onto every bid he made to MMCRC, and he said that others did it, too. "We call it the 'Midtown factor.' We figure we deserve at least that much for all the extra grief we've got to put up with when we work with [MMCRC's director]."

Other things that cost MMCRC money were the inexperience of the small developers and MMCRC's desire to create some pretty expensive housing for Tiffany. Some developers simply did shoddy work that MMCRC's own people had to improve upon, I was told. Others underestimated the amount of time it would take to complete a job, and MMCRC had to soothe the bruised feelings of several home buyers by adding nice little "extras" to their new house. These "extras" cost the redevelopment corporation many thousands of dollars.

When MMCRC was not losing money on the houses it rehabilitated, it was losing money on the syndication packages it put together and the land it held. It does not seem unfair to conclude that MMCRC was a poorly run business. By the end of 1985, MMCRC had more than $300,000 in unpaid bills and its deficit was growing quickly. Its fifteen employees were earning $100,000 per month, and this alone had translated over the past few years into a yearly deficit of $200,000. Had the hospitals not been increasing their yearly contributions to cover the mounting debt and the city not floated an emergency loan to the redevelopment corporation in 1985, MMCRC would have been in much worse financial shape by the time it was reorganized.

Clearly, the plan to recast Tiffany as a racially and economically mixed neighborhood ran headlong into some painful economic facts of life. People who knew that MMCRC was underfunded hoped that the "profits" earned by MMCRC as a property manager and real estate syndicator would make up whatever shortfall existed, which did not happen. When it did not happpen, MMCRC did some things to make sure that the plan for Tiffany might still be carried out. By playing tough with Tiffany's tenants and homeowners, however, MMCRC came close to subverting the very goal its supporters had said they wanted to achieve.

The surprising thing is this: Despite all of the controversy and questionable business deals that took place, Tiffany is more racially and economically mixed than at any other time in its history. The neighborhood does look much better, and the population is more stable.[9]

The Tiffany neighborhood was stuck somewhere between its past and future, when MMCRC took over. The past was represented by what one found west of 39th Street, a neighborhood in which eleven people were murdered between May 1982 and August 1984.[10] Its future could be seen in the abandoned homes and vacant lots that already littered Terry Park and Compton-Grand. Something had to be done, and MMCRC did it. This more than anything else may explain why people allowed MMCRC to go on as long as it did.

What Will Come of Midtown?

It is hard today to imagine the desperate situation that persons living and working in the area faced during its worst times. They were overwhelmed by events not of their making and tried to cope as best they could. The warning signs were there long before things became intolerable. Yet, no one thought or cared to do much about them.

The area's white population had begun to decline during the 1960s.[11] Blacks, who already had a sizable presence, increased their share of the population. The number of working residents actually increased a bit; but the character of the workforce changed along with the population. Persons who worked in industrial or manufacturing jobs their whole lives found little reason to stay. They were at or near retirement age and their children had moved on to start families of their own. New residents in the area tended to hold clerical, sales, and service jobs. There even was a modest increase in the number of residents who held relatively skilled technical and professional jobs.

Bigger changes came during the 1970s. The eastern half of the area lost even more people and housing. Fewer than 300 persons now lived there, and over 70 percent of them were black. The situation in the western half, where Tiffany is located, was different. Its population declined a little more; but now it had more people than the eastern section. What mattered was that a complete reversal occurred in the racial composition of its population. Blacks now were the dominant population in the area. The percentage of young persons also jumped up, as did the average size of households. Housing vacancies increased a good deal, but comparatively few units were lost to demolition.

By the end of the 1970s, supporters of MMCRC could find only two things to give them hope that this situation might change. First, the number of reported crimes had begun to drop as some black families with troublesome children were moved out. And, second, the number of residents employed in the professions actually had increased a bit.

One wonders why, in the face of such problems, the institutions affiliated with MMCRC had to be nudged into action by James Conway, the mayor of St. Louis at that time. Given their initial reluctance to become involved, however, it should not have been much of a surprise that MMCRC's board failed to pay much attention to what its director was doing.

MMCRC's new board of directors was composed of relatively tough-minded people. Several had a good deal of experience with institutions that have financed and overseen commercial and residential redevelopment projects. Though none was a developer, each had a feel for the problems and possibilities that come with this kind of work. Whom they chose to lead MMCRC would say a good deal about what might happen in this part of the city. In Thomas Mangogna, they had someone with good political skills. Prior to becoming Mayor Schoemehl's chief of staff in July 1984, Mangogna had headed a local foundation dealing with former criminals and handled rough chores for Schoemehl as a board member on the city's Land Reutilization Authority and Public Housing Authority. He had a reputation as a tough, skillful administrator who did not suffer incompetence or fools well.

Much work remained to be done. One project already under construction involved seventy-four units scattered across Tiffany, and included some commercial buildings. An effort was going to be made to renegotiate that deal because, as one outside observer noted, "the way it's set up MMCRC will lose money even if the project is a success." However, people were not optimistic that this could be done without involving MMCRC in a rather nasty legal fight. Another project involving forty to fifty more units was under consideration as of May 1986. MMCRC probably would be the general partner in that deal, even if it meant obtaining only 1 percent of the proceeds, just so MMCRC could manage the units afterward. The situation for homebuyers was not much better. An individual interested in rehabilitating a single-family residence could pay between $10,000 and $12,000 for an abandoned house in 1986. By the time one finished rehabilitating the residence, it probably would have cost between $60,000 and $75,000. A home buyer who paid much more than that paid too much to buy into this neighborhood, well-informed observers told me. It will be recalled, however, that several of the houses rehabilitated and sold by MMCRC itself cost considerably more than that. Persons who hoped to realize a profit on their purchase were going to have to wait some time before prices in the neighborhood rose to the level of $85,000.

Housing prices in the Ranken Neighborhood, which is part of WUMCRC's territory, would be comparable. This is not surprising, inasmuch as Tiffany and Ranken look very similar and have similar populations. Indeed, a number of the low-income black families displaced from Tiffany were moved into Ranken by their patron, Joe Roddy. Similar rehabilitated houses on the blocks closer to the Washington University Medical Center could be sold in 1986 for more than $100,000. This is one illustration of how much stronger was the housing market in WUMCRC's best blocks in comparison to MMCRC's by 1986.

As late as 1988, there still had been no housing market in the Compton-Grand and Terry Park neighborhoods. The failure of MMCRC to do anything except hold the title to 150 empty lots and abandoned buildings in those neighborhoods had been a matter of no small concern to several of MMCRC's institutional sponsors. In the year that followed, however, MMCRC found a developer to build twenty-six new townhouses behind the St. Louis University Medical School. Each cost $89,000, and by the spring of 1989, nine already had been sold to medical school personnel.

The thirty-one subsidized apartment units awarded to MMCRC in 1983 by the city also were to have been located in this area. However, MMCRC's new board wisely decided to delay the construction or rehabilitation of any units that could have used those subsidies. They likely will continue to wait until a more comprehensive redevelopment scheme for this part of the Midtown area can be fashioned. Those thirty-one units are about the only incentive MMCRC could offer a prospective developer.

The most difficult task facing MMCRC was to "heal the wounds" between it and Tiffany's residents. Nearly thirty homeowners, both white and black, still had a standing suit against MMCRC in 1986. These were people whose homes had been condemned by MMCRC or who expected such an action to be taken against them. Only a few were so embittered by their experience that they probably wanted MMCRC to wither away; most were nice people who simply were afraid of losing their homes. Much of that fear would dissipate if MMCRC made it clear that single-family residences would no longer be the object of condemnation suits. Plans to establish a low-interest loan fund for exterior home improvements would help reinforce that point. Whatever design standards eventually are applied probably would be consistent with those required for houses in this type of "historic district." They would not be as demanding or frivolous as those required by MMCRC's former director, I was told.

Middle-class people have found housing in Tiffany, and more probably will in the future. It is hard to imagine a set of circumstances, however, in which most of the residents would be more well-to-do. The housing available to be rented or purchased is not fancy enough to attract middle-class people in numbers that would tip the neighborhood in that direction.

People and business are not rushing to the neighborhood, in any case. MMCRC's most recent offering, a set of fifty-six apartments whose rehabilitation cost $5.2 million, had difficulty drawing renters at first. The CDA agreed to pay up to $62,500 to defray MMCRC's deficits in maintaining the empty units, once those deficits reached $162,500. As of April 1987, the project had not yet reached that level of indebtedness.[12] Fortunately, by 1989 all but one of the units had been filled. The eight commercial properies that had been rehabilitated as part of the same project remained empty.

Only part of Tiffany's current problems can be traced to MMCRC's past financial dealings and political controversies. The area at times still can be a dangerous place in which to live. In November 1986, for instance, a security guard killed one of two men who tried to rob him while he was patrolling the 39th Street business strip on Tiffany's western border. Six months later someone poured gasoline through the mail slot in the front door of an apartment in Tiffany and set the place on fire. One woman was killed in the incident, which was attributed to a domestic dispute.[13]

In the spring of 1989 a number of young black men from the area just west and south of Tiffany began loitering in the neighborhood and committing some robberies and assaults. MMCRC's director hired several off-duty police officers to harass and arrest these young men. Lest this be viewed as a racist reaction by more well-to-do whites to the presence of young black men in their neighborhood, it should be noted that the Cochran and Carr Square TMCs did the same thing to maintain a safe environment for its black residents. The point of all this for the Midtown Medical Center area, however, is that such events do not make the neighborhood a more attractive place in which to live. It is because the area has come back as far as it has that such incidents receive much attention today. Not too long ago they would have seemed unexceptional. MMCRC, for all its problems, has made the neighborhood safer and more attractive.

The redevelopment corporation also has come closer to fashioning a racially and economically mixed residential population than many people probably realize. Though this was an explicit goal of MMCRC, some things the redevelopment corporation did seemed to frustrate its realization. The practical effect of all the controversies swirling around the organization, however, was to make it more likely that the goal could be reached in the future.

The clearest indication yet that more established but less well-to-do homeowners would find a place in Tiffany was provided in November 1987. Nineteen homeowners settled their suit against MMCRC, thereby ending four years of litigation. The redevelopment corporation dropped its efforts to have these properties condemned and set aside $45,000 to help homeowners pay for some basic repairs to their houses. The suit had been filed after MMCRC's original director demanded that many expensive cosmetic changes be made to these houses and offered no assistance to pay for them. Now, as long as the condition of the houses satisfies all city building codes, MMCRC will not move against the owners.[14]

To the extent that the area's redevelopment continues on a slow, yet steady course, Tiffany could become a full-service neighborhood. It will be many years before the shopping area along 39th Street is filled with shops catering to area residents. Nevertheless, the neighborhood has been shown to be a place where people from different backgrounds can live together and, after a fashion, learn how to practice the difficult art of politics together.

One suspects that contemporary theorists would have predicted a much different conclusion to this area's redevelopment. The hospital administrators, more aggressive and shrewd than they have been shown to be, would never have negotiated with neighborhood residents much less given in to their demands. They would have allowed the area to deteriorate to the point that no opposition, organized or otherwise, could have been mounted against them or be taken seriously. There would have been more displacement and clearance. Redevelopment work in the area certainly would be farther along than it is.

That these things did not not happen speaks to the inablility of contemporary ecologists and Marxists to predict with any certainty how redevelopment will work in any given spot and who will benefit from it. The residential population in Tiffany today is more racially and economically mixed than at any time in its history and more stable than it has been in nearly thirty years. Given the area's history, this is a remarkable achievement.

Pluralism did not come easily to the area. It had to be worked for, and the labor involved was substantial. Residents helped to establish rules to guide the redevelopment process, and they helped to amend that process when it was found wanting. They acquired a degree of equality by being recognized and a degree of efficacy by making others behave differently. Such things were noteworthy by their absence in the redevelopment of Pershing-Waterman.

In a real sense, what happened in Pershing-Waterman helped to shape both the style and substance of redevelopment in the Midton Medical Center area. Persons were more attentive to what would be done in redevelopment areas, and conditions in Tiffany made it easier to be attentive. There was more home ownership and at least the remnant of a strong community. It would not have been as easy for a developer to buy every piece of property or buy out long-time residents. There simply were too many of them in Tiffany. One had no choice but to rehabilitate the neighborood around its established residents.

Many of those persons were black and not especially well-to-do. Ways were found to keep most of them in the neighborhood. A refuge of sorts was found for them in Tiffany. They have remained in the redevelopment area to a great extent; and recent Asian immigrants have been added to their number. The employment opportunities for these people are not known. Should hospital administrators seek to build a stronger bond with the neighborhood, however, these persons could be given training and preferential treatment when jobs became available in the institutions.

The redevelopment of the Midtown Medical Center area made other contributions to the rebuilding of St. Louis. Most persons would not view these contributions favorably, and not without cause. What happened in the Midtown area was a great embarrassment to many persons and brought them unwanted attention. On the other hand, St. Louisans again were forced to deal with sensitive problems associated with redeveloping an older city neighborhood. Though many St. Louisans involved with redevelopment work might disagree, it could be argued that the public interest was served well by the heated argument over Midtown's reclamation. If nothing else, it confirmed that room for low-income minorities would have to be made in future redevelopment plans and neighborhoods. The underclass would have a place in postindustrial St. Louis.

RACE, REDEVELOPMENT, AND THE NEW COMPANY TOWN

G ood books pose important and interesting questions. This book began
with an important but seemingly uninteresting question: Can cities be
rebuilt in a way that accommodates both the rich and poor? The answer would
tell us much about the urban society we expect to create, and this is what made
the question important. What might seem to make it uninteresting is the
possibility that we already knew the answer. That is cities can be rebuilt, but
not in ways that accommodate the interests of both rich and poor.

Older industrial cities may not have been pretty a good part of the time, but
they were places both persons who ran things and persons who made things
could find a home. Cities are different today. Fewer things are made there.
More is managed, traded, or simply consumed. Thus, cities still can be
congenial places for persons who run things or serve those who do. Cities no
longer are congenial places for persons who make things or service the
companies where they work, or so it is commonly thought.

Not all confirmed city observers believe that this should be the case. Some
would like to see cities rebuilt so that both the rich and poor still could find a
home there. Yet in most contests over who stays and who goes, they would
accept at face value that it is the less well-to-do and poor who are required to
leave and the well-off who are invited to stay. For this reason, perhaps, other
city watchers propose that low-income minority residents be relocated to
places where they can find work and decent housing. This would help them

and the cities they left, it is reasoned. Areas vacated by such persons could then be redeveloped in ways better suited to fit in a postindustrial world.

Much of what these city watchers say makes sense, if one accepts the premise that low-income minority people can find no good place to rest inside modern cities. That premise was challenged in this book. Recounted here was the story of how parts of St. Louis were redeveloped in ways that enabled minority residents to stay and benefit from the rebuilding going on around them.

At this point, one could reasonably ask two questions. First, how widely can or should the lessons of St. Louis's redevelopment be applied? The manner in which St. Louisans addressed the obsolescence of their city and the role different parties would play in its revival may have been unique and incapable of being replicated elsewhere. Even if St. Louis could export its redevelopment secrets, however, the long-term implications of those secrets may not be good. Persons might take strong exception to what was accomplished and the idea that city residents really benefit all that much from the rebuilding that occurred.

This brings us to a second and in some ways more important question. What kind of city will St. Louis ultimately become? It is clear enough that St. Louis and most large U.S. cities have shed their industrial coats and are growing something new. Their postindustrial coats are a good deal shinier, at least for the moment, but are they better? We do not yet know whether postindustrial cities are capable of teaching us anything useful about ourselves as a people, where we ought to be going, or how to arrive there in good shape. What happened in St. Louis does not provide any complete or fully satisfying answers to such questions, but it does give some tantalizing glimpses into what the postindustrial city could become. These are the issues we will address in the final chapter.

Can the St. Louis Surprise Be Copied?

St. Louis' redevelopment received a good deal of attention from the media, in part because many observers had declared the city dead. City boosters are proud of what has been accomplished in a comparatively short period of time. A group of developers, city officials, and institutional sponsors of redevelopment came together in the mid-1980s and had a report written that highlighted these successes and their contribution to the entire process. It was published along with similar reports from Louisville, Boston, and Pittsburgh by the Urban Land Institute in 1987.[1]

Three things proved crucial to St. Louis' revival, the authors maintained. First, successive mayoral administrations had cultivated a redevelopment industry. Second, public officials allowed "the private sector" to choose where building would occur. Third, work began in the Central Corridor before moving on to weaker areas.

The authors were correct in noting how public officials had gone out of their way to create, subsidize, and promote the work of a redevelopment industry in St. Louis. It was literally the case that St. Louis had no homegrown developers in the late 1960s and early 1970s. There were companies that would work in the city, to be sure. Yet there was no one around to help rehabilitate old housing or to build new housing appropriate for city living on the scale that it was needed. Public officials in collaboration with interested private parties, among them would-be developers, established procedures and incentives that would encourage developers to do that work. Together they fashioned a progrowth coalition or redevelopment regime that helped to rebuild many parts of St. Louis.[2]

The authors suggest that the "private sector" made the decisions on where to build. These decisions were based primarily on market conditions. Inasmuch as the city's housing market was not good at that time, developers worked in areas where the market could be made attractive. Once a coalition or regime supporting redevelopment was put together, the "private sector" allegedly took the lead in making important redevelopment decisions. Government merely helped to keep the rebuilding industry fed and running smoothly.

This is a most interesting argument because it confirms what many theoreticians say about the way redevelopment games are played inside cities. Private corporations and development firms tell government what they want to do and government helps them do it. Contemporary ecologists would be pleased. They see cities as places where most big decisions and changes are made in the private sector. Governments produce little and coordinate a lot in the world envisioned by ecologists; and the testimony of some leaders in St. Louis's revival would seem to support this argument. It also is consistent with the work of contemporary Marxists who argue that big business decides when and where a city shall be rebuilt and who will benefit from it. Nothing, I dare say, would please Marxists more than to have private leaders admit to directing the redevelopment process in a given city. Leaders in St. Louis would seem to have confirmed what Marxists have been saying all along about the games capitalists play.

What makes the admission of some St. Louis redevelopment leaders all the more interesting in this case is that it is not true. Indeed, it is little more than self-aggrandizing puff. The history of St. Louis's redevelopment shows quite clearly that public officials laid much of the groundwork, both good and bad, on which private developers built. Areas selected for redevelopment often had little inherent strength or no established sponsor. This was the case in both Pershing-Waterman and DeSoto-Carr where public officials had to bring parties together that could carry out projects or return from time to time to keep carefully laid plans from unraveling. Sometimes, private institutions had to be prodded into working in an area. Such was the case for the Midtown Medical Center. In all the areas described in this book, local officials had to encourage developers to pursue one type of rebuilding effort over another.

It simply was not the case that the "private sector" always took the lead, made decisions based on sound businesslike reasoning, or, for that matter, behaved in a disinterested way toward less well-to-do persons. The city government not only fed developers and kept the progrowth coalition together, it also nudged and sometimes coerced the members of that group to behave in a particular way. St. Louis officials often revealed at least as much entrepreneurial flair as the developers and corporations that now claim to have steered the city's redevelopment bandwagon.

An important corollary to the myth of private sector dominance in the redevelopment of St. Louis is that work began in the city's Central Corridor and eventually fanned out into weaker areas. Part of this idea is based in fact: Revitalizing the Central Corridor was an early element in efforts to transform St. Louis into a postindustrial city. It also is true that more time and resources have been spent in this part of town than in any other part. However, much time and money were allocated to projects a good distance away from the Central Corridor. Some of these efforts worked out better than others, but they all contributed to the line of reasoning laid out by the authors of the ULI report: Build on the inherent strength of the Central Corridor; fashion a postindustrial St. Louis around the institutions and residential areas in that part of town.

The prospects for continuing the redevelopment boom much beyond the friendly confines of the city's midsection are not especially good. Federal support for urban redevelopment has decreased, and both black and white local politicians have cooled toward big rebuilding projects. Neither wants neighborhoods disrupted in their part of town.

In his first term as mayor, Vince Schoemehl decided to use the city's discretionary income from sources such as federal block grants to subsidize smaller neighborhood projects. Bigger developers who wanted to work on commercial projects in or around the Central Corridor would have to go after Urban Development Action Grants, which are more competitive and doled out from Washington, not St. Louis. It was a shrewd political move designed to ease the fears of neighborhood leaders and help them stop the deterioraton of their areas before it was necessary to take more drastic action.

Though politically sound, the plan has yet to produce much rehabilitated housing. It takes a long time to assemble enough property to make a package attractive to a developer; and low-interest loan money for rehabilitating small numbers of houses has been difficult to acquire. The overall effect of the policy has been to retard rather than increase the amount of rebuilding in St. Louis neighborhoods. (It also has had the effect of maintaining the existing populations inside neighborhoods waiting to be redeveloped and, at least indirectly, of slowing down the pace of racial integration in areas outside the Central Corridor.) This may change in the future as the housing market improves and money becomes easier to get. In the meantime, however, tracking down the owners of individual pieces of abandoned property has proven a most difficult chore.

Schoemehl's policy is socially conservative. It is less likely to disrupt the current mix of residents inside a neighborhood than the policies pursued by his predecessors John Poelker and Jim Conway. Yet, Conway and Poelker were hardly radicals. They may have supported integration as a matter of principle, but no one ever expected every neighborhood to become integrated. Conway especially used federal money to promote integration. Had such funds not been available, however, perhaps he would not have pushed so hard. It also is instructive to note that both Poelker and Conway promoted redevelopment efforts that had the effect of displacing low-income minority residents from their homes. If Schoemehl's approach to neighborhood redevelopment is socially conservative, it is not much more conservative than Poelker's or Conway's was.

Two facts remain. First, residential integration was feasible and complemented the kinds of institutional and corporate redevelopment that persons wanted in the Central Corridor. Second, conditions are not right for doing this kind of work elsewhere in the city at this time. Contrary to what the authors of the ULI report said, little new or different is likely to happen outside the Central Corridor any time soon.

Approximately 11,000 new and rehabilitated housing units were produced between 1977 and 1985. This did not compensate for the loss of some 60,000 units between 1960 and 1980, but it was a start.[3] Some 6,000 of the units produced were new. Most were built in or around the Central Corridor. Nearly half of the rehabilitated units were in or around LaSalle Park, Tiffany, Pershing-Waterman, and the Washington University Medical Center area. The remaining units were spread among ten or more other neighborhoods across the city.[4]

The redevelopment of St. Louis is not over. Of the $3.2 billion invested in the downtown area since 1958, half has come during the 1980s.[5] It is neighborhood redevelopment that is likely to suffer. It would have been difficult to sustain a high level of housing redevelopment even under good conditions. Both developers and public officials were reluctant to pursue housing projects at the end of the 1980s, however, because of changes in federal tax laws and a poor real estate market. It became more profitable to do commercial projects. A number of firms, especially Pantheon, had difficulty filling units they had built. New housing projects such as the one proposed for the area just west of DeSoto-Carr suddenly were being reconsidered. Projects already underway were facing the prospect of filling more slowly than expected. The houses that developer Mark Conner was building in DeSoto-Carr and LaSalle Park, for instance, essentially were competing for the same customers. Moreover, new Conner houses were keeping the resale value of older Conner houses lower because of the reduced demand for housing in the downtown area.

Especially during this lull, perhaps, it is important to keep two things in mind. First, the racial and economic mixing taking place in the Central Corridor will not be easily exported to neighborhoods with more stable and racially homogeneous populations. Second, had the institutional machinery to support such work not been in place by the mid-1970s, it is most unlikely that new and rehabilitated housing would have been produced so quickly and in neighborhoods set apart from the downtown area. The Land Clearance for Redevelopment Authority was able to rehabilitate only a few apartments during the late 1960s, and it had plenty of money. The old urban renewal program did not call for things to rehabilitated, simply torn down. The LCRA simply did not know how to do rehabilitation work. There was no private development industry in St. Louis at that time. Such and industry was created over the course of the next five to seven years. *Local public officials created that industry, subsidized it, and gave it some direction.*

One runs the risk of attributing to public officials the same kind of shrewd and thorough plotting that only corporate directors and cagey developers are supposed to be able to carry out. This would be a big mistake. A good deal of the time they backed their way into solutions to problems without fully appreciating what they were doing. How Mayor Conway's staff put together some of the institutional machinery that allowed so much housing to be produced during and after their tenure is a good illustration of this point.

Only after 1974 was an effective and self-perpetuating "growth coalition" inside St. Louis built. This was not easy to accomplish. St. Louis bankers did not have much experience making investments in risky inner-city neighborhoods. Indeed, their record of divesting themselves of any obligation to such neighborhoods was a good deal stronger. (FHA policies effectively kept loan money out of inner-city neighborhoods until 1968. Bankers were not the only persons who knew little about city real estate markets.) Bankers also had a tendency to distrust politicians or at least be wary of making loan commitments involving the city government that might last beyond one mayoral administration, I was told. Gaining the trust of city bankers would be necessary, if those bankers were expected to provide lines of credit to developers sent by city officials. The problem was to find a satisfactory way to guarantee that redevelopment projects could be mounted and carried out in a timely fashion.

No one ever sat down and said, "This is a problem we need to work on." Nor did public officials go about solving it in any systematic way. They arrived at a solution almost by accident, as Mayor Conway's staff worked to solidify control over redevelopment activities in the mayor's office.

The city's Board of Aldermen and comptroller were the biggest impediments to putting redevelopment projects "on track" quickly. The former has the authority to appropriate the funds spent by the mayor. The latter is supposed to ensure that appropriated funds are spent wisely and that city agencies do not spend more money than they have been allocated. The comptroller did not trust the mayor to curb the improvident spending habits of agency officials, including those in charge of the CDA. The Board of Aldermen fretted about redevelopment projects going over budget—not an unreasonable fear given their knowledge of urban renewal and model cities programs—and they doubted Conway's commitment to low-income housing. (One former official noted that the members of the Board of Aldermen really were much more concerned about having their pet projects approved, and that is why they made it difficult for the mayor to implement his rebuilding projects.) Together, the aldermen and comptroller managed to stall some of Mayor Conway's early redevelopment initiatives by keeping too close an eye on how redevelopment funds were being spent.

During the summer of 1978, Conway's staff decided that they had to do something to make the comptroller pay legitimate bills submitted by developers to the city. "By exercising a pocket veto," said one former Conway assistant, "the comptroller was threatening to undercut any hope of getting private developers to work in the city. Developers simply would not put up with that kind of [nonsense]. What we did was sign a 'master agreement' with Mercantile Bank, which was the only one interested in our idea." The banks in effect, became the city's fiscal watchdog. "We put about $3 million of CDA's money into an escrow account. Attached to the master agreement would be a series of 'third party agreements' with Merc standing between the developer and another bank interested in that developer's project. Money in the escrow account was disbursed by Merc only as directed by CDA and only after Merc's lawyers determined that it was a legal expenditure."

Everyone seemed to like the plan, except perhaps the comptroller. "The Board of Aldermen approved the plan. It avoided the pocket veto, and it helped establish a good relation with a big bank," a former official said. The irony was that "we never would have thought of this arrangement, if it hadn't been for the comptroller's stubbornness. We probably would have hired fifteen accountants to oversee all of the projects, and they wouldn't have done as good a job as the bank." Not only did the city save money this way, but it made money from interest earned by the federal funds reserved in Merc's escrow account. Merc was paid for its services, and the developers no longer worried about paying their bills.

After Conway's people took care of the comptroller, they had to deal with the Board of Aldermen. The aldermen came after Mayor Conway's redevelopment plans from the appropriation's end of the process rather than the expenditure's end, but the effect was the same. Projects were delayed. The aldermen accomplished this "by getting into the details of how much money Conway proposed to spend on really tiny things, like garden rakes," I was told. At that rate, "it would take well over a year to get specific expenditures approved. And this would kill any developer, because they have their own bills to pay." This did not seem to bother many aldermen who had their own personal complaints about this mayor, and they refused to budge.

That changed when the regional director of HUD threatened to take back all of the federal money the aldermen were unwilling to let the mayor spend. Several people told me that HUD's intervention was no accident. "Conway's people set it up. What's more, they pulled it off. It was a nice piece of work. All they had to do was stand there, shrug their shoulders, and say, 'We told you so.'" Then, Conway's CDA director, Don Spaid, "walked into the aldermen's offices and cut a deal that allowed them to approve spending money for a given project, but left the specifics up to the CDA." This arrangement "sped up the whole process," and it still enabled the aldermen's fears to be addressed. As one former official in Conway's administration told me, "months still separated Board approval and the actual expenditures. So, money changed hands only after the approved work was being carried out. No one got ahead of the budgeted money." He added that "having the 'TPA' (third party agreement) with Merc really helped to soothe the aldermen and made it easier for them to accept this arrangement."

There was one other nice outcome of this fight that was not anticipated. It forced Conway to reconcile his personal opposition to funding "another low-income housing program" with the demands of some aldermanic leaders to do something for the poor. The bargain that was struck led to the creation of something Conway's people called *Housing Implementation Program* run by the CDA. Mixing subsidized and nonsubsidized housing units within the same project, at a ratio of approximately 1:4, became a central tenet of that program and a hallmark of Conway's whole approach to neighborhood revitalization.

HUD officials generally were pleased that more money was being spent and that more housing was going to be produced in the city. They were less than pleased, however, that the city government was earning interest on the federal money it had laying around in bank accounts waiting to be spent. Now, HUD was on Conway's back and demanding that the city spend available and newly appropriated funds more quickly. Conway's staff was not terribly keen on this idea. They liked the extra money the city "earned" in this way. They also were not at all sure that they could spend it as quickly as HUD wanted it spent. Remember, there were only a few developers in St. Louis by the mid-1970s. "Well," said one former Conway staffer, "this is how we handled that little problem. The law says that expenditures must begin forty days after the project is approved. The law doesn't say by when the last money has to be spent. We'd have some architect's drawings done or some other small thing like that, and we'd spend some money. Then they'd leave us alone. After that, we strung the whole process out so that we could earn more interest on the federal funds."

Revealed in the way Conway and his staff solidified their control over redevelopment efforts was a willingness to experiment with the law. This is not a trait peculiar to that administration, however. "They all do it," one current city official told me. "They pull and stretch a law until they think it says they can do what they wanted to do, then they do it." Usually, they succeed. Sometimes, the laws actually are changed so that the politician's questionable actions suddenly acquire a scent of propriety. One of the Conway administration's most notable innovations in this regard was its "creative" use of CDBG and UDAG funds for housing development projects that probably were ineligible for assistance. Whether it was providing "public improvements" around housing sites, subsidizing rehabilitation efforts before it was legal, or using a rather broad definition of what constituted economic development and a low-income neighborhood to justify its actions, the Conway administration "massaged" federal policies until those policies were amended to include the kinds of things Conway had been supporting all along.[6]

On most occasions, though, the Conway administration simply found perfectly legal things to do before most other big city mayors did. For instance, St. Louis was among the first cities that used CDBG funds to assist families in purchasing or refinancing a rehabilitated home. This usually was accomplished by using federal money to lower the effective rate of a home mortgage. There were instances, however, when the money was passed along to a developer or buyer as a loan or an outright gift. No matter how the money was spent, it always served to lower the eventual cost of renting an apartment or buying a home. It was the kind of advantage that city developers and public leaders believed they needed to compete with suburban home builders and apartment managers. It also showed private lenders that the city was making a serious long-term commitment to neighborhood redevelopment.

The Conway administration may not have invented the idea of leveraging, but it certainly learned how to increase the return on its redevelopment investments a good deal sooner and more effectively than leaders in many other cities. It did not come by its knowledge of leveraging and real estate investments by accident. Conway's staff, like Poelker's before it and Schoemehl's after it, was in constant and close contact with the city's bankers and whatever developers they could attract and trust. Together, they fashioned Conway's Housing Incentive Program and For-Sale Incentive Program. (The latter was introduced as mortgage interest rates began to climb during the late 1970s, and developers such as Pantheon faced almost certain extinction if they did not get some public assistance to make their housing affordable.) Together, they tried to figure out which areas to redevelop and how to proceed with rehabilitation efforts or new construction. Clearly, more than a little thought went into the creation of the institutional machinery that allowed so much housing to be built and rehabilitated in such a short time. A lot of blind experimenting and no small amount of creative bookkeeping also contributed to it, however. These lessons as much as anything else need to be understood and copied, if leaders in other cities want to create their own redevelopment surprises.

Should St. Louis's Redevelopment Be Copied?

Quite apart from whether St. Louis can be copied is the question of whether it is a good thing to be copying. Given the economics and social costs attached to urban redevelopment, is this the way to rebuild cities or are there better ways to do it? Important as it is to ask ourselves this question, it is all but impossible to answer satisfactorily. Each of us may have some notion in our head of what the postindustrial city should look like, who should live in it, and what part it should play in the larger society. On the other hand, we may have no idea whatsoever what kind of a city we should be building.

What political scientist Clarence Stone has said about urban redevelopment and the common good bears repeating.

The common good is something that doesn't just happen. It is something that must be brought into being, albeit imperfectly, by a set of political actors.

[Yet] those who are endowed with authority may use their capacity in pursuance of a partial view of the common good...[and] conception[s] of the common good can fall out of favor as conditions change.

For this reason, any policy, no matter how sincerely put forward as being in the public interest, is inescapably shaped by those who carry it out.[7]

The common good is something for which we strive but cannot fully comprehend or reach. It is an elusive goal, and we should not be surprised when our best efforts fall substantially short of the mark.

This admonition safely planted, we begin to search for ways to distinguish good redevelopment from bad redevelopment. Contemporary theorists working in the Marxist and ecological traditions provide some help. They are pretty good at telling us what areas inside cities usually are repaired and why these areas among all others tend to be chosen. Although the five areas described in this book did not match perfectly the kinds of places theorists expect to be redeveloped, both ecologists and Marxists could provide a quite reasonable explanation as to why these areas were rebuilt. Each area was itself a site of major postindustrial development or quite close to such a site. These sections of St. Louis could be rebuilt to complement the professional, technical, and service institutions that had become crucial to every city's economic recovery.

Contemporary ecologists and Marxists were much less help when it came to describing how areas were redeveloped and who benefitted from it. In general, they would have expected most if not all low-income persons to be replaced by relatively well-to-do white homeowners. This did not happen in the areas described here. The Pershing-Waterman area was a place from which almost all low-income blacks were moved, and even it came to house a racially and economiclly mixed population. If it can be said that some benefit accrues to living in a neater and safer neighborhood, then the low-income and minority persons living in these areas today benefitted from urban redevelopment.

How the redevelopment process unfolded in each area also was something of a surprise. The biggest surprise, at least for contemporary Marxists, would have been that corporations and institutions either chose to stay in a rundown city or could not easily move from it. Ralston Purina could have moved to land it owned in St. Louis County, but its directors chose to remain on the site where the company was founded. St. Louis University Medical School turned down an offer to move to St. Louis County in part because such a move would have interrupted if not reduced its subsidies to St. Louis University. Washington University owns a good deal of property across the city, and the value of that property would have diminished had the medical center disbanded. Finally, the survival of Pantheon depended upon its leaders' ability to revive the neighborhoods in which it worked. Beyond the fact that such organizations would have a commitment to the city, it is surprising that they would be responsive to public pressure and even amend their plans to suit the needs of relatively powerless groups. It happened in the five parts of St. Louis whose redevelopment was described. This includes the Pershing-Waterman area where the Pantheon Corporation chose to retreat from plans to redevelop the blocks around Nina Place because of resistance from neighborhood leaders and advocates for the poor.

One other thing about the redevelopment of these areas rarely comes to the public's attention but is crucial to the operation of a progrowth regime: the favors that coalition members do for each other. Clarence Stone calls such things "side payments."[8] Side payments do *not* include things such as tax breaks and government subsidies to businesses or contributions from developers to local politicians.[9] Important as these may be, requesting and receiving that kind of assistance is part of an established routine in the business of rebuilding cities. It also is the type of assistance that both the media and critics of redevelopment are likely to discuss when they want to point out the cozy relation between developers and politicians.

A side payment is a favor that one member in a progrowth coalition does for another. It need not involve an exchange of money. A side payment is just as important and perhaps more important as social collateral. Its value lies in the trust it creates among parties who must learn to cooperate, if they are to succeed in a risky venture. These favors provide a basis for mutual support and, when necessary, for disciplining a coalition member. Side payments are a means of inducing socially responsible public behavior through the manipulation of resources that go to private parties. In St. Louis's redevelopment, there are many illustrations of side payments being used to secure socially beneficial public ends.

It is more than good business, for instance, that keeps the Carr Square and Cochran Gardens TMCs working with developer Richard Baron. Baron spent long hours with these groups during and after the 1969 rent strike. He came to respect the groups, and the groups trusted him. In a sense, Baron's whole development business was a side payment to him from the TMCs. He reciprocated by advancing them the initial money they would need to invest in the O'Fallon development. The TMCs, in turn, used much of the money they later earned from that project to maintain their sites, even though they were not obligated to do so. In effect, the TMCs helped the city by supplementing funds spent on modernizing Cochran and maintaining both it and Carr Square. Such investments were not overlooked by city officials who worked hard to secure public and private funds to help the TMCs in other ventures.

Side payments showed up in the other redevelopment areas as well. When the Midtown Medical Center Redevelopment Corporation ran into trouble, for example, representatives of the city's business community were placed on its board of directors. Civic Progress, a group composed of St. Louis business leaders, had loaned MMCRC money through several of its member corporations. Ralston Purina executive Fred Perabo, who was in charge of LaSalle Park's redevelopment, was one of the new board members. Having such persons on the board helped to reassure nervous city leaders that MMCRC might be saved and that the city would be spared any further embarrassment.

On the other hand, part of MMCRC's problem had been that its charter required it not to displace anyone. MMCRC did displace persons, though fewer than had been displaced from other redevelopment areas and probably fewer than needed to be moved to rebuild the area more efficiently. The nondisplacement provision was "imposed" on MMCRC, I was told, by the Board of Aldermen whose members did not want to be held responsible for creating another Pershing-Waterman. MMCRC accepted this restriction but was unable or unwilling to behave in accordance with it. "Everyone would have understood it, if MMCRC had displaced some of its residents," one former city official told me. "All of these corporations break thier contracts with the city in one way or another. It's just that MMCRC went too far." The agreement not to displace persons was a favor that backfired.

A favor granted by the Pantheon Corporation to the city in 1979 has met a similar fate. The company agreed to redevelop a neighborhood whose reclamation had proven as unprofitable as it was prolonged. Lafayette Town sits on the edge of an area that was cleared during the urban renewal period. Little redevelopment had occurred because of its poor location. City officials hoped that Pantheon, which had been given so much assistance in the Pershing-Waterman area, would be good enough to help them out in this area. Pantheon has not accomplished much in Lafayette Town. Since 1979, several projects have gone forward. In general, Pantheon did little beyond serving as the area's land broker. Neighborhood residents became angry over the lack of progress. In 1988, they demanded that the right to rebuild Lafayette Town be passed on to a developer that would do more than charge other firms outrageous amounts of money to build on nearly worthless property. It was likely that some action would be taken to remove Pantheon as the area's developer. In return, however, Pantheon was demanding a favor of its own. It wanted to be paid $1.4 million for its investment in the area and for the new developer to assume Pantheon's outstanding debt of $1 million.[10]

The favor WUMCRC did in accepting the Ranken neighborhood under its redevelopment umbrella has worked out much better, of course. So, too, has the arrangement between the city and Mercantile Bank that had the bank processing bills submitted by developers. This made no profit for the bank, but it did facilitate the entire redevelopment process.

Side payments accomplish something different from tax breaks, subsidies, and contributions: They are social collateral. Recipients of redevelopment assistance either are expected to help the city more or come to assume a bigger role in its improvement than has been agreed to contractually. Sometimes the favors work out well; other times they do not. Nevertheless, stringing together concessions, compromises, and favors sustains a coalition and lets redevelopment work proceed in an efficient manner. Persons who want to undertake risky projects make side payments to reassure their "business partners" that they are reliable and willing to make sacrifices to complete a job.

The willingness of local business persons to assume such additional and sometimes expensive obligations cannot be explained easily by contemporary ecologists and Marxists. Nor can such theorists easily account for the ability of low-income groups to influence the redevelopment process or receive some benefit from it. Although both ecologists and Marxists assume that modern corporations are mobile, Marxists make much more of this point to help account for the seemingly extraordinary power business has over government. Yet, at least in St. Louis, several corporations and institutions that could have left decided to help rebuild the city instead. The kind of work they sponsored indicates that something more than blind greed or a fear of social unrest at the hands of the underclass was motivating their leaders.

All of these things would be hard for contemporary theorists to explain. This raises the possibility that their standard explanations of whether urban redevelopment serves a public interest also may be flawed. After all, if Marxists and ecologists cannot account for how the redevelopment process works, one must assume that their explanations for why it allegedly works in a particular way are suspect. One must consider the possibility that urban redevelopment can achieve something that benefits more than those who typically are thought to profit from it. It is to a fuller description of what that something may be that we now turn.

The City as Polity

The ancient Greeks, a people who knew something about politics and building cities, never worried about urban renewal programs, public-private partnerships, tax credits, and social scientists, so far as we know. They were quite preoccupied, however, with discovering how to build a good community. They thought the most likely place to build one would be in a city. Cities have people in sufficient number and variety to produce a mix of ideas and customs. Such things being necessary to enrich public life, the Greeks sought to bring the best of these customs, ideas and people together to build a city that could benefit all citizens.

They tried and failed to build such a place. Unfortunately, the Greeks had a fairly limited view of who could be a citizen. The pursuit of the common good was reserved for uncommon persons. Slaves, barbarians, members of the laboring classes, women, and non-Greeks would have been excluded from the ideal political community. This, no doubt, contributed to their failure. Centuries later, Pullman tried to build a fit and viable community from the persons who worked for his company. His vision of who could be a citizen was similarly limited, too. Notwithstanding such notable failures, city builders never stopped trying and failing to create a city where people could live in relative harmony and practice the art of politics together.

In the second half of the twentieth century, many persons have all but conceded that this is an impossible dream. A number of them advocate the removal of lower-income minority residents from cities and the relocation of such persons to more dispersed communities. Such a strategy has many serious and generally unacknowledged problems. On the other hand, those who could be expected to oppose such an idea, most notably contemporary Marxists, provide no novel or realistic way of building a city where both the rich and poor can be accommodated on a long-term basis.[11] A great deal of their writing is dedicated, after all, to demonstrating just how impoverished and corrupt local politics is. This is especially clear in matters related to urban redevelopment, where Marxists allege much mischief is afoot and offer tantalizing glimpses of how the rebuilding of cities is rigged to favor big corporations and well-to-do white persons.

We would seem to be stuck in a situation where the only realistic strategy is to continue what we have been doing. Some parts of cities will be rebuilt. Some persons gradually will leave the city or move back to it. Most low-income minority residents will sit more or less where they are and remain unproductive. Life will go on.

Some thirty years ago, at least one person thought that the situation could have turned out differently. Political scientist Norton Long had hoped that business leaders would find a responsible way to reassert themselves in the daily affairs of cities. He viewed the modern corporation as competing with the city itself for the loyalty of its personnel; and he worried about the loss of civic-minded stewards who could help guide the city. He thought that if unions and companies found an agreeable way to invigorate the political process, it might be possible to build a more united community and a set of ethical standards everyone could adopt.

Long's view of citizenship and politics was borrowed from the Greeks and more recent urban reformers. They all worried about how to build a community from a mass of people who had very different backgrounds. Long resurrected the nineteenth century American idea that the city's business leaders could be instrumental in drawing everyone else together.[12] Today, few students of urban politics and economics would hold such a view. Most would reject it outright. There is little in the recent history of U.S. cities to indicate that business leaders are much interested in doing this. There is more evidence that quite the opposite is true.

In this book, we saw that Long's vision was neither impaired nor destined to turn cities into a plutocrat's playground. The areas in St. Louis whose redevelopment was featured here not only look better today, they also have racially and economically mixed populations. The political debates inspired by redevelopment work promoted by corporations did not ignore the problems inherent in building a more pluralistic city. Indeed, the behavior of public and private leaders fueled speculation about such problems and how they could be addressed.

On the surface, it would appear that what took place in parts of St. Louis could pass for "good redevelopment." It is time to reexamine what criteria were used in making such a judgement and how well the St. Louis case satisfies those criteria. It is easiest to do this by reintroducing the criteria in the form of four questions.

1. Did redevelopment promote pluralism?

2. Were the interests of powerless groups considered?

3. Were the goals of powerless groups realized?

4. Was redevelopment pursued with these questions placed squarely before the public?

Redevelopment and Pluralism

Those parts of St. Louis that have been redeveloped most also tend to have more racially and economically mixed populations. This is true of the Central Corridor generally. It is especially true of the five areas in it or contiguous to it whose redevelopment was described here.

Other parts of St. Louis city also have a degree of racial or economic integration. Some have been redeveloped in a self-conscious way; others simply have become that way as persons moved in or out of the area. The point is not that racial and economic integration is possible only through the intervention of large corporations and institutions. Rather, it is that such intervention can facilitate and even cause integration to occur where none was thought possible.

The population losses and reshuffling that began shortly after World War II have not ended, but they have slowed down considerably. Efforts to rebuild St. Louis followed and in many instances contributed to this movement of persons. The northern third of St. Louis became overwhelmingly black. The southern third has remained almost as white as it once was. The middle third of the city is more racially and economically mixed than the other parts of St. Louis. The fact and manner of its redevelopment contributed to making it so.

Redevelopment promoted pluralism. It prompted a debate over whether integration was something to be pursued as an end in itself or merely embraced as a by-product of other changes occurring in the city. Although the final outcome of that debate remains in doubt, its basic outline is not. Integration is something that can be achieved on a workable scale in a variety of settings. It can be an integral part of one's plans for rebuilding a neighborhood or even a broad portion of a city. Integration is not something so crucial to the future of the whole city, however, that every part needs to hold a racially and economically mixed population. It is self-evident that not every part can be integrated and that many persons from different races and social classes do not see residential and social integration as necessary for them to carry on useful and happy lives.

In some cases, it is better for certain individuals to live among people more like themselves. This kind of segregation, whether it is imposed or chosen voluntarily, can help to create small communities within which people not only feel better about themselves but also act together to promote their own economic and political interests. If this seems an apology for middle-class parochialism, it is not. For it is the same principle embraced by the leaders of tenant management in St. Louis and in public housing sites across the United States. At some point they may be prepared to move more boldly into a completely integrated world. On the other hand, they may elect never to become fully assimilated into all parts of American society. What our five areas in St. Louis clearly demonstrate, however, is that the assimilation of individuals typically thought to be unprepared or unfit for life in the post-industrial city can be facilitated through aggressive redevelopment undertaken by public officials and modern corporations.

Redevelopment and Political Equality

Many people and organizations have a real and immediate interest in urban redevelopment. Most of them are not heard from on a regular basis, however. Those who are consulted or usually make their influence felt tend to be more well-to-do or better connected to a city's business and political leaders. Among those ordinarily excluded from this process are poor and minority people and the established residents in a neighborhood. To the extent that urban redevelopment helps to invigorate local politics, and maybe serve more pluralistic ends, such parties would be involved in the rebuilding process.

Not much was heard from these parties during the urban renewal phase of St. Louis's redevelopment. More recently, a good deal has been heard from them. The degree to which they were heard varied from one to another redevelopment area. The two tenant management groups were quite successful in making themselves heard. They both resisted efforts to move their people and later made their positions known on how DeSoto-Carr should be rebuilt. What they did and how they did it capture almost ideally what some contemporary Marxists would view as effective grassroots organizing.

There was grassroots organizing in LaSalle Park and the two medical center areas. The remnants of LaSalle Park's resident population welcomed, even solicited early urban renewal plans. They wanted to leave. Residents in the two medical center areas resisted some plans to redevelop their areas. Other parties, selected by the redevelopment corporations, helped to monitor and plan rebuilding efforts. Neighborhood residents in LaSalle Park have been consulted and advised on plans to rebuild their neighborhood from time to time, but they have not tried to initiate any plans of their own.

No neighborhood group formed in Pershing-Waterman. A few residents came together and complained about rent increases several years ago, but nothing came of it. Black residents who were displaced found a voice only through the lawyers who sued Pantheon in their name. The story was different in Nina Place and Lafayette Town, where residents and outside groups resisted Pantheon's efforts to do more work in those areas. Pantheon remained unopposed inside Pershing-Waterman, however.

Direct citizen involvement varied in these areas. It was expressed best and most consistently in DeSoto-Carr. In all five areas, though, some room was made to accommodate the interests of low-income persons. One would have to conclude that redevelopment politics in some of the present neighborhoods moved the city a little in the direction of granting minorities greater political equality. Low-income groups organized and became involved in the policy-making process. They were effective in having their interests considered.

Redevelopment and Efficacy

The matter of their organizing aside, the goals espoused by less powerful groups often were realized. Again, this was clearest in DeSoto-Carr, where the tenant management groups have consistently expanded both the number and variety of tasks they undertook and completed. The area that had the next clearest record of successful citizen involvement was the Midtown Medical

Center area. There, local citizens were involved in both creating and amending the area's redevelopment plan. The interests of less powerful groups were acted on in the Washington University Medical area and in LaSalle Park. Minority and low-income whites were not excluded from the areas. If anything, their presence became more secure.

In general, however, there is little indication that low-income or minority groups exercised much influence over the basic direction and timing of redevelopment efforts in the city. Virtually all of the important decisions were made by public and private leaders who at times accommodated their interests to the interests of organized residents.

Only in DeSoto-Carr has there been any progress made in exploring ways to involve low-income blacks in the city's economy. The plans to build an industrial park just west of DeSoto-Carr offer hope that more can be done to expand further these employment opportunities. However, no sustained effort has been made to increase the job prospects of low-income blacks in any of the other redevelopment areas. To his credit, the original director of the Midtown Medical Center Redevelopment Corporation subsidized a job-training operation in his area, but it was not continued for long.

Additional efforts must be made to train and place low-income blacks into jobs that will enable them to create a secure niche for themselves inside a postindustrial St. Louis. Otherwise, the possible long-term benefits of redevelopment that could accrue to minorities would be wasted. In the absence of such efforts, it becomes more difficult to argue against plans to relocate minority people to places outside of central cities where employment opportunities might be greater.

The important point that can be made in this book is that postindustrial development does not necessarily create an environment hostile to low-income minority residents. They can find a home in the rebuilt city. It would be hard work to take the next step toward integrating them more fully into the city's rebuilt economy. The alternatives, however, are likely to be more expensive and not as likely to produce a community in which pluralism is possible.

Redevelopment and a Public Dialogue

Urban redevelopment is a means to many ends. For some persons it is primarily a way to make money or acquire a measure of political power; for others it is merely another way to lose their home. The argument made in this book has been that redevelopment can serve broader, more socially desirable ends. If this is to occur, some theorists believe we must face quite openly what is gained and lost as a result of redevelopment work. There must be a public dialogue about the consequences of rebuilding cities that can inform and guide the rebuilding process. Moreover, that dialogue needs to be framed in fairly explicit moral terms. It is not enough for parties with a real or alleged interest in the way cities are rebuilt to quietly agree on the merits of a particular plan. They should lay their arguments out before the public so that everyone has a chance to render a judgment on how good or bad that plan is. Only then can we be relatively certain that the plan can serve the common good.

This kind of dialogue entails a substantial risk. Every society has built-in stresses and strains. In every society distinctions are made among people, and some persons are rewarded more than others. And in every society much effort goes into masking such inequalities or softening some of their effects.[13] It is an exceptional occurrence when the people of a society create a situation where those stresses, strains, and inequities can be laid bare and addressed. Yet, this is precisely what can happen when corporations try to redevelop inner-city neighborhoods and mix together people from different races and social classes.

This is what happened in St. Louis. What some St. Louisans did was not always successful, and thus far their solutions have not been copied widely. This does not make them less valuable; it only makes them less useful to the enterprising theorist. The theorist's lot in this case is a hard one: a search for signs that St. Louisans thought and argued about redevelopment in a principled way. The principle in question was the building of a community composed of different people who could practice politics together.

Did St. Louisans think and argue about redevelopment with this principle in mind? Sometimes, they did; more often, they did not. Public discussion over good and bad redevelopment in St. Louis did seem to increase in the early 1980s, but not to the point that it had a profound impact on the direction and timing of redevelopment in different parts of the city. The expanded dialogue occurred at a time of much residential redevelopment. People were sensitive to what had happened in Pershing-Waterman and still was happening in the Midtown Medical Center area. The irony, of course, is that this surge in public debate occurred just before residential redevelopment began to taper off.

Neither ecologists nor Marxists would be especially surprised by this. The former consider local politics today a trivial pursuit and would think no more (or less) of urban redevelopment were it discussed in this way. The latter wish for such a dialogue but believe that the world conspires against it. The dialogue came almost too late to have any effect on the way neighborhoods were redeveloped. A fuller explanation of why St. Louisans were not more high-minded about their redevelopment requires us to borrow a little from these two competing views of the urban world and a lot from U.S. history.

This much can be said in defense of people who fret about the emptiness of local politics or simply accept it as a historical fact. Nineteenth century urban Americans were more self-conscious about the problem of uniting a divided and fractious public. They also experimented more with reforms intended to draw together the city's different races, ethnic groups, and classes. They may have succeeded no more than we do today, but they certainly worked harder at it.

Their attempts to build a new urban community failed in part because reformers could hardly keep up with the pace of city growth. Leaders were preoccupied with their city's expansion. They literally had bigger things on their minds. A more important reason for the failure to build a united public may have been that reformers were approaching the problem from the wrong direction. They hoped to ensure the city's prosperity by creating some idea of the common good that all residents would adopt. Once everyone shared the same vision, the reformers thought that civil order could be secured and economic progress would be virtually guaranteed. Unfortunately, this approach did not work. Most people simply did not accept the reformer's version of what was in their best interest. People remained rowdy. The city grew despite their bad behavior, and many reformers moved to the suburbs.

Contemporary St. Louisans who wanted to save their city took a different approach. They were not worried about building a bigger or more ideal city. They certainly had no expectations that their redevelopment projects would help unite all St. Louisans or provide them with a common understanding of their proper place in the city. (Too many people were moving around for anyone to know where his or her place was.) The St. Louis reformers discussed in this book worried about losing what little was left of the city. To be sure, they wanted to leave something of value for all St. Louisans. Their primary interest, though, was in seeing to it that there was enough of the city left for them to use. Their approach was to secure the common good, however one wished to define it, by preserving the city's economic vitality, not the other way around.

They had no particular moral vision for all St. Louisans in mind. Integration was a nice idea, perhaps, but it was not the idea that drove politicians and developers to do what they did. Their primary interest was in rebuilding the city, or at least the middle part of it. The financing of redevelopment deals was easier and nicer when it included housing for low- and moderate-income residents. Later on, when it became clear that such projects worked out well, they were not timid about expanding the use of subsidized housing to leverage bigger and better deals.

They accepted the creation of racially and economically mixed neighborhoods as an accomplishment, but they did so with a certain detached satisfaction. Some were convinced that it was a good thing to do. Others were just happy that their social engineering did not flop. None thought that integration is so great a moral imperative that every neighborhood or housing project should be economically and racially mixed. These are practical men and women. They may have strong beliefs about integration, and they may go out of their way to pursue a good business deal that encourages it. However, they will not chase a bad deal just to achieve more racial and economic mixing in a neighborhood.

This much of the explanation as to why St. Louisans did not speak more often or loudly about a broader public good that could be served by redevelopment belongs to contemporary ecologists. They believe that people will do what is necessary to make a community's economy complement things happening outside the city. They also would accept the do-gooding of nineteenth century reformers as a well-meaning but fundamentally flawed response to the big changes occurring in cities at that time. Some persons may have been helped for a little while. Efforts to unite the city's different people probably were more important in providing some friendly camouflage for those who were trying to make the city grow.

The latter part of this explanation really belongs to contemporary Marxists. They believe that the world is organized in ways that frustrate any serious treatment of the things that keep some people on top and the rest of us on the bottom fighting among ourselves. They would see mischief behind the do-gooding of nineteenth century reformers, and they would see it in our century, too.

Reformers in the second half of this century may have been less eclectic than their nineteenth century counterparts, but they managed to keep busy. Of particular interest to them were various ways to help black people become better integrated into the mainstream economic and political life of the United States. In St. Louis, this was expressed most consistently and powerfully through attempts to desegregate public schools in the area. Several participants in the city's rebuilding campaign spoke candidly about all the fuss over school desegregation. They thought it helped to take attention off of efforts to rebuild St. Louis, and they appreciated it. They were not unaware of the fact that they were helping to create some neighborhoods where white and black people actually would live together. They also knew, however, that most persons would look at the displacement of poor and black residents as a more important issue. At least in the short run, residential development often made the gap between the races more apparent. So, they pursued their work as quietly as they could.

Often they could not avoid publicity. Yet a surprising amount of the basic work that went into building St. Louis' development industry was never reported or openly discussed. People involved with that industry are still reluctant to talk about some things that they did, but they can be quite candid about what others did. From what they say, it is clear that the redevelopment game was highly structured and favored some players over others. The basic decisions on what parts of town were to be improved, who would do the work, and how much assistance they would receive, were not made in an open forum.

The present study shows that the redevelopment process in St. Louis was made possible and directed a great deal by the local government. Redevelopment was not exclusively or even primarily the product of corporate leaders who had big plans and immediate access to public and private financing to carry out those plans. The work of politicians and government enabled "civic concerns" to be interjected into the development process. They were not slaves to corporate interests.

The degree of cooperation among public and private leaders in St. Louis was unprecedented, but there was no conspiracy among corporate leaders, bankers, politicians, and developers. Initially, only a few politicians pushed for these changes. Only one bank president had the nerve to step forward. The city's only developer was not very big, and only one corporation had initiated any kind of neighborhood revitalization campaign. Several business leaders willingly admitted that they had little idea of the trouble they were creating for themselves by undertaking such work; none had any experience with large-scale rehabilitation efforts. Greedy capitalists were not waiting in the wings to surprise everyone with a redevelopment boom. With few exceptions, they had to be convinced that anything outside of the central business district that had not already been knocked down was worth saving.

The rewards for a corporation undertaking residential redevelopment projects were not all that attractive. Several St. Louis corporations actually declined the opportunity to become involved in this kind of civic improvement effort. One northside company turned down several requests by Mayor Conway's staff to "adopt" a nearby neighborhood. Efforts by residents to rehabilitate the neighborhood had been relatively successful. Yet the area lacked a substantial tenant that could serve as an anchor for these efforts and help sponsor additional work. City officials could not convince the owners of this industrial plant to undertake the project. Historically, neighborhood residents had trekked down a big hill to work in this plant. Today, a highway provided a visual buffer between the plant and neighborhood. City officials thought this made it easier for the corporation's directors to turn down their requests. Another and possibly more important reason may have been that plant workers no longer lived in that neighborhood. This kind of company had much less in common with the neighborhood than had once been the case.

A second large corporation on the Near Southside had made known its willingness to serve as a sponsor for the redevelopment of the neighborhood surrounding it. Few existing residents may have been working in the plant and corporate headquarters today. Nevertheless, the corporation had a long history of civic involvement in the city. Its offer of assistance was rejected by a vocal segment of the resident population. These persons apparently feared that many elderly and poor people would be displaced. The critics did not fall into either category, and they wanted to preserve the neighborhood's current mix of young professionals, rehabbers, and the poor. In this case, an articulate and vigorous group of people succeeded in discouraging their corporate neighbor from leading revitalization efforts.

The redevelopment of these two neighborhoods has proceeded, despite the lack of corporate involvement. Both benefitted from the rehabilitation boom in the late 1970s and early 1980s. The Northside neighborhood had 455 housing units repaired in 110 buildings. The neighborhood on the Near Southside had 608 units rehabilitated in 188 buildings.

However, the reclamation of these areas has lagged behind that of neighborhoods where institutional sponsors were found for redevelopment projects. Many buildings in both of the unadopted areas have not yet been repaired. In the case of the Near Southside neighborhood, for example, the income tax credits for historic rehabilitation work helped in the renovation of only one-third of the structures that could have been repaired.[14] Now that the real estate market is a bit weaker, this neighborhood's reclamation will be retarded further. In just this kind of situation, local observers noted, the presence of a corporate sponsor "with deep pockets" could have helped complete some projects and promote all the work being done. It certainly would have made it easier for local officials to set aside low-income housing subsidies for apartments in the area. Those subsidies often went to areas that had an established redevelopment sponsor.

The idea that a redevelopment juggernaut led by corporations was ready to roll over a decaying central city simply does not fit what happened in St. Louis. The redevelopment process created in St. Louis more closely resembles an old commercial airliner constructed out of spare parts from many different planes and slapped together with gum, string, glue, and a few spare rivets. No one, least of all the pilots of the shaky craft, knew that the thing would ever get off the ground, much less fly.

Lessons from St. Louis

The validity of this observation aside, we are left with two straightforward but important questions: Why did St. Louis's redevelopment regime work this way? What lessons can leaders of other cities take from St. Louis and apply in their own community?

When assessing the success of redevelopment in St. Louis it helps to keep certain facts in mind. The most important facts are these. To grow and complement the city's commercial base, the St. Louis economy has continued to change. It is moving ever closer toward corporations that provide services and farther from those that manufacture products. The city's population continues to shrink, albeit at a much slower pace, and minority residents occupy a more prominent niche in that population. This is most apparent in the public schools where black youngsters predominate and white youngsters are a distinct numerical minority. A political and governmental structure that was fragmented and weak in 1950 is not much stronger or better coordinated today. The corporate community, insofar as one exists, still is rather conservative and more likely to react to a crisis than to formulate long-term strategies to cope with longstanding problems. In short, St. Louis remains a troubled city despite some dramatic progress in rebuilding most of the downtown business district, a fair part of the Central Corridor, and a number of other neighborhoods outside of these areas.

That redevelopment proceeded in the face of such problems testifies to the ability of city leaders to take strong action, once they are convinced that something drastic and far-reaching must be done. The deterioration of St. Louis called for such a response, and public and private leaders worked consistently and hard to reverse the most obvious signs of physical blight in the city. One might expect that the experience and success they enjoyed in redeveloping the city up to this point could spill over into other areas. Although it is not yet clear that this will happen, it certainly is possible.

The important lesson is this: St. Louis leaders were terribly concerned about the condition of their city, and they were willing to try almost anything to save it. To that end they experimented with a number of different strategies to address the city's physical decline and the erosion of its economy and population. Some things that they tried worked better than others, but none worked so poorly so as to discourage city leaders from continuing their rebuilding campaign. They worked to overcome the political and government barriers placed before them or they discovered clever ways to exploit those same barriers in the furtherance of their plans.

Local political and corporate entrepreneurs made redevelopment happen. They built a coalition of business leaders, elected officials, civil servants, and some grassroots leaders. Parts of this coalition worked on different redevelopment projects. In the process of trying to put together these projects, they also had to fashion a set of practices, understandings, and more formal agreements among themselves that enabled them to carry out their work in a relatively predictable, if not entirely secure, political and economic environment. Some individuals made a great deal of money or acquired much influence. Others made little or no money, found their influence waning, or lost their position and reputation in the community. Regardless of who happened to be in the coalition at any particular moment, the rebuilding of St. Louis continued. St. Louisans created a redevelopment regime in which the practice of politics figured prominently.

The importance of this regime was most apparent when federal policies changed and made certain types of projets less feasible or when market conditions swung wildly. It was then that members of the local progrowth coalition turned to each other to bring back a bit more stability into their deliberations and deals. Sometimes a business leader like Leon Strauss might benefit from sympathetic bankers and bureaucrats when he could not pay his bills or sell his properties. On another occasion it might be a grassroots leader such as Loretta Hall, whose plan for purchasing Carr Square was aided when officials dropped a requirement that new units be constructed as replacements for those being acquired by the tenant organization. The replacement units would come from rehabilitated apartments in another housing development. By making such allowances, the important work of the redevelopment regime was able to go forward. Big bumps in the path of redevelopment plans were reduced to more manageable ruts for both corporate *and* grassroots leaders.

The areas described in this book are not significant because a progrowth coalition facilitated their rebuilding: Other persons have shown the influence that such coalitions can wield. Nor is it surprising that these areas were rebuilt: Plans to redevelop both DeSoto-Carr and LaSalle Park had been laying around for many years, and one could have expected the two medical centers to do something with their areas sooner or later. What is surprising was the way in which these areas were rebuilt once a full-blown coalition was in place. Contrary to what we expect in redevelopment areas, we find a mix of corporate expansion and residential construction. Moreover, the persons living in these areas represent a broad range of income levels and several races. These areas show what a progrowth coalition can do when its members listen to a variety of views and take advantage of public funds set aside to encourage the construction or rehabilitation of low-income housing.

The "contrived communities," to borrow Gerald Suttles's phrase, created in these five areas are neither complete nor perfect. Some individuals have cordial relations with neighbors of a different race or social class. Most of them probably do not, content instead to live peacefully in the neighborhood and to leave these different people alone. Someday they may join in a common social or political cause. The fact that they have come this far together is no small accomplishment, however, given the history of racial and class antagonisms in this country. The fact that modern corporations and institutions sponsored or facilitated the creation of these neighborhoods is noteworthy. Such entities are not supposed to be adventurous, particularly when no clear profit and much potential trouble could be realized in such a risky venture.

Two things happened in St. Louis that made a difference. First, local political entrepreneurs provided corporations and housing developers with substantial incentives to build or rehabilitate dwellings that would appeal to a diverse population. Second, any number of private leaders quietly expressed an interest in fostering integration. They thought it important to see whether something could be done to make the city less segregated even as they were rebuilding large parts of it.

A number of positive lessons can be drawn from this experience. The most important are these:

1. The situation facing a community must be sufficiently desperate before public and private leaders are likely to experiment with novel ways to rebuild a city.

2. Political entrepreneurs can help to fashion and direct a coalition of parties whose primary interest is to protect their own corporate assets or political base.

3. That coalition sometimes can accommodate the interests of both corporate and grassroots leaders.

4. It is possible to rebuild residential areas around a large institution or corporation so that they hold a diverse population.

5. Public assistance in the form of federal grants and loans can be used to leverage much larger sums of private money that go to projects that serve a relatively broad public interest.

6. One could wait a lifetime for individuals to do "the right thing" *for the right reasons*; it is better and certainly more efficient to put one's faith in the redemptive power of fear and greed to get "right things" done.

The kinds of public and private sector cooperation that have been evident in St. Louis could be reproduced in other cities. How similar the results would be remains to be seen. It is clear, however, that corporations and institutions can redevelop residential areas. Moreover, the neighborhoods in question can be tolerant places in the sense that a variety of people find them comfortable places in which to live. Finally, what happens in these places tends to excite people and make them more involved in local affairs. Even when redevelopment proceeds relatively smoothly, which is rare, residents pay at least a little more attention to what is going on in their neighborhood. Sometimes they pay a whole lot more attention to what is going on around them. Redevelopment can help to enrich and energize local politics.

Conservative advocates of community action would expect such a process to be led by a "steward class" of business leaders. This idea would not appeal to advocates of community action with a more left-of-center bias. Yet, what happened in St. Louis could not be viewed as a plutocrat's dream come true, even though real and would-be plutocrats helped fashion it. There was much more public arguing about redevelopment and mixing of odd combinations of people than a self-respecting plutocrat would have tolerated. The whole enterprise was handled much too sloppily and its results were far too novel.

The public and private leaders responsible for building St. Louis's development industry and nudging it into action were aware that they were doing something different. They did not spend much time worrying about the historical significance of their work, however; events were moving much too quickly. They left it to others to make sense of their work. In that regard, it seems fair to say that these persons created an updated version of the company town. Private institutions and corporations immersed themselves in city politics and neighborhood issues in a way that has not been seen since the nineteenth century. They created an environment that was secure and complemented the institutions that they represented. To this end they invested substantial money and time in activities that were bound to cause them more trouble. More often than not, that is exactly what happened. Nevertheless, they enjoyed a fair amount of success. Far from acting like footloose entrepreneurs, these modern institutions sunk their roots deeper into the community and made it possible for persons from different social classes and races to live together. They did not run away from the problems endemic to urban America. Pullman, Illinois, was never like this.

Modern corporations and institutions can help to create a postindustrial city in which different people can live and learn to practice politics together. To do so, however, they need the assistance of public officials. There are people who believe, as a matter of principle, that it is not the proper role of government to help build or rebuild cities. They would be right if they said the same about a host of other things that have become tax-deferred industries thanks to the generosity of federal legislators and creative accountants. When it comes to cities, they are wrong.

The simple fact is that there would be no cities in the United States, if governments had not subsidized them into existence. The settlement of the original thirteen colonies was an exercise in town and city building promoted by greedy monarchs who had to do something with all the religious dissenters, malcontents, and extra people they had hanging around. Later, the former colonists settled the West in much the same way. Legislators and businessmen, usually working in cahoots, found ingenious ways to create new towns. The federal government often became involved by providing land for eager entrepreneurs and nascent "urban institutions" such as the common or public schools. Contemporary urban America shows the effect of this process. Many of our Sunbelt cities would still be dusty patches of mesquite populated by little crawly things, if the federal government had not seen fit to spend our tax dollars there on new defense-related industries during and after World War II.

Whether the federal government today should continue to subsidize the process of city building as much as it has in the past is a reasonable question. The idea that government has no proper role to play in the process of rebuilding cities is without merit. If acted upon, it would condemn our cities and the people who live in them to a kind of purgatory where the only hope is for eventual escape.

As we have seen in the story of St. Louis's rebuilding, such an outcome is neither inevitable nor in the public interest. Our cities can again become places capable of producing a rich and varied civic culture from which all of us benefit. It also is possible to rediscover the "virtue of a polity" within our cities.[15] Moreover, this discovery can be linked to the process of urban redevelopment.

It is all well and good to say this about St. Louis. It may even prove true for other cities. Yet, it also is important to keep in mind some of the less positive lessons that can be drawn from the experience of rebuilding St. Louis. The following are the most important of these lessons:

1. It is not clear that private leaders will push for continued neighborhood improvements, once their own areas are relatively secure.

2. It is difficult to sustain the most progressive progrowth coalitions over a long period of time.

3. It is much more difficult to rebuild a neighborhood with many persons still living in it.

4. Displacement of many, if not all, existing residents from an area may be necessary, if that area is to be rebuilt in a timely and effective way.

5. The absence of long-term federal assistance to promote racial and economic mixing in neighborhoods is likely to reduce the chances that integration can be sustained over an extended period.

6. There probably are limits to how much integration can be achieved in a redeveloped neighborhood and on how many neighborhoods can be integrated across a city.

7. Despite some impressive redevelopment efforts, rebuilt neighborhoods and

the city as a whole remain vulnerable; overlooked problems do not vanish and may grow to threaten otherwise good works.

Most corporations and institutions that become involved with redevelopment are not in the business of rebuilding cities. They are hospitals, food manufacturers, computer firms, or any number of things other than a development corporation. The caretakers of these organizations are interested primarily in making their part of the city more attractive and safe. They rebuild the area around their headquarters and then try to retire from the redevelopment game. There are times when corporate officials with some redevelopment experience are asked to advise the sponsors of another rebuilding campaign, and corporations may contribute to a fund to help promote that campaign. It is difficult, however, for them to sustain their interest in work conducted in other parts of the city and sometimes even in their own part.

For this reason, perhaps, a progrowth coalition is a fairly brittle thing. There may be some consensus that growth is good, but that does not take the members of that coalition terribly far. Often there are fundamental disagreements over where the city's limited public funds should be spent and on what type of projects. Even the most adept political entrepreneur will have difficulty keeping coalition members interested in new projects and areas when resources are thin and the areas in question are thought to be unattractive.

The individuals living in or around a redevelopment site often are among its least attractive features. They can be troublemakers or merely troublesome to developers who would rather not have to work around established residents or to pay to have them relocated. This is why most or virtually all of an area's residents usually are moved out of an area before the developer moves in. The response is not unique to wealthy developers or big corporations, as the behavior of the two tenant management firms demonstrated. The only mitigating factor is that other low-income people can take the place of the original residents and do quite nicely in the redeveloped area.

Low-income individuals may fit in a rehabilitated neighborhood, but they are not likely to stay unless they continue to receive some kind of assistance to pay for housing. Otherwise, they will not be able to afford the rents that typically rise as a neighborhood is improved. Unfortunately, the federal government has cut back on the subsidy programs that proved so helpful in integrating several St. Louis neighborhoods. Private owners are not likely to pass along much of the cost of housing low-income individuals to their more well-to-do tenants. No matter how successful racial and economic integration is in redeveloped neighborhoods, therefore, it may be only a temporary feature in the city unless housing subsidies are continued.

Other problems must be overcome as well when one builds a racially or economically mixed neighborhood. Most important, perhaps, is the reluctance of persons to live among people different from themselves. The success of areas like DeSoto-Carr and LaSalle Park notwithstanding, it is hard for developers to attract and hold a diverse residential population. Moreover, even as parts of St. Louis's midsection were becoming integrated, the northern and southern thirds of the city generally remained racially segregated.

The limits to which one can foster or push racial integration are evident in St. Louis. Many minority youngsters from the city have a difficult time adjusting to the suburban schools they attend as part of a metropolitan desegregation plan, and often they are not well integrated into their new schools. Inside the city, the story is different. Minority students already outnumber whites in nearly every school, and in many instances groups of black youngsters terrorize not only their peers but also the faculty and staff.

Youth gangs became a prominent feature in St. Louis during the mid-1980s. Since then, however, some two dozen gangs with over 700 known members have been making their presence felt in the city's neighborhoods and public schools. Most gangs engage in one or another form of illegal activity, and all have demonstrated a willingness to use violence. More to the point of the present book, gangs are in both of the tenant-managed public housing sites and can be found in neighborhoods contiguous to the other four redevelopment areas. Two particularly aggressive groups on the Near Southside are composed of young men who were children in the Midtown Medical Center Redevelopment Corporation area. Their families were displaced from the redevelopment area and took up residence where the gangs are located today.

The impact of these gangs in the schools and neighborhoods they occupy cannot be overstated. The gangs also threaten the areas around their home turf. Some of the neighborhoods in this latter category are potential redevelopment sites. City officials are justifiably concerned about the prospects for rebuilding an area and attracting new residents when rival gangs begin to operate around it.

Much of the work that has gone into rebuilding St. Louis during the last forty years could be jeopardized by the spread of violent youth gangs and the drugs they sell. There would be great irony in this, inasmuch as most gangs have emerged from neighborhoods that once were relocation sites for people displaced from different redevelopment and urban renewal areas. The consequences of "uneven development" in St. Louis and other cities would be visited back on those who are alleged to have profitted most from it.[16]

In the face of this grim appraisal two final lessons are to be drawn from St. Louis's redevelopment history. First, there is no such thing as a guaranteed success or "sure thing" in rebuilding cities. Contrary to what many critics of redevelopment think, politicians and big corporations do not have the redevelopment game so well rigged that their pet projects are assured success even as the city around them continues to decline. Second, the very alliances between business leaders and public officials that critics of redevelopment decry may prove instrumental in addressing the lingering effects of poverty and despair left in the shadow of St. Louis's rebirth. Though they might be reluctant to admit it, there was no easy way for business persons to return to the comparative safety of their corporate headquarters once they revived the idea that they could act as stewards of the city's future.

The redevelopment of St. Louis was the most important problem facing public and private leaders in 1950, and this is no less true today. The difference is that they have had a lot of practice working together during the last forty years. Their work is not yet completed. The public-private partnerships they fashioned to rebuild the city now face their most severe test. Leaders will have to discover ways to share the responsibility of living in a modern city with individuals who have yet to taste its opportunities. Should these leaders succeed, St. Louis will become a living tribute to the men and women who helped to rebuild it. Should they fail, the shinier parts of St. Louis eventually will take on the appearance of a cheap tin whistle.

Appendix

S tatistical information about the five redevelopment areas described in this book is presented in this appendix. This information was obtained from three different sources: U.S. Census Bureau; Community Development Agency; St. Louis Police Department. In no case did the boundary lines of the redevelopment areas correspond perfectly to the census tracts, program areas, or Pauly Blocs used by these agencies in the course of their work. The CDA's "program areas" are bigger than the redevelopment areas. The census tracts and Pauly Blocs are smaller.

An effort was made to match the census tract data to the redevelopment areas' boundary lines, but the match was not always perfect. Sometimes, only a portion of a tract, say 50 percent, fell within the boundary lines of the redevelopment area. On such an occasion, half of that tract's population would have been added into that of the redevelopment area's. When this is done, we assume that the people in that tract are pretty well spread throughout it. To take two examples, we would be assuming that all of the white people do not live in one corner of the tract or that all of the people holding professional jobs are not bunched together in another corner. We expect white people holding professional jobs to be pretty evenly spread throughout the census tract. This may not be entirely true; but it is an assumption we must make, if we are to get any reasonable picture of who lived in these areas over a thirty year period.

The CDA used this same process in order to arrive at its picture of who lived in one of the city's "program areas." The CDA built its demographic profiles for these areas from data aggregated for U.S. census tracts. The crime data from the city police department's Pauly blocs were reassembled to match the five redevelopment areas in much the same way.

TABLE A1
Approximate Costs and Subsidies for Redevelopment

Area of City		Project Development Costs[1]				Public Subsidies[2]				
Redevelopment Area	CDA Program Area	Chapter 99	Chapter 353	Chapter 100	UDAG	FOR-SALE Incentive	HUD 108	Industrial Revenue Bonds	SBA 503	Other
DeSoto-Carr	DeSoto-Carr	94,322,024 / 22 9%		7,081,000 / 3 4%	4,300,000 / 2 5%		720,000 / 2 33%	17,686,266 / 7 5%		
LaSalle Park	LaSalle Park	20,079,079 / 21 2%				516,644 / 6 13%		3,220,000 / 7 .8%	715,541 / 5 5%	550,000 / 1 7%
Washington University Medical Center	Central West End	22,744,096 / 6 2%	137,303,294 / 91 8%	20,877,246 / 10 12%	4,480,000 / 2 5%	524,126 / 13 13%	194,040 / 2 9%	32,755,000 / 12 9%	959,600 / 13 7%	30,000 / 1 .4%
	Ranken		10,411,800 / 29 .6%	4,864,750 / 7 3%		56,474 / 2 1%	110,000 / 1 5%	6,225,000 / 7 2%	688,250 / 6 5%	
Midtown Medical Center	Chouteau		2,158,000 / 6 .1%	2,602,000 / 8 2%	110,000 / 1 .1%	90,562 / 3 2%	222,000 / 2 10%	2,240,000 / 4 .6%	529,000 / 3 4%	1,947,150 / 6 25%
	Eads		48,072,369 / 31 3%	4,856,000 / 4 3%		464,487 / 12 12%	629,272 / 2 29%	4,100,000 / 3 1%	1,000,000 / 2 7%	60,000 / 2 .8%
Pershing-Waterman	Skinker-DeBaliviere	27,887,000 / 6 3%	89,847,314 / 26 5%	10,875,000 / 2 6%	5,375,000 / 3 6%	238,791 / 10 6%		24,248,150 / 6 6%	217,000 / 3 1%	442,500 / 1 6%
Central Business District	Central Business District	726,866,000 / 33 72%	1,362,350,476 / 72 77%	38,035,000 / 9 23%	51,351,457			73,479,284 / 20 20%	1,972,730 / 12 14%	216,000 / 1 3%
Other Parts of St. Louis		113,220,625 / 49 12%	121,717,142 / 50 6.3%	78,655,840 / 27 47%	18,753,551 / 15 23%	2,059,088 / 66 23%	305,000 / 4 14%	207,516,000 / 106 56%	8,252,127 / 78 58% 26 57.8%	4,562,983 / 26 57.8%
Citywide Totals		1,005,038,824 / 137 100%	1,771,860,395 / 305 100%	167,846,836 / 68 100%	84,370,008 / 33 100%	3,950,172 / 112 100%	2,180,312 / 13 100%	371,469,700 / 172 100%	14,334,248 / 123 100%	7,808,633 / 38 100%

Table Notes:

1. Project development costs represent the overall cost of projects between 1964 and 1985. They include the projected profits to be earned by the developer and subsidies provided by federal, state, and local government agencies. The costs under each category (i.e., Chapter 99, Chapter 353, and Chapter 100) are not mutually exclusive. For instance, a portion of the $7,081,000 committed in Chapter 100 projects for DeSoto-Carr might also be included in the $94,322,024 committed to Chapter 99 projects. Chapter 99 projects are those sponsored under the old urban renewal program. Chapter 353 projects were sponsored under Missouri's urban redevelopment program. Chapter 100 funds go to commercial and "industrial" projects.

2. These incentives were available under Chapters 99, 353, and 100 of the Missouri statutes. The city of St. Louis has extensive experience using the redevelopment laws of Missouri. Although each law provides slightly different powers to the developer, in all cases an area must be designated "blighted" and a proposed development plan approved. The approval process requires analysis and a recommendation by the St. Louis Community Development Agency to the city's Board of Aldermen and mayor who have ultimate approval authority.

The Land Clearance for Redevelopment Authority (Chapter 99) of the city of St. Louis is authorized by Section 99.300 to 99.175 of the revised statutes of Missouri to redevelop areas of the city after such areas are blighted by the Board of Aldermen and a redevelopment plan has been approved by the board. Redevelopment activity can include utilization of the power of eminent domain to acquire property, relocation assistance, construction of public improvements, tax abatement from city taxes on improvements for up to twenty-five years, and revenue bond financing.

Urban Redevelopment Corporations (Chapter 353) may acquire real property or secure options in their own name or, in the name of nominees, they may acquire real property by gift, grant, lease, purchase or otherwise. Additionally, corporations may be authorized by the city of St. Louis to utilize the power of eminent domain and to receive abatement on improvements for up to twenty-five years.

The Urban Redevelopment Program is open to qualified corporations for areas of the city that fulfill the requirements for blighting. Generally eight to twelve months are required for the entire proces, which entails designating the area blighted, advertisement for and acceptance of a development plan or competing proposals, review and recommendation of the Community Development Commission, approval of the plan and ordinance by the Board of Aldermen, signature by the mayor and developer, and execution of a contract between the city and the selected redeveloper.

The Planned Industrial Expansion Authority (Chapter 100) is authorized by the City of St. Louis to utilize the power of eminent domain, to issue tax exempt revenue bonds, and to provide abatement from city taxes on improvements for up to twenty-five years. Industrial and commercial projects are eligible. Bond financing for 100 percent of project costs is available; no equity injection is required. Maximum bond amount is $10 million, with maturity up to twenty-five years based upon assets financed. Interest rates may be significantly below "prime."

Money can be applied to land acquisition, building acquisition, machinery, equipment fixtures, construction, renovation, or "soft costs" (e.g., architectural, legal, installation costs).

The Urban Development Action Grant is a federally funded program established in the late 1970s to assist distressed central cities alleviate physical and economic deterioration. Essentially, the UDAG provides "gap financing" to attract private development to projects generating new permanent jobs and tax revenues. The individual grants are awarded three times a year on a highly competitive basis to eligible cities, which apply on behalf of a participating developer. When a city is successful in obtaining a UDAG, the funds are loaned to the project developer on favorable financing terms.

The For-Sale Incentive Program is designed to assist developers in the city of St. Louis market new or substantially rehabilitated homes to owner-occupant purchasers. On approved projects, the city will commit to make these funds available to developers. The FSIP assistance is intended to provide a direct benefit to the prospective purchasers of a developer's units. The decision to provide assistance and the amount, if any, will be determined in accordance with CDA's assessment of the status of the for-sale market in the project neighborhood.

The For-Sale Incentive funds are intended to provide an adjunct to traditional financing for the benefit of purchasers. The developer, the purchaser and the lender will negotiate the specific use of the incentive funds, which are restricted to the following eligible use categories: payment of closing costs, payment of points, and interest rate reduction.

There are two components to the HUD 108 Loan Program. First, the *108 Regular Program* consists of borrowing against the CDBG entitlement for a specific project, which is paid back over a six year period through withholding the entitlement. Interest for the payback is established yearly at ⅛ percent above the Treasury Bill rates.

Second, the *Special 108 Program* is specifically for business expansion. The city can borrow a lump sum amount, which it can use to fund a number of yet to be determined business expansion activity. The interest payment is the same. The city can borrow up to three times its annual entitlement, or about $60 million. The maximum loan amount for the HUD portion of the project is $500,000. The HUD loan can fund up to 50 percent of a project cost, with private equity or other financing making up the remaining 50 percent. City policy stipulates that 108 fund a maximum of 40 percent. Eligible projects are existing businesses who must acquire and may also rehabilitate property for business expansion. The project should meet slum and blight or low- and moderate-income housing criteria.

The major differences between the Special and Regular 108 Programs is the payback period, six years for regular and twenty years for special. There is more flexibility with what can be funded with the regular program. To receive additional funds under either program, the Block Grant Application or Statement will need to be amended.

Financing is available for commercial and industrial development through tax exempt issued by the Planned Industrial Expansion Authority. The maximum bond issuance for a single project is $10 million with maturity up to twenty-five years. Because of the tax-exempt status of the bonds, this financing generally is available at interest rates of 2-4 percent below conventional rates. The financing can be applied to land or machinery purchases, construction, renovation, and related development costs (e.g., architectural fees, legal expenses). It is possible to obtain up to 100 percent financing with no required equity.

Under existing federal legislation (SBA 503), the Local Development Company in conjunction with the Small Business Administration and a participating private lender can lend up to 42.5 percent of the total cost of a project at a fixed interest rate for up to twenty-five years. The financing can be applied to the purchase of land or building, acquisition of machinery and equipment construction, renovation and related expenses (e.g., legal expenses, architectural fees). The structure of the actual loan is normally 50 percent participating bank (borrower's choice), 40 percent LDC debenture guaranteed by the SBA, and 10 percent local equity contributing with the borrower providing 7.5 percent.

The Rental Rehabilitation Program differs from the HIP program in two significant ways: funding for the rental rehabilitation program is to be utilized for all projects involving only moderate levels of property rehabilitation; priorities for finding proposals are not primarily restricted to operation impact areas, as is the case with the HIP program. Essentially, however, the goals are the same for the two programs: to stimulate the development of multifamily units emphasizing the needs of low- and moderate-income families. Like the HIP program, any necessary project can be covered that would either not be included in a private mortgage loan or if included would value the project economically infeasible. If the Rental Rehabilitation Program application is approved, financing is furnished in the form of a deferred payment loan to the developer.

TABLE A2
Population for St. Louis
City and County, 1960-1980

Year	Outer Suburbs of St. Louis County	Inner Suburbs of St. Louis County	St. Louis City
	(North Section)	(North Section)	(North Section)
1960	33,527	242,462	330,966
1970	62,725	299,509	275,332
1980	62,063	279,436	188,312
	(Central Section)	(Central Section)	(Central Section)
1960	39,266	210,253	148,654
1970	116,137	207,747	113,111
1980	156,984	177,391	74,583
	(South Section)	(South Section)	(South Section)
1960	42,290	137,525	260,370
1970	56,265	164,810	229,327
1980	86,619	147,593	187,277
Percent	(North Section)		
Change	85.1	15.2	-43.1
	(Central Section)		
	299.8	-15.6	-49.8
	(South Section)		
	104.8	7.3	-28.1

Source: *U.S. Census of Population* 1960, 1970, 1980.

TABLE A3
Black Population of St. Louis
City and County, 1960-1980

Year	Outer Suburbs of St. Louis County	Inner Suburbs of St. Louis County	St. Louis City
	(North Section)	(North Section)	(North Section)
1960	1,172	7,176	182,617
1970	1,392	15,771	210,614
1980	2,377	61,244	169,220
	(Central Section)	(Central Section)	(Central Section)
1960	697	6,603	29,545
1970	559	23,482	41,545
1980	2,508	38,142	31,698
	(South Section)	(South Section)	(South Section)
1960	591	2,667	1,612
1970	927	3,225	1,169
1980	1,328	3,190	4,344

Source: *U.S. Census of Population* 1960, 1970, 1980.

TABLE A4
Percent of Housing Twenty Years or Older in
St. Louis City and County, 1960-1980

Year	Outer Suburbs of St. Louis County	Inner Suburbs of St. Louis County	St. Louis City
	(North Section)	(North Section)	(North Section)
1960	9.6	23.4	91.2
1970	5.3	27.7	87.3
1980	22.7	56.7	89.5
	(Central Section)	(Central Section)	(Central Section)
1960	27.9	97.3	93.3
1970	11.8	83.1	80.5
1980	15.6	78.9	78.2
	(South Section)	(South Section)	(South Section)
1960	42.1	32.0	83.3
1970	35.4	35.9	84.4
1980	32.9	64.1	92.5

Source: *U.S. Census of Population* 1960, 1970, 1980.

TABLE A5
Percent of Renter-Occupied Housing in
St. Louis City and County, 1960-1980

Year	Outer Suburbs of St. Louis County	Inner Suburbs of St. Louis County	St. Louis City
	(North Section)	(North Section)	(North Section)
1960	11.2	11.9	64.3
1970	19.3	22.9	60.8
1980	22.1	26.1	54.9
	(Central Section)	(Central Section)	(Central Section)
1960	16.2	29.2	79.3
1970	17.0	35.0	74.1
1980	23.5	35.0	74.2
	(South Section)	(South Section)	(South Section)
1960	20.3	10.9	47.4
1970	21.9	18.8	48.6
1980	21.8	22.2	46.7

Source: *U.S. Census of Population* 1960, 1970, 1980.

TABLE A6
Number of Employees and Businesses
in St. Louis County and City in 1970, 1977, and 1984

	1970		1977		1984	
	Employees	Businesses	Employees	Businesses	Employees	Businesses
St. Louis County:						
Total	237,437	12,166	346,104	19,524	447,397	25,404
Agriculture	867	119	1,494	214	1,875	296
Mining	537	21	364	31	456	37
Construction	14,467	1,294	19,845	1,838	26,945	2,025
Manufacturing	87,674	764	97,499	1,182	107,526	1,356
Transportation/						
Utilities	10,196	321	18,806	583	32,333	824
Wholesale	14,435	1,157	26,232	2,137	35,733	2,568
Retail	55,533	3,149	78,425	5,044	90,228	5,909
Finance	13,423	1,615	20,516	2,253	30,133	2,560
Services	39,653	3,569	82,520	6,000	119,227	8,370
St. Louis City:						
Total	376,113	15,023	280,639	10,816	260,203	10,194
Agriculture	105	28	99	25	307	40
Mining	1,144	21	903	7	678	7
Construction	12,801	783	9,427	528	8,835	549
Manufacturing	132,575	1,677	97,127	1,258	67,176	1,056
Transportation/						
Utilities	32,235	466	25,412	464	24,463	426
Wholesale	37,920	1,948	24,167	1,364	22,354	1,134
Retail	50,719	3,457	34,514	2,670	32,070	2,418
Finance	28,287	2,055	23,303	1,049	20,491	815
Services	79,793	4,477	65,540	3,338	82,634	3,288

Source: *County Business Patterns* 1971, 1977, and 1984 for Missouri; U.S. Department of Commerce, Bureau of the Census.

TABLE A7
Place of Employment for Workers
Living in St. Louis SMSA, 1970 and 1980
(by age, race, and education)

	1970, Working in			1980, Working in		
	SMSA	St. Louis County	St. Louis City	SMSA	St. Louis County	St. Louis City
Age:						
16 or older	803,525	283,832	338,671	905,901	365,139	305,892
	(100%)	(35.3%)	(42.1%)	(100%)	(40.3%)	33.7%)
16-19	53,226	21,927	18,260	64,424	30,908	13,156
	6.6%	7.7%	5.4%	7.1%	8.5%	4.3%
20-24	93,774	34,276	40,040	122,629	51,269	39,714
	11.7%	12.1%	11.8%	13.5%	14.0%	12.9%
25-54	504,875	182,571	209,216	577,777	231,296	200,290
	62.8%	64.3%	61.8%	63.8%	63.3%	65.5%
55-64	118,686	35,487	55,514	112,364	40,934	42,530
	14.8%	12.5%	16.4%	12.4%	11.2%	13.9%
65 or older	32,784	9,571	15,641	28,637	10,732	10,202
	4.1%	3.4%	4.6%	3.2%	2.9%	3.3%
Race:						
White	703,247	258,851	276,837	784,443	330,117	237,333
	87.5%	91.2%	81.7%	86.6%	90.4%	77.6%
Black	97,706	24,160	60,446	112,756	31,431	65,117
	12.1%	8.5%	17.8%	12.4%	8.6%	21.3%
Education:						
College	198,962	80,595	79,844	339,426	149,268	115,546
	24.8%	28.4%	23.6%	37.5%	40.9%	37.8%

Source: *County Business Patterns* 1971, 1977, and 1984 for Missouri; U.S. Department of Commerce, Bureau of the Census.

TABLE A8
Place of Employment for Workers
Living in St. Louis SMSA, 1970 and 1980
(by earnings)

	1970, Working in			1980, Working in		
	SMSA	St. Louis County	St. Louis City	SMSA	St. Louis County	St. Louis City
$0-9,999	601,439	207,397	256,284	373,309	157,092	109,422
	76.5%	74.7%	77.0%	42.1%	43.9%	36.5%
$10,000-14,999	129,624	47,419	53,781	169,409	66,482	62,172
	16.5%	17.1%	16.1%	19.1%	18.6%	20.7%
$15,000-24,999	40,783	17,076	16,246	237,511	90,755	89,607
	5.2%	6.1%	4.9%	26.8%	25.4%	29.9%
$25,000+	14,563	5,553	6,676	105,557	43,292	38,600
	1.8%	2.0%	2.0%	11.9%	12.1%	12.9%
Total Earners	786,409	277,445	332,987	885,786	357,621	299,801
	(100%)	(100%	(100%)	(100%)	(100%)	(100%)

Source: *County Business Patterns* 1971, 1977, and 1984 for Missouri; U.S. Department of Commerce, Bureau of the Census.

TABLE A9
Place of Employment for Workers
Living in St. Louis SMSA, 1970 and 1980
(by occupation)

	1970, Working in			1980, Working in		
	SMSA	St. Louis County	St. Louis City	SMSA	St. Louis County	St. Louis City
Professional/ Technical/ Manager	186,670	74,195	74,751	239,896	103,470	84,252
	23.4%	26.2%	22.1%	26.7%	28.4%	27.7%
Finance	42,364	15,134	20,096	55,451	25,463	19,440
	5.5%	5.3%	5.9%	6.2%	7.0%	6.4%
Business Service	23,049	7,958	11,022	40,020	18,924	13,820
	3.0%	2.8%	3.3%	4.4%	5.2%	4.5%
Personal Service	30,763	12,078	11,944	26,439	11,770	7,720
	4.0%	4.3%	3.5%	2.9%	3.2%	2.5%
Professional Service	135,185	47,215	54,727	187,506	72,757	61,989
	17.5%	16.7%	16.2%	20.9%	19.9%	20.3%
Public Administration	46,217	12,109	25,066	46,077	11,961	22,445
	6.0%	4.3%	7.4%	5.1%	3.3%	7.4%
Transportation/ Communication	63,996	13,990	35,001	76,117	21,851	37,167
	8.3%	4.9%	10.4%	8.5%	6.0%	12.2%
Clerical/Sales	225,888	83,787	101,523	269,689	120,275	90,054
	29.3%	29.6%	30.1%	30.0%	33.0%	29.6%
Wholesale/ Retail	171,690	70,586	65,319	193,419	91,305	50,427
	22.3%	24.9%	19.3%	21.5%	25.0%	16.5%
Construction	37,563	15,311	11,374	41,351	17,928	11,536
	4.9%	5.4%	3.4%	4.6%	4.9%	3.8%
Manufacturing	230,279	83,630	99,314	210,795	85,841	76,650
	29.9%	29.5%	29.4%	23.5%	23.5%	25.2%
Crafts	280,504	88,844	121,290	259,426	89,618	93,921
	32.5%	31.3%	35.9%	28.9%	24.6%	30.8%
Service	98,393	35,408	39,367	119,479	48,993	35,367
	12.8%	12.5%	11.7%	13.3%	13.4%	11.6%
Other	27,896	6,912	5,289	38,201	9,627	5,624
	3.6%	2.4%	1.6%	4.2%	2.6%	1.8%
Total Workers	796,932	283,325	337,412	897,965	364,644	304,517
	(100%)	(100%)	(100%)	(100%)	(100%)	(100%)

Source: *County Business Patterns* 1971, 1977, and 1984 for Missouri; U.S. Department of Commerce, Bureau of the Census.

TABLE A10
Place of Employment for Workers
Living in St. Louis County, 1970 and 1980
(by age, race, and education)

	1970, Working in			1980, Working in		
	SMSA	St. Louis County	St. Louis City	SMSA	St. Louis County	St. Louis City
Age:						
16 or older	350,835	202,583	137,616	424,676	273,848	137,569
	(100%)	(57.7%)	(39.2%)	(100%)	(64.5%)	(32.4%)
16-19		17,995	5,284		26,646	4,492
		8.9%	3.8%		9.7%	3.3%
20-24		23,414	14,306		37,656	15,075
		11.5%	10.4%		13.7%	10.9%
25-54		128,863	91,362		169,615	94,904
		63.6%	66.3%		61.9%	69.0%
55-64		25,270	21,292		31,267	18,859
		12.5%	15.5%		11.4%	13.7%
65 or older		7,041	5,372		8,664	4,239
		3.5%	3.9%		3.2%	3.1%
Race:						
White		194,588	130,081		252,698	115,659
		96.0%	94.5%		92.3%	84.1%
Black		7,334	6,905		18,478	20,087
		3.6%	5.0%		6.7%	14.6%
Education:						
College		66,147	42,026		120,478	65,411
		32.6%	30.5%		44.0%	47.5%

Source: *County Business Patterns* 1971, 1977, and 1984 for Missouri; U.S. Department of Commerce, Bureau of the Census.

TABLE A11
Place of Employment for Workers
Living in St. Louis County, 1970 and 1980
(by earnings)

	1970, Working in		1980, Working in	
	St. Louis County	St. Louis City	St. Louis County	St. Louis City
$0-9,999	138,319	86,620	122,913	36,835
	69.9%	63.7%	45.9%	27.1%
$10,000-14,999	34,979	31,664	47,030	26,596
	17.7%	23.3%	17.5%	19.5%
$15,000-24,999	14,960	12,174	62,510	42,835
	7.6%	8.9%	23.3%	31.5%
$25,000+	5,119	5,416	35,413	26,758
	2.3%	4.0%	13.2%	19.7%
Total Earners	197,877	135,874	267,866	136,024
	100%	100%	100%	100%

Source: *County Business Patterns* 1971, 1977, and 1984 for Missouri; U.S. Department of Commerce, Bureau of the Census.

TABLE A12
Place of Employment for Workers
Living in St. Louis County, 1970 and 1980
(by occupation)

	1970, Working in		1980, Working in	
	St. Louis County	St. Louis City	St. Louis County	St. Louis City
Professional/ Technical/ Manager	60,520	43,493	83,862	48,928
	29.9%	31.7%	30.7%	35.8%
Finance	12,050	8,925	20,640	8,920
	5.9%	6.1%	7.5%	6.5%
Business Service	5,995	4,643	14,262	6,100
	3.0%	3.2%	5.2%	4.4%
Personal Service	7,670	2,819	8,448	2,367
	3.8%	1.9%	3.1%	1.7%
Professional Service	37,384	20,380	59,474	26,948
	18.5%	14.0%	21.7%	19.7%
Public Administration	8,282	9,444	8,897	9,401
	4.1%	6.5%	3.2%	6.9%
Transportation/ Communication	9,060	15,332	14,537	18,907
	4.5%	11.2%	5.3%	13.8%
Clerical/Sales	65,738	42,141	95,871	40,960
	32.5%	30.8%	35.0%	29.9%
Wholesale/ Retail	55,339	27,756	72,274	22,677
	27.3%	20.3%	26.4%	16.6%
Construction	10,739	5,552	12,713	5,697
	5.3%	4.0%	4.6%	4.2%
Manufacturing	52,161	40,882	56,995	34,416
	25.8%	29.8%	20.8%	25.1%
Crafts	52,176	43,399	55,294	37,341
	25.8%	31.7%	20.2%	27.3%
Service	23,210	7,830	36,661	9,272
	11.5%	5.7%	13.4%	6.8%
Other	4,604	1,994	7,419	2,451
	2.3%	1.4%	2.7%	1.8%
Total Workers	202,345	136,974	273,499	136,816
	100%	100%	100%	100%

Source: *County Business Patterns* 1971, 1977, and 1984 for Missouri; U.S. Department of Commerce, Bureau of the Census.

TABLE A13
Place of Employment for Workers
Living in St. Louis City, 1970 and 1980
(by age, race, and education)

	1970, Working in			1980, Working in		
	SMSA	St. Louis County	St. Louis City	SMSA	St. Louis County	St. Louis City
Age:						
16 or older	199,271	38,454	157,194	149,280	33,149	113,431
	(100%)	(19.3%)	(78.9%)	(100%)	(22.2%)	(76.0%)
16-19		1,868	10,689		1,529	6,738
		4.8%	6.8%		4.6%	5.9%
20-24		4,946	19,435		5,721	16,877
		12.9%	12.4%		17.2%	14.9%
25-54		23,534	87,760		19,713	66,260
		61.2%	55.8%		59.5%	58.4%
55-64		6,364	29,651		4,693	18,136
		16.5%	18.9%		14.1%	16.0%
65 or older		1,742	9,659		1,493	5,420
		4.5%	6.1%		4.5%	4.8%
Race:						
White		23,227	106,209		21,028	71,364
		60.4%	67.6%		63.4%	62.9%
Black		15,151	50,292		11,707	40,811
		39.4%	32.0%		35.3%	36.0%
Education:						
College		6,436	26,783		10,824	34,027
		16.7%	17.0%		32.6%	30.0%

Source: *County Business Patterns* 1971, 1977, and 1984 for Missouri; U.S. Department of Commerce, Bureau of the Census.

TABLE A14
Place of Employment for Workers
Living in St. Louis City, 1970 and 1980
(by earnings)

	1970, Working in		1980, Working in	
	St. Louis County	St. Louis City	St. Louis County	St. Louis City
$0-9,999	33,245	136,464	16,196	57,882
	88.2%	88.7%	50.0%	52.7%
$10,000-14,999	3,642	13,794	7,927	24,789
	8.7%	9.0%	24.5%	22.6%
$15,000-24,999	592	2,586	7,046	22,281
	1.6%	1.7%	21.8%	20.3%
$25,000+	210	1,024	1,167	4,845
	.5%	.7%	3.6%	4.4%
Total Earners	37,690	153,823	32,336	109,797
	(100%)	(100%)	(100%)	(100%)

Source: *County Business Patterns* 1971, 1977, and 1984 for Missouri; U.S. Department of Commerce, Bureau of the Census.

TABLE A15
Place of Employment for Workers
Living in St. Louis City, 1970 and 1980
(by occupation)

	1970, Working in		1980, Working in	
	St. Louis County	St. Louis City	St. Louis County	St. Louis City
Professional/ Technical/ Manager	5,699	24,769	6,807	24,128
	14.8%	15.8%	20.5%	21.3%
Finance	1,707	7,855	1,927	5,901
	4.4%	5.0%	5.8%	5.2%
Business Service	1,091	4,632	1,903	5,313
	2.8%	2.9%	5.7%	4.7%
Personal Service	3,466	8,334	2,058	4,651
	9.0%	5.3%	6.2%	4.1%
Professional Service	5,707	31,367	6,931	29,631
	14.8%	20.0%	20.9%	26.2%
Public Administration	2,182	12,688	1,420	9,610
	5.7%	8.1%	4.3%	8.5%
Transportation/ Communication	2,180	13,458	2,106	9,415
	5.7%	8.6%	6.3%	8.3%
Clerical/Sales	8,815	45,588	8,731	33,076
	22.9%	2.9%	26.4%	2.7%
Wholesale/ Retail	7,827	30,462	6,990	20,309
	20.3%	19.4%	21.1%	17.9%
Construction	1,582	3,808	1,450	3,200
	4.1%	2.4%	4.4%	2.8%
Manufacturing	11,966	42,526	7,743	23,729
	31.1%	27.1%	23.4%	20.9%
Crafts	15,321	57,144	10,360	32,666
	39.8%	36.4%	31.3%	28.8%
Service	8,549	29,233	7,064	22,896
	22.2%	18.6%	21.3%	20.2%
Other	788	2,258	781	2,137
	2.0%	1.4%	2.3%	1.9%
Total Workers	38,454	156,928	33,122	113,231
	(100%)	(100%)	(100%)	(100%)

Source: *County Business Patterns* 1971, 1977, and 1984 for Missouri; U.S. Department of Commerce, Bureau of the Census.

TABLE A16
DeSoto-Carr Population, 1960-1980

| | Race | | | | Age | | |
	Total	White	Black	Other	0-19	20-64	65+
CDA Program Area:							
1960	27,584	2,615	24,914	55	55%	38%	7%
1970	15,338	737	14,567	34	55%	36%	9%
1980	5,254	135	5,108	11	44%	45%	11%
1960	100%	9%	90%	1%			
1970	100%	5%	94%	1%			
1980	100%	3%	97%				
Census Tract 1257:							
1960	7,638	1,960	5,678				
1970	4,968	841	4,127				
1980	3,340	142	3,198				
1960	100%	26%	74%				
1970	100%	17%	83%				
1980	100%	4%	96%				

Source: *U.S. Census of Population* 1960, 1970, 1980.

TABLE A17
DeSoto-Carr Housing, 1960-1980

	Total Units	Vacant Units	Average Household	Renter Occupied	In Multiple Unit Buildings
1960	7,983	783 (10%)	3.8	97%	91%
1970	6,566	2,271 (35%)	3.5	97%	87%
1980	2,448	556 (23%)	2.7	100%	81%

Note: Total units, vacant units, and average household data are for the DeSoto-Carr CDA Program Area. Percent renter occupied or in multiple unit buildings are for census tract 1257.

Source: *U.S. Census of Population* 1960, 1970, 1980.

TABLE A18
DeSoto-Carr Occupations, 1960-1980 (for census tract 1257)

	Total	Professional, Technical	Clerical, Sales	Agricultural, Industrial	Service
1960	846	57	140	463	186
1970	1,367	292	274	450	351
1980	932	150	234	241	307
1960	100%	7%	16%	55%	22%
1970	100%	21%	20%	33%	26%
1980	100%	16%	25%	26%	33%

Source: *U.S. Census of Population,* 1960, 1970, 1980.

TABLE A19
DeSoto-Carr Crimes, 1971 and 1983 (for Pauly blocs 71, 72, 73, 74)

	Total Crimes	Crimes against Persons	Crimes against Property
1971	597	138	459
1983	328	104	224
Percent change	-45%	-25%	-51%

Source: St. Louis Metropolitan Police Department.

TABLE A20
LaSalle Park Population, 1960-1980

	Race				Age		
	Total	White	Black	Other	0-19	20-64	65+
LaSalle Park CDA Program Area:							
1960	12,892	11,239	1,515	139	46%	47%	7%
1970	9,287	3,244	5,945	99	53%	39%	8%
1980	6,108	786	5,269	53	50%	44%	6%
1960	100%	87%	12%	1%			
1970	100%	35%	64%	1%			
1980	100%	13%	86%	1%			
Census Tracts .5 of 1224; .5 of 1234							
1960	10,372	9,680	692				
1970	6,453	3,919	2,534				
1980	3,622	1,424	2,198				
1960	100%	93%	7%				
1970	100%	61%	39%				
1980	100%	39%	61%				

Source: *U.S. Census of Population* 1960, 1970, 1980.

TABLE A21
LaSalle Park Housing, 1960-1980

	Total Units	Vacant Units	Average Household	Renter Occupied	In Multiple Unit Buildings
1960	4,194	382 (9%)	3.3	88%/84%	78%/76%
1970	3,509	893 (25%)	3.4	89%/80%	91%/89%
1980	2,487	554 (22%)	3.1	91%/67%	71%/80%

Note: Total units, vacant units, and average household data are for the LaSalle Park CDA
Program Area. Percent renter occupied or in multiple unit buildings are for census tracts
1224/1234.
Source: *U.S. Census of Population* 1960, 1970, 1980.

TABLE A22
LaSalle Park Occupations, 1960-1980 (census tracts: .5 of 1224; .5 of 1234)

	Total	Professional, Technical	Clerical, Sales	Agricultural, Industrial	Service
1960	1,761	89	176	1,356	140
1970	1,513	92	281	803	337
1980	1,175	253	240	379	303
1960	100%	5%	10%	77%	8%
1970	100%	6%	19%	53%	22%
1980	100%	22%	20%	32%	26%

Source: *U.S. Census of Population* 1960, 1970, 1980.

TABLE A23
LaSalle Park Crimes, 1971 and 1983 (by Pauly blocs: .5 of 24 and 35; .25 of 36)

	Total Crimes	Crimes against Persons	Crimes against Property
1971	297	59	238
1983	141	32	109
Percent change	-52%	-45%	-54%

Source: St. Louis Metropolitan Police Department.

TABLE A24
Washington University Medical Center Area Population, 1960-1980

	Race				Age		
	Total	White	Black	Other	0-19	20-64	65+
Central West End CDA Program Area:							
1960	23,106	19,366	3,541	199	22%	65%	13%
1970	18,196	12,749	5,269	178	22%	59%	19%
1980	13,688	9,014	4,372	302	12%	62%	26%
1960	100%	84%	15%	1%			
1970	100%	70%	29%	1%			
1980	100%	66%	32%	2%			
Ranken CDA Program Area:							
1960	9,198	8,843	334	21	31%	60%	9%
1970	6,513	5,815	654	45	31%	57%	12%
1980	4,660	2,327	2,257	76	34%	56%	10%
1960	100%	96%	4%	0%			
1970	100%	89%	10%	1%			
1980	100%	50%	48%	2%			
Census tracts: .25 of 1186, .6 of 1191							
1960	7,520	7,337	183				
1970	6,037	4,626	1,413				
1980	4,658	2,903	1,755				
1960	100%	98%	2%				
1970	100%	77%	23%				
1980	100%	62%	38%				

Source: *U.S. Census of Population* 1960, 1970, 1980.

TABLE A25
Washington University Medical Center Area Housing, 1960-1980

	Total Units	Vacant Units	Average Household	Renter Occupied[1]	In Multiple Unit Buildings[1]
Central West End CDA Program Area:					
1960	10,768	801 (7%)	2.1	74%/90%	76%/93%
1970	9,071	1,174 (13%)	2.0	66%/93%	82%/93%
1980	9,016	1,494 (17%)	1.6	71%/90%	78%/94%
Ranken CDA Program Area:					
1960	3,351	210 (6%)	2.8		
1970	2,985	258 (9%)	2.5		
1980	2,362	540 (23%)	2.6		

[1]Census tracts 1186/1191.
Source: *U.S. Census of Population* 1960, 1970, 1980.

TABLE A26
Washington University Medical Center Area Occupations, 1960-1980

	Total	Professional, Technical	Clerical, Sales	Agricultural, Industrial	Service
1960	1,816	440	259	947	170
1970	2,656	840	689	741	386
1980	1,979	893	474	237	375
1960	99%	24%	14%	52%	9%
1970	100%	32%	26%	28%	14%
1980	100%	45%	24%	12%	19%

Source: *U.S. Census of Population* 1960, 1970, 1980.

TABLE A27
Washington University Medical Center Area Crimes, 1971 and 1983
(by Pauly blocs: .4 of 22; .25 of 23; .75 of 24; .75 of 25, 29; .5 of 30)

	Total Crimes	Crimes against Persons	Crimes against Property
1971	1,707	84	1,623
1983	1,058	75	983
Percent change	-38%	-11%	-39%

Source: St. Louis Metropolitan Police Department.

TABLE A28
Pershing-Waterman Population, 1960-1980

	Race				Age		
	Total	White	Black	Other	0-19	20-64	65+
Skinker-DeBaliviere CDA Program Area:							
1960	14,501	14,286	120	95	19%	64%	17%
1970	14,168	5,342	8,725	101	36%	50%	14%
1980	7,610	2,626	4,879	105	27%	58%	15%
1960	100%	98%	1%	1%			
1970	100%	38%	61%	1%			
1980	100%	34%	64%	2%			
Census Tracts: .8 of 1052, .5 of 1121:							
1960	9,137	9,057	80				
1970	8,909	3,057	5,852				
1980	4,361	1,334	3,027				
1960	100%	99%	1%				
1970	100%	34%	66%				
1980	100%	31%	69%				

Source: *U.S. Census of Population* 1960, 1970, 1980.

TABLE A29
Pershing-Waterman Housing, 1960-1980

	Total Units	Vacant Units	Average Household	Renter Occupied	In Multiple Unit Buildings
1960	6,940	474 (7%)	2.2	82%/88%	84%/89%
1970	6,863	1,326 (19%)	2.5	78%/86%	84%/90%
1980	4,951	1,655 (33%)	2.3	56%/68%	78%/83%

Note: Total units, vacant units, and average household data are for the Skinker-DeBaliviere CDA Program Area. Percent renter occupied or in multiple unit buildings are for census tracts 1052/1121.

Source: *U.S. Census of Population* 1960, 1970, 1980.

TABLE A30
Pershing-Waterman Occupations, 1960-1980 (census tracts: .8 of 1052, .5 of 1121)

	Total	Professional, Technical	Clerical, Sales	Agricultural, Industrial	Service
1960	2,122	743	551	660	168
1970	3,546	811	898	927	910
1980	1,767	690	404	312	361
1960	100%	35%	26%	31%	8%
1970	100%	23%	25%	26%	26%
1980	100%	39%	23%	18%	20%

Source: *U.S. Census of Population* 1960, 1970, 1980.

TABLE A31
Pershing-Waterman Crimes, 1971 and 1983 (by Pauly blocs: 37, 41, .33 of 42)

	Total Crimes	Crimes against Persons	Crimes against Property
1971	1,071	253	818
1983	266	45	221
Percent change	-75%	-82%	-72%

Source: St. Louis Metropolitan Police Department.

TABLE A32
Midtown Medical Center Area Population, 1960-1980

	Race				Age		
	Total	*White*	*Black*	*Other*	*0-19*	*20-64*	*65+*
Chouteau CDA Program Area:							
1960	5,370	5,222	139	10	32%	59%	9%
1970	4,123	3,860	234	29	35%	54%	11%
1980	3,526	531	2,958	37	47%	47%	6%
1960	100%	97%	2%	1%			
1970	100%	94%	5%	1%			
1980	100%	15%	84%	1%			
Eads CDA Program Area:							
1960	12,182	5,841	6,308	33	41%	52%	7%
1970	7,536	1,150	6,340	45	45%	45%	10%
1980	2,707	392	2,292	23	38%	48%	14%
1960	100%	48%	52%	0%			
1970	100%	15%	84%	1%			
1980	100%	14%	85%	1%			
Census tracts: .6 of 1173; .75 of 1185:							
1960	9,788	7,036	2,752				
1970	7,046	3,075	3,971				
1980	3,729	1,023	2,706				
1960	100%	72%	28%				
1970	100%	44%	56%				
1980	100%	27%	73%				

Source: *U.S. Census of Population* 1960, 1970, 1980.

TABLE A33
Midtown Medical Center Area Housing, 1960-1980

	Total Units	Vacant Units	Average Household	Renter Occupied	In Multiple Unit Buildings
Chouteau CDA Program Area:					
1960	1,951	923 (5%)	2.9	70%/73%	85%/78%
1970	1,721	206 (12%)	2.7	72%/72%	82%/76%
1980	1,521	397 (26%)	3.1	69%/63%	75%/58%
Eads CDA Program Area:					
1960	3,897	226 (6%)	3.3		
1970	2,918	704 (24%)	3.4		
1980	1,097	186 (17%)	2.9		

Note: Total units, vacant units, and average household data are for the Choteau and Eads
    CDA Program Areas. Percent renter occupied or in multiple unit buildings are for
    census tracts 1173/1185.
Source: *U.S. Census of Population* 1960, 1970, 1980.

TABLE A34
Midtown Medical Center Area Occupations, 1960-1980 (census tracts: .6 of 1173; .75 of 1185)

	Total	Professional, Technical	Clerical, Sales	Agricultural, Industrial	Service
1960	2,013	261	286	1,268	198
1970	2,308	341	446	998	523
1980	1,201	363	250	286	302
1960	100%	13%	14%	63%	10%
1970	100%	15%	19%	43%	23%
1980	101%	30%	21%	24%	25%

Source: *U.S. Census of Population* 1960, 1970, 1980

TABLE A35
Midtown Medical Center Area Crimes, 1971 and 1983 (by Pauly blocs 12, 18, .33 of 28, 29, 30)

	Total Crimes	Crimes against Persons	Crimes against Property
1971	881	101	780
1983	446	49	397
Percent Change	-49%	-51%	-49%

Source: St. Louis Metropolitan Police Department.

NOTES

Preface

1. Daniel J. Monti, *A Semblance of Justice: St. Louis School Desegregation and Order in Urban America* (Columbia: University of Missouri Press, 1985). Daniel J. Monti, "A Bit Less Separate, and Still Not Equal," *Metropolitan Education,* no. 4 (Spring 1987): 53-69.

2. Daniel P. Moynihan, "Toward a National Urban Policy," in Daniel P. Moynihan, ed., *Toward A National Urban Policy* (New York: Basic Books, 1970), pp. 3-25. President's Commission for a National Agenda for the Eighties, *Urban America in the Eighties* (Washington, D.C.: U.S. Government Printing Office, 1980). William Julius Wilson, *The Truly Disadvantaged: The Inner City, the Underclass, and Public Policy* (Chicago: University of Chicago Press, 1987).

3. Norton Long, *The Polity* (Chicago: Rand McNally, 1962), pp. 135 and 185.

Chapter 1. Can Cities Be Rebuilt for Rich and Poor Alike?

1. Stephen Steinberg, *The Ethnic Myth: Race, Ethnicity, and Class in America* (New York: Atheneum, 1981).

2. John Mollenkopf, *The Contested City* (Princeton, N.J.: Princeton University Press, 1983).

3. See the following for examples: Clarence Davies, *Neighborhood Groups and Urban Renewal* (New York: Columbia University Press, 1966). Haywood Sanders, "Urban Renewal and the Revitalized City: A Reconsideration of Recent History," in Donald Rosenthal, ed., *Urban Revitalization,* vol. 18, Urban Affairs Annual Reviews (Beverly Hills, Calif.: Sage Publications, 1980), pp. 103-126. Jeffrey Henig, *Neighborhood Mobilization* (New Brunswick, N.J.: Rutgers University Press, 1982). Dennis Gale, *Neighborhood Revitalization and the Postindustrial City* (Lexington, Mass.: D.C. Heath and Co., 1984). Joe Feagin, *The Urban Real Estate Game* (Englewood Cliffs, N.J.: Prentice-Hall, 1983). Biliana Cicin-Sain, "The Costs and Benefits of Neighborhood Revitalization," in Rosenthal, *Urban Revitalization,* pp. 49-75. Martin Anderson, "The Sophistry that Made Urban Renewal Possible," in Jewel Bellush and Murry Hausknecht, eds., *Urban Renewal: People, Politics, and Planning* (Garden City, N.Y.: Anchor Books, 1967), pp. 52-66. Barrett Lee and Paula Mergenhagen, "Is Revitalization Detectable?

Evidence from Five Nashville Neighborhoods," *Urban Affairs Quarterly* 19, no. 4 (June 1984): 512. Dennis Gale, "Neighborhood Resettlement: Washington, D.C.," in S. Laska and D. Spain, eds., *Back to the City,* (New York: Pergamon, 1980), pp. 95-115. M. LeFaivre and N. Smith, "A Class Analysis of Gentrification," in J. Palen and B. London, eds., *Gentrification, Displacement and Neighborhood Revitalization* (Albany: SUNY Press, 1984), pp. 43-64. James Hudson, "SoHo: A Study of Residential Invasion of a Commercial and Industrial Area," *Urban Affairs Quarterly* 20, no. 1 (September 1984): 46-63. M. Chernoff, "Social Displacement in a Renovating Neighborhood's Commercial District: Atlanta," in Laska and Spain, *Back to the City,* pp. 204-219. Roman Cybriwsky, "The Fashioning of Gentrification in Philadelphia," *Urban Resources* 3, no. 3 (Spring 1986): 27-32. Michael White, "Racial and Ethnic Succession in Four Cities," *Urban Affairs Quarterly* 20, no. 2 (December 1986): 165-183. Harvey Molotch, "The City as a Growth Machine: Toward a Political Economy of Place," *American Journal of Sociology* 82, no. 2 (September 1976): 309-332. Bruce London, Barrett Lee, and S. Gregory Lipton, "The Determinants of Gentrification in the United States: A City-Level Analysis," *Urban Affairs Quarterly* 21, no. 3 (March 1986): 369-388. Michael Schill and Richard Nathan, *Revitalizing America's Cities* (Albany: SUNY Press, 1983). T. Maher, A. Haas, B. Levine, and J. Liell, "Whose Neighborhood? The Role of Established Residents in Historic Preservation Areas," *Urban Affairs Quarterly* 21, no. 2 (December 1985): 267-281. P. Clay, "Urban Reinvestment: Process and Trends," in P. Clay and R. Hollister, eds., *Neighborhood Policy and Planning* (Lexington, Mass.: Lexington Books, 1983), pp. 21-33. R. Taub, D. Taylor, and J. Dunham, *Paths of Neighborhood Change: Race and Crime in Urban America* (Chicago: University of Chicago Press, 1984). F. DeGiovanni and N. Paulson, "Household Diversity in Revitalizing Neighborhoods," *Urban Affairs Quarterly* 20, no. 2 (December 1984): 211-232. Michael Long, "Measuring Economic Benefits from Gentrification," *Journal of Urban Affairs* 8, no. 4 (Fall 1986): 27-39. Chava Nachmias and John Palen, "Neighborhood Satisfaction, Expectations, and Urban Revitalization," *Journal of Urban Affairs* 8, no. 4 (Fall 1986): 51-61. W. Dennis Keating, "Urban Displacement Research: Local, National, International," *Urban Affairs Quarterly* 21, no. 1 (September 1985): 132-136. William Peterman and Sherri Hannan, "Influencing Change in Gentrifying Neighborhoods: Do Community-Based Organizations Have a Role?" *Urban Resources* 3, no. 3 (Spring 1986): 33-36. Frank DeGiovanni, "An Examination of Selected Consequences of Revitalization in Six U.S. Cities," in Palen and London, *Gentrification,* pp. 67-89. Mark Baldassare, "Evidence for Neighborhood Revitalization: Manhattan," in Palen and London, ibid., pp. 90-102. Daphne Spain and Shirley B. Laska, "Renovators Two Years Later: New Orleans," in Palen and London, ibid., pp. 103-127. John Palen and Chava Nachmias, "Revitalization in a Working-Class Neighborhood," in Palen and London, ibid., pp. 128-139. David Varady, *Neighborhood Upgrading: A Realistic Approach* (Albany: SUNY Press, 1986). Matthew Crenson, *Neighborhood Politics* (Cambridge, Mass.: Harvard University Press, 1983). Robert Beauregard, "Politics, Ideology, and Theories of Gentrification," *Journal of Urban Affairs* 7, no. 4 (Fall 1985): 51-62.

4. See, for example, T. Maher et al., "Whose Neighborhood?"; and Daphne Spain and Shirley Laska, "Renovators Two Years Later."

5. Biliana Cicin-Sian, "Costs and Benefits," p. 53. Clay, "Urban Reinvestment."

6. Peter J. Steinberger, *Ideology and the Urban Crisis* (Albany: SUNY Press, 1985), pp. 26-150.

7. Amos Hawley, *Urban Society: An Ecological Approach* (New York: Ronald Press, 1971). Brian Berry and John Kasarda, *Contemporary Urban Ecology* (New York: Macmillan, 1977). Paul Peterson, *City Limits* (Chicago: University of Chicago Press, 1981). George Sternlieb and James Hughes, "The Uncertain Future of the Central City," *Urban Affairs Quarterly* 18, no. 4 (June 1983): 455-472. President's Commission for a National Agenda for the Eighties, *Urban America in the Eighties* (Washington, D.C.: U.S. Government Printing Office, 1980). John Kasarda, "Entry-Level Jobs, Mobility, and Urban Minority Unemployment," *Urban Affairs Quarterly* 19, no. 1 (September 1983): 21-40. Jack Kasarda, "The Implications of Contemporary Redistribution Trends for National Urban Policy," unpublished paper, University of North Carolina, 1980). Paul Peterson, "Technology, Race and Urban Policy," in Paul Peterson, ed., *The New Urban Reality* (Washington, D.C.: Brookings Institution, 1985), pp. 1-32. John Kasarda, "Urban Change and Minority Opportunities," in Peterson, ibid., pp. 33-68. Brian Berry, "Islands of Renewal in Seas of Decay," in Peterson, ibid., pp. 69-98. Gary Orfield, "Ghettoization and Its Alternatives," in Peterson, ibid., pp. 161-196. William Julius Wilson, "The Urban Underclass in Advanced Industrial Society," in Peterson, ibid., pp. 129-160. William Julius Wilson, *The Truly Disadvantaged: The Inner City, the Underclass, and Public Policy* (Chicago: University of Chicago Press, 1987). Daniel P. Moynihan, "Toward a National Urban Policy," in Daniel P. Moynihan, ed., *Toward a National Urban Policy* (New York: Basic Books, 1970), pp. 3-25. Harold Wolman, "The Reagan Urban Policy and Its Impacts," *Urban Affairs Quarterly* 21, no. 3 (March 1986): 311-335. Ed Marciniak, *Reclaiming the City* (Washington, D.C.: National Center for Urban Ethnic Affairs, 1986). Royce Hanson, ed., *Rethinking Urban Policy: Urban Development in An Advanced Economy* (Washington, D.C.: National Academy Press, 1983). Ivan Szelenyi, "Urban Policies of the New Right—Critical Responses," in Ivan Szelenyi, ed., *Cities in Recession: Critical Responses to the Urban Policies of the New Right* (Beverly Hills, Calif.: Sage, 1984), pp. 1-25. Herbert Gans, "American Urban Theories and Urban Areas: Some Observations on Contemporary Ecological and Marxist Paradigms," in Szelenyi, ibid., pp. 278-308. Harvey Molotch, "The City as a Growth Machine," pp. 309-332. Frances Fox Piven and Richard A. Cloward, "The New Class War in the United States," in Szelenyi, *Cities in Recession,* pp. 26-45. Richard Child Hill, "Transnational Capitalism and Urban Crisis: The Case of the Auto Industry and Detroit," in Szelenyi, ibid., pp. 141-161. Brian Elliot and David McCrone, "Austerity and the Politics of Resistance," in Szelenyi, ibid., pp. 192-216. Glenn Yago, "Urban Transportation Policy for Whom? Determinants and Consequences of Transit Change in the United States and Germany," in Szelenyi,

ibid., pp. 99-140. Joe Feagin, "The Corporate Center Strategy: The State in Central Cities," *Urban Affairs Quarterly* 21, no. 4 (June 1986): 617-628. Harvey Molotch and John Logan, "Urban Dependencies: New Forms of Use and Exchange in U.S. Cities," *Urban Affairs Quarterly* 21, no. 2, (December 1985): 143-169. Susan Fainstein and Norman Fainstein, "Economic Restructuring and the Rise of Urban Social Movements," *Urban Affairs Quarterly* 21, no. 2 (December 1985): 187-206. Andrew Kirby, "Nine Fallacies of Local Economic Change," *Urban Affairs Quarterly* 21, no. 2 (December 1985): 207-220. Erick Monkkonen, "The Sense of Crisis: A Historian's Point of View," in M. Gottdiener, ed., *Cities in Stress: A New Look at the Urban Crisis,* vol. 30, Urban Affairs Annual Reviews (Beverly Hills, Calif.: Sage, 1986), pp. 20-37. Dennis Judd, "Electoral Coalitions, Minority Mayors, and the Contradictions in the Municipal Policy Agenda," in Gottdiener, ibid., pp. 145-170. Jeffrey Henig, "Collective Responses to the Urban Crisis: Ideology and Mobilization," in Gottdiener, ibid., pp. 221-245. Todd Swanstrom, "Urban Populism, Fiscal Crisis, and the New Political Economy," in Gottdiener, ibid., pp. 81-109. Manuel Castells, "Space and Society: Managing the New Historical Relationships," in M. Smith, ed., *Cities in Transformation,* vol. 26, Urban Affairs Annual Reviews (Beverly Hills, Calif.: Sage, 1984), pp. 235-260. Timothy Kinsella, "The Future of Downtown as a Center for Business Knowledge Activity: A Review of the Literature in the Context of Organizational Theory," *Economic Development Quarterly* 1, no. 3 (August 1987): 279-292. Larry Sawers, "New Perspectives on the Urban Political Economy," in William K. Tabb and Larry Sawers, eds., *Marxism and the Metropolis* (New York: Oxford University Press, 1984), pp. 3-20. David Gordon, "Capitalist Development and the History of American Cities," in Tabb and Sawers, ibid., pp. 21-53. Richard LeGaters and Karen Murphy, "Austerity, Shelter, and Social Conflict in the United States," in Tabb and Sawers, ibid., pp. 123-151. Nancy Kleiniewski, "From Industrial to Corporate City: The Role of Urban Renewal," in Tabb and Sawers, ibid., pp. 205-222. William Tabb, "The Failures of National Urban Policy," in Tabb and Sawers, ibid., pp. 255-297. William Tabb, "A Pro-People Urban Policy," in Tabb and Sawers, ibid., pp. 367-382. Pierre Clavel, *The Progressive City* (New Brunswick, N.J.: Ritgers University Press, 1986). June Manning Thomas, "Redevelopment and Redistribution," in Paul Porter and David Sweet, eds., *Rebuilding America's Cities: Roads to Recovery* (New Brunswick, N.J.: Center for Urban Policy Research, 1984), pp. 143-159. Norman Krumholz, "Recovery: An Alternate View," in Porter and Sweet, ibid., pp. 173-190. Dennis Judd and Randy Ready, "Entrepreneurial Cities and the New Politics of Economic Development," in George Peterson and Carol Lewis, eds., *Reagan and the Cities* (Washington, D.C.: Urban Institute Press, 1986), pp. 209-248. Richard Child Hill, "Market, State, and Community: National Urban Policy in the 1980s," *Urban Affairs Quarterly* 19, no. 1 (September 1983): 5-20. Roger Friedland, "The Politics of Profit and the Georgraphy of Growth," *Urban Affairs Quarterly* 19, no. 1 (September 1983): 41-54. Glen Yago, "Urban Policy and National Political Economy," *Urban Affairs Quarterly* 19, no. 1 (September 1983): 113-132. Neil Smith and Michele LeFaivre, "A Class Analysis of Gentrification," in John Palen and Bruce London, eds., *Gentrification, Displacement and Neighborhood Revitalization* (Albany: SUNY Press, 1984), pp. 43-64. Joe Feagin, *The Urban Real Estate Game* (Englewood Cliffs, N.J.: Prentice-Hall, 1983). Robert Beauregard, "Structure, Agency, and Urban Redevelopment," in Smith, *Cities in Transformation*, pp. 51-72. David Perry, "Structuralism, Class Conflict, and Urban Reality," in Smith, ibid., pp. 219-234. Richard Child Hill, "Urban Political Economy: Emergency, Consolidation, and Development," in Smith, ibid., pp. 123-137. Michael P. Smith and Dennis R. Judd, "American Cities: The Production of Ideology," in Smith, ibid., pp. 173-196. M. Gottdiener, *The Decline of Urban Politics* (Beverly Hills, Calif.: Sage, 1987). Richard Sennett, *The Fall of Public Man* (New York: St. Martin's Press, 1979). Ira Katznelson, *City Trenches: Urban Politics and the Patterning of Class in the United States* (New York: Pantheon Books, 1981). Manuel Castells, *The City and the Grassroots: A Cross-Cultural Theory of Urban Social Movements* (Berkeley: University of California Press, 1983). Michael P. Smith, *The City and Social Theory* (New York: St. Martin's Press, 1979). Paul Kantor, "The Dependent City: The Changing Political Economy of Urban Economic Development in the United States," *Urban Affairs Quarterly* 22, no. 4 (June 1987): 493-520. Todd Swanstrom, "The Limits of Strategic Planning for Cities," *Journal of Urban Affairs* 9, no. 2 (1987): 139-158. Marc Levine, "Downtown Redevelopment as an Urban Growth Strategy: A Critical Appraisal of the Baltimore Renaissance," *Journal of Urban Affairs* 9, no. 2 (1987): 103-124. Marc Levine, "Economic Development in Baltimore: Some Additional Perspectives," *Journal of Urban Affairs* 9, no. 2 (1987): 133-138.

8. Joe R. Feagin and Mark Gottdiener, "The Paradigm Shift in Urban Sociology," *Urban Affairs Quarterly* 24, no. 2 (1988): 163-187.

9. The theoretical underpinnings of this plan for action come less from classical Marxism than from two schools of thought that political philosopher Peter Steinberger calls "managerialism" and "communalism" (Steinberger, *Ideology*, pp. 27-36). Contemporary Marxists borrow ideas from each. The idea that a rationally planned polity can avoid the evils of private power was taken from managerialism. So, too, was the notion that government can solve problems and act in behalf of a broadly representative "public interest." Contemporary Marxists tone down the elitist elements of managerialism by finding a place for less trained and more passionate citizens to influence government. Yet, as conceived by Manuel Castells, the leading proponent of Marxism as applied to urban affairs, the places reserved for direct citizen involvement would be the neighborhood and in public meetings. At higher levels of government, the average citizen would be involved through voluntary organizations that advise leaders and serve on "ad hoc" committees (Castells, "Space and Society," p. 251). Marxists would build into government all of the conflicts and antagonisms found in the larger community. This is an idea quite at odds with the managerial approach, where the object is to have policies and programs developed by professionals insulated somewhat from the hurly-burly of local politics.

The last element in the Marxist plan for action derives quite nicely from the communalist approach to local politics (Steinberger, *Ideology*, pp. 63-39). Advocates of this approach are especially interested in the process by which policies and programs are conceived and carried out. A government insulated from the people it serves may be efficient, the argument goes, but it is less likely to produce things thought to serve the common good. People must participate in politics, especially at the neighborhood level, if government is to act in the public's interest.

Whether neighborhood councils and local activists would make important decisions or simply exercise more discretion in administering decisions handed down from higher levels of government is not known. One would suppose that Marxists would favor more local autonomy. Still, it is not clear that Castell's scheme would guarantee such an outcome. It is quite possible that more well-to-do persons would end up exercising just as much control as they once did. Indeed, conservative advocates of communalism see community action as "a process of rediscovery in which traditional approaches and ties are uncovered under the leadership of a steward class" (Steinberger, ibid., p. 78). (It is likely that the corporately sponsored redevelopment discussed in this book could be commended or criticized on such grounds.)

Regardless of their political persuasion, critics of communalism fear it would breed parochialism and frustrate efforts to plan things in a rational way and on a communitywide basis. They also suspect that such schemes will not produce better or more citizen involvement. Although there is some evidence to support each point, it is not overwhelming. Moreover, these criticisms largely miss the points made by advocates of communalism: Conflict can be helpful, exclusivity can be a virtue, professionalism can anesthetize politics, and a "communitywide" perspective often masks efforts to ignore more parochial concerns (Steinberger, ibid., pp. 79-8f1; Janet Hook, "Selling the Idea of Virtue to an Amoral Society," *Chronicle of Higher Education* (March 9, 1983), p. 26. Alasdair MacIntyre, *After Virtue* (Notre Dame, Ind.: University of Notre Dame Press, 1981).

One supposes that contemporary Marxists hope to avoid the drawbacks of managerialism and communalism. They would do this by adopting only those parts that play to their interest in both neighborhood activism and regional planning. This may or may not be the best way to ensure that democracy prevails within urban areas, but it most certainly is not the stuff of which revolutions are made.

10. Albert Reiss, *Louis Wirth: On Cities and Social Life* (Chicago: University of Chicago Press, 1964). Claude S. Fischer, *The Urban Experience* (New York: Harcourt Brace Jovanovich, 1976). David A. Karp, Gregory P. Stone, and William C. Yoels, *Being Urban* (Lexington, Mass.: D.C. Heath and Company, 1977). Marc Weiss, *The Rise of the Community Builders* (New York: Columbia University Press, 1987). Carol O'Connor, *A Sort of Utopia: Scarsdale, 1891-1981* (Albany: SUNY Press, 1983). Gwendolyn Wright, *Moralism and the Model Home: Domestic Architecture and Cultural Conflict in Chicago, 1873-1913* (Chicago: University of Chicago Press, 1980). Andrew Lees, *Cities Perceived: Urban Society in European and American Thought, 1820-1940* (New York: Columbia University Press, 1985).

11. Paul Boyer, *Urban Masses and Moral Order in America: 1820-1920* (Cambridge: Harvard University Press, 1978).

12. Smith, *The City and Social Theory*, p. 35.

13. Almont Lindsay, *The Pullman Strike* (Chicago: Phoenix Books, 1967), p. 35.

14. Ibid., p. 72.

15. Hook, "Selling the Idea of Virtue."

16. Gerald Suttles, *The Social Construction of Communities* (Chicago: University of Chicago Press, 1973), pp. 82-107.

17. MacIntyre, *After Virtue*, p. 154.

18. Steinberger, *Ideology*, p. 140.

19. Clarence Stone, "The Study of the Politics of Urban Redevelopment," in Clarence Stone and Heywood Sanders, eds., *The Politics of Urban Redevelopment* (Lawrence: University of Kansas Press, 1987), pp. 10-11.

20. William J. Wilson, "The Urban Underclass."

21. J.D. Wacquant and William J. Wilson, "The cost of Racial and Class Exclusion in the Inner City," *The Annals* 501 (January 1989): 8-25. John D. Kasarda, "Urban Industrial Transition and the Underclass," *The Annals* 501 (January 1989): 26-47.

22. Wilson, "The Urban Underclass," p. 180.

23. Jennifer Hochschild, *Race, Class and Power,* Working Paper 10, Natioal Conference on Social Welfare, Washington, D.C., 1986. Jennifer Hochschild, *The New American Dilemma* (New Haven, Conn.: Yale University Press, 1984). Daniel J. Monti, *A Semblance Of Justice: Saint Louis School Desegregation and Order in Urban America* (Columbia: University of Missouri Press, 1985). Daniel J. Monti, "A Bit Less Seperate and Still Not Equal," *Metropolitan Education,* no. 4 (Spring 1987): 53-69.

24. Jamshid Momeni, ed., *Race, Ethnicity, and Minority Housing in the United States* (New York: Greenwood Press, 1986). Gary Tobin, ed., *Divided Neighborhoods: Changing Patterns of Racial Segregation* (Beverly Hills, Calif.: Sage, 1987). Allen Goodman, "Neighborhood Impacts on Housing Prices," in Ralph Taylor, ed., *Urban Neighborhoods: Research Policy* (New York: Praeger, 1986), pp. 123-143.

25. R. Allen Hays, *The Federal Government and Urban Housing* (Albany: SUNY Press, 1985). J. Paul Mitchell, ed., *Federal Housing Policy and Programs* (New Brunswick, N.J.: Center for Urban Policy Research, 1985).

26. See the following, for example. Eugene J. Meehan, *Public Housing Policy: Convention versus Reality* (New Brunswick, N.J.: Center for Urban Policy Research, 1975). Eugene J. Meehan, *The Quality of Federal Policy: Programmed Failure in Public Housing* (Columbia: University of Missouri Press, 1966). Clarence Davies, *Neighborhood Groups and Urban Renewal* (New York: Columbia University Press, 1966). Heywood Sanders, "Urban Renewal and the Revitalized City: A Reconsideration of Recent History," in Rosenthal, *Urban Revitalization,* pp. 103-126.

Chapter 2. The Decline and Reclamation of St. Louis

1. "Urban Decay in St. Louis" (St. Louis: Institute for Urban and Regional Studies, Washington University, 1972), pp. 13-14.

2. The data summarized in this portion of the chapter are presented in the statistical appendix at the end of the book. Footnotes in the text will lead the reader to specific tables where information relevant to a particular point can be found.

3. See Table A2 in the Appendix.

4. See Table A3 in the Appendix. John Farley, "Metropolitan Housing Segregation in 1980: The St. Louis Case," *Urban Affairs Quarterly* 18, no. 3 (March 1983): 347-359.

5. See Table A3 in the Appendix.

6. See Tables A4 and A5 in the Appendix.

7. See Table A6 in the Appendix.

8. Only 37 percent had been so employed in 1970, whereas 48.9 percent were in 1984. The percentage of employees working in such businesses in St. Louis County grew from 26.6 to 40.5 percent during the same period. The county's economic base is more diversified.

9. See Tables A7-A9 in the Appendix.

10. See Tables A10-A12 in the Appendix.

11. See Tables A13-A15 in the Appendix.

12. "Analysis of the 1970 and 1980 U.S. Census—City of St. Louis" (St. Louis: Community Development Agency, 1983). At least between 1970 and 1980, the number of single-parent families remained about 38,400. However, the total number of families in St. Louis declined over 27 percent. The percentage of single-parent families in the city grew from 26 to 36 as a result. Some 6 percent of the city's 1970 population was unemployed in 1970; the figure had grown to 11 percent by 1980. Estimates placed the unemployment figure for blacks in 1983 to be in

excess of 20 percent, and that figure probably was conservative. Finally, between 1970 and 1980, the percentage of households receiving public assistance grew from 11 to 14 and the percentage receiving social security grew from 33 to 37.

13. The data were provided to the author by the Community Development Agency, which divides the city into seventy "program areas." Program areas in predominately white or racially mixed areas generally had between 20 and 40 percent of their populations in the 0-19 years age category in 1960. They had per capita incomes ranging between $3,000 and $5,000. By 1980, they had 16 and 26 percent of their population in the 0-19 years age category and their per capita incomes ranged from $6,000 to $11,000. The percentages for the juvenile population in predominately black program areas in 1960 ranged from 25 to 41. By 1980, the range went from 25 percent to 45 percent with many more areas having percentages in the high 30s and low 40s than had been the case in 1960. The per capita incomes had grown from $1,000 to $2,000 in 1960 to $3,000 and $5,000 in 1980, essentially where the predominately white and racially mixed areas had been twenty years earlier.

14. Brian Berry and John Kasarda, *Contemporary Urban Ecology* (New York: Macmillan, 1977), pp. 241-243. Berry and Kasarda observed in thirty-four SMSAs that a slightly smaller percentage of black workers lived and worked in suburban communities in 1970 than in 1960 (i.e., 14.7 percent versus 15.3 percent). More generally, they found that 49 percent of all blacks working in the suburbs of those SMSAs in 1970 were commuting from the central city. They took this as a sign that the housing markets for blacks in those SMSAs were intensely segregated. The figures presented here for St. Louis between 1970 and 1980 reveal that some things were different and certainly changed, at least in this SMSA. Recalling that black migration from St. Louis city did not begin until the mid-1960s, 67.4 percent of all blacks working in St. Louis county in 1970 were commuting from the city. This figure dropped to 38.8 percent by 1980. During the same period, the percentage of all black workers who lived and worked in St. Louis county doubled (i.e., from 9.2 percent in 1970 to 20.3 percent in 1980). These changes reflect the growing availability of suburban housing for blacks in St. Louis county. Ignored in Berry and Kasarda's analysis, however, was the fact that more blacks in 1970 were commuting from suburbs to central cities for jobs than had been the case in 1960 (i.e., 1,854 for 3.6 percent in 1960 and 2,792 for 4.5 percent in 1970). By 1970, the comparable statistic for St. Louis county already was 8.7 percent, and that figure grew to 22 percent in 1980. Furthermore, the number and percentage of black St. Louis workers living in the city and commuting to the suburbs dropped between 1970 and 1980 (i.e., 15,151 for 19 percent in 1970 to 11,707 for 12.8 percent in 1980). The city was exporting fewer black workers and attracting more from the suburbs. The transformation of St. Louis city into a postindustrial center was not discouraging all black workers. No work familiar to the author shows how widely the changes described in St. Louis were witnessed in other SMSAs.

15. No attempt will be made here to chronicle the failure and accomplishments

of urban renewal programs and other federally sponsored efforts to rebuild cities during the years 1950-1974. Many authors have described this work in great detail. A small sample of these authors would include the following. Scott Greer, *Urban Renewal and American Cities* (Indianapolis, Bobbs-Merrill Co., 1965). Jewel Bellush and Murray Hausknecht, eds., *Urban Renewal: People, Politics and Planning* (Garden City, N.Y.: Anchor Books, 1967). Clarence Davies, *Neighborhood Groups and Urban Renewal* (New York: Columbia University Press, 1966). Langley Keyes, *The Rehabilitation Planning Game* (Cambridge: MIT Press, 1969). William Worthy, *The Rape of Our Neighborhoods* (New York: William Morrow and Co., 1976). Herbert Gans, *The Urban Villagers* (New York: Free Press, 1962). R. Allen Hays, *The Federal Government and Urban Housing* (Albany: SUNY Press, 1985). Marc A. Weiss, "The Origins and Legacy of Urban Renewal," in J. Paul Mitchell, ed. *Federal Housing Policy and Programs* (New Brunswick, N.J.: Center for Urban Policy Research, 1985), pp. 253-276. Brian Boyer, *Cities Destroyed for Cash* (Chicago: Follet Publishing Company, 1973). Heywood Sanders, "Urban Renewal and the Revitalized City: A Reconsideration of Recent History," in Donald Rosenthal, ed., *Urban Revitalization,* vol. 18, Urban Affairs Annual Reviews (Beverly Hills, Calif.: Sage, 1980), pp. 103-126. The last piece is especially useful in showing how massive clearance programs had become less favored and rehabilitation work more favored by the early 1970s. It also shows how much of the land that had been cleared eventually was refilled with housing, a good deal of it set aside for low- and moderate-income people.

16. St. Louis Redevelopment Authority, "Brief Facts on St. Louis Redevelopment Authority," (pamphlet, St. Louis Redevelopment Authority, 1984).

17. *St. Louis Globe-Democrat* (March 19, 1984).

18. Martin Anderson, "The Sophistry that Made Urban Renewal Possible," in Bellush and Hausknecht, *Urban Renewal,* pp. 52-66.

19. Land Clearance for Redevelopment Authority, "Annual Report for 1974," mimeograph, Land Clearance for Redevelopment Authority, 1974, p. 11.

20. St. Louis Development Program Staff, "History of Renewal for St. Louis, Missouri," mimeograph, St. Louis City Plan Commission, 1971, pp. 15-16.

21. Team 4, Inc., "Citywide Implementation Strategies: The Draft Comprehensive Plan" (St. Louis: Team 4 Inc., 1976), pp. 7-8. Further adding to the conspiratorial tone of this whole affair was a report written by Anthony Downs and published by the Department of Housing and Urban Development in 1975. In it, downs presented an argument remarkably similar to that contained in the Team 4 report. Only, he urged that the idea of building on areas with market strength be adopted as a national policy when it came to cities spending the new block grant funds. The report did not escape the attention of St. Louisans. See Anthony Downs, "Using the Lessons of Experience to Allocate Resources in the Community Development Program," in Jon Pynoos, Robert Schafer, and Chester Hartman,

eds., *Housing Urban America* (New York: Aldine Publishing Co., 1980), pp. 522-535.

22. *St. Louis Post-Dispatch* (July 24, 1988).

23. Clarence Stone, "The Study of the Politics of Urban Redeveloment," in Clarence Stone and Heywood Sanders, eds., *The Politics of Urban Development* (Lawrence: University of Kansas Press, 1987), pp. 3-24.

24. Heywood Sanders, "The Politics of Development in Middle-Sized cities: Getting from New Haven to Kalamazoo," in Stone and Sanders, ibid., pp. 182-198.

Chapter 3. The Politics of Compromise: DeSoto-Carr

1. St. Louis Development Program Staff, "History of Renewal for St. Louis, Missouri," mimeograph St. Louis City Plan Commission, 1971, p. 4.

2. Eugene Meehan, *Public Housing Policy: Convention versus Reality* (New Brunswick, N.J.: 1975), p. 30.

3. Richard Baron, "Community Organizations: Antidote for Neighborhood Succession and Focus for Neighborhood Improvement," *Saint Louis University Law Journal* 21, no. 2 (1978): 648.

4. Ibid., pp. 650-651.

5. Ibid., p. 653.

6. Joel Fleishman, "Not without Honor: A Prophet Even in His Own Country, A Case Study of the Resolution of the St. Louis Public Housing Tenant Strike of 1969," mimeograph, Ford Foundation Dispute Resolution Project, 1979, p. 59.

7. Ibid., p. 60.

8. Meehan, *Public Housing Policy.* Eugene Meehan, *The Quality of Federal Policymaking* (Columbia: University of Missouri Press, 1966).

9. Meehan, *Quality of Policymaking.* Baron, "Community Organizations." Fleishman, "Not without Honor."

10. Meehan, *Public Housing Policy.*

11. Baron, "Community Organizations," p. 660.

12. *St. Louis Post-Dispatch* (May 27, 1984).

13. Carlos G. Velez-Ibanez, *Bonds of Mutual Trust* (New Brunswick, N.J.: Rutgers University Press, 1983), pp. 140-141. Ivan Light, *Ethnic Enterprise in America: Business and Welfare among Chinese, Japanese, and Blacks* (Berkeley: University of California Press, 1972).

14. *St. Louis Post-Dispatch* (March 12, 1986).

15. Jesse M. Chancellor, "A Critique of the St. Louis Application to the Department of Housing and Urban Development's Public Housing Homeownership Demonstration Submitted by the Tenant Management Corporation of Cochran Gardens," unpublished masters thesis, University of Missouri—St. Louis, 1986.

16. *St. Louis Post-Dispatch* (July 6, 1988).

17. Stewart Perry, *Communities on the Way* (Albany: SUNY Press, 1987), pp. 184-197.

18. See Tables A16-A19 in the Appendix.

19. Donald Warren, *Black Neighborhoods: An Assessment of Community Power* (Ann Arbor: University of Michigan Press, 1975).

20. Michael Lipsky, *Protest in City Politics: Rent Strikes, Housing, and the Power of the Poor* (Chicago: Rand McNally, 1970), p. 122.

Chapter 4. The Reluctant Giant: LaSalle Park

1. The St. Louis Development Program Staff, "History of Renewal for St. Louis, Missouri," mimeograph, St. Louis Plan Commission, 1971, p. 40.

2. Land Clearance for Redevelopment Authority, "LaSalle Park Urban Renewal Plan," mimeograph, Land Clearance for Redevelopment Authority, 1969, pp. 1-2.

3. Ibid., pp. 11-12.

4. Land Clearance for Redevelopment Authority, "Annual Report for 1974," mimeograph, Land Clearance for Redevelopment Authority, 1974, p. 32.

5. LCRA, "LaSalle Park Urban Renewal Plan," p. 3.

6. Ibid., p. 5.

7. Nini Harris, "The Rebirth of LaSalle Park," *St. Louis Commerce* (September 1983), p. 25.

8. Ibid., p. 26.

9. Raynor Warner, Sibyl McCormac Groff, and Ranne Wanner, "Ralston Purina Company," in Frank Stella, ed., *Business and Preservation* (New York: Publishing Center for Cultural Resources, 1978), p. 156.

10. Ibid.

11. John P. Baird, "LaSalle Park: Success Story of Corporate Involvement in Urban Renewal," speech made at Cleveland State University on occasion of Ralston Purina's reception of George S. Dively Award for Corporate Leadership in Urban Redevelopment, February 4, 1984, p. 17.

12. Claudia Burris, "Square Plans for Future Construction," *Square Talk* (St. Louis: Ralston Purina, Summer 1984), p. 2.

13. Harris, "Rebirth," p. 28.

14. Warner et al., "Ralston Purina Company," p. 158.

15. *St. Louis Post-Dispatch* (March 30, 1980).

16. Ibid.

17. *St. Louis Post-Dispatch* (March 31, 1980).

18. *St. Louis Post-Dispatch* (April 3, 1980).

19. Harris, "Rebirth," p. 28.

20. See Tables A20-A23 in the Appendix.

Chapter 5. Bedside Manor: The Washington University Medical Center Redevelopment Corporation Area

1. Richard C. Ward and Jack H. Pyburn, "Can Doctors Heal the City?" *Practicing Planner* (September 1977): 36.

2. Ibid., p. 40.

3. *The Rehabber* (May 1982). Samuel B. Guze, "The State of the Medical Center," *Outlook Magazine* (Summer 1983), pp. 20-21.

4. S. Jerome Pratter and William Conway, "Washington University Medical Center," in National League of Cities, ed., *Dollars from Design* (Washington, D.C.: National League of Cities, 1981), p. 35.

5. *St. Louis Business Journal* (December 5-11, 1983).

6. Pratter and Conway, "Washington University Medical Center."

7. Urban Land Institute, "Project Reference File: Washington University Medical Center Redevelopment, St. Louis, Missouri" (Washington, D.C.: Urban Land Institute, October-December 1980), p. 2.

8. Ibid.

9. Prater and Conway, "Washington University Medical Center," p. 36.

10. National Council for Urban Economic Development, "Establishing and Operating Private Sector Development Organizations: A Technical Guide Based on Model Approaches" (Washington, D.C.: U.S. Department of Housing and Urban Development, July 1984), pp. 40-45.

11. Washington University Medical Center Redevelopment Corporation, "Revised Development Plan" (St. Louis: WUMCRC, April 1985), p. 16.

12. *St. Louis Post-Dispatch* (October 6, 1985).

13. *St. Louis Globe-Democrat* (February 27, 1976; September 30, 1976). *St. Louis Post-Dispatch* (June 27, 1979).

14. *Westend World* (May 1987).

15. See Tables A24-A27 in the Appendix.

Chapter 6. Packaged Rehabilitation: The Pershing-Waterman Area

1. *St. Louis Globe-Democrat* (December 5, 1979).

2. *St. Louis Post-Dispatch* (May 30, 1976).

3. *St. Louis Globe-Democrat* (December 5, 1976).

4. *St. Louis Post-Dispatch* (June 13, 1979; November 17, 1978). *St. Louis Post-Dispatch* (September 6, 1979).

5. Barry Checkoway, "Large Builders, Federal Housing Programs, and Postwar Suburbanization," in W. K. Tabb and L. Sawers, eds., *Marxism and the Metropolis* (New York: Oxford University Press, 1984), pp. 152-173.

6. Ibid., pp. 158-159.

7. Gary Tobin and Dennis Judd, "A Multi-Year Study of Demographic Change in Three Revitalization Projects in St. Louis," paper presented at annual meeting of the Association of Collegiate Schools of Planning, New York City, October 19, 1984.

8. *Westend World* (June 1979). *St. Louis Post-Dispatch* (February 17, 1985).

9. See Tables A28-A31 in the Appendix.

Chapter 7. Broken Promises: The Midtown Medical Center Redevelopment Area

1. Midtown Medical Center Redevelopment Corporation, "Proposal for

Redeveloping the Midtown Medical Center Area," unpublished report Midtown Medical Center Redevelopment Corporation, 1977, p. 4.

2. Richard Ward, "Neighborhood Strategy Application," unpublished report, Team 4, Inc., 1978.

3. Ibid., p. 21.

4. Ibid.

5. Ibid. Data reported by St. Louis Community Development Agency, unpublished table, 1986. Richard Ward, "Neighborhood Strategy." *The Rehabber* (November 1983).

6. *St. Louis Post-Dispatch* (September 25, 1983).

7. *The Neighborhood News* (October 19, 1983).

8. *St. Louis Post-Dispatch* (October 9, 1983).

9. *St. Louis Globe-Democrat* (August 25, 1984).

10. *St. Louis Post-Dispatch* (March 1, 1986).

11. See Tables A32-A35 in the Appendix.

12. *St. Louis Business Journal* (April 13-19, 1987).

13. *St. Louis Post-Dispatch* (November 21, 1986; May 7, 1987).

14. *St. Louis Post-Dispatch* (November 11, 1987).

Chapter 8. Race, Redevelopment, and the New Company Town

1. Richard Ward, Robert Lewis, and S. Jerome Pratter, "St. Louis," in Rachelle Levitt, ed., *Cities Reborn* (Washington, D.C.: Urban Land Institute, 1987).

2. Clarence Stone, "The Study of the Politics of Urban Development," in Clarence Stone and Heywood Sanders, eds., *The Politics of Urban Development* (Lawrence: University of Kansas Press, 1987), pp. 10-11. John Mollenkopf, *The Contested City* (Princeton, N.J.: Princeton University Press, 1983).

3. Ward et al., "St. Louis," pp. 153-154.

4. Ibid., p. 168.

5. Ibid., pp. 153-154.

6. Eugene Eisman, "Leveraging Maximizes the Effectiveness of State and

Federal Housing Program Funds," in David Listokin, ed., *Housing Rehabilitation* (New Brunswick, N.J.: The Center for Urban Policy Research, 1983), pp. 284-285.

7. Stone, "Politics of Urban Development," pp. 10-11.

8. Ibid.

9. Conflicting reports on the impact of tax abatements on redevelopment in St. Louis have been issued in the 1980s. The first one showed that the loss in tax revenues because of abatements was more than compensated for by increases in other types of revenue attributed to redevelopment (Daniel Mandleker, Gary Feder, Margaret Collins, *Reviving Cities with Tax Abatement,* New Brunswick, N.J.: Rutgers University Press, 1980). The second showed that this was not the case and suggested that the use of tax abatements in the city be curtailed (Arthur Denzau and Charles Leven, *Report on Alternative Revenue Sources: Local Revenue Generation,* a report to the Saint Louis Board of Education's Community Advisory Committee, Department of Economics, Washington University, May 1985). Part of the disagreement between these two reports can be attributed to how each set of authors chose to measure lost and recaptured revenues. However, there is no denying that the liberal use of tax abatements in the city, at least in the short run, has reduced the revenues received by the city school system. Tax abatements have been a rather sore point in ongoing discussions over the financial plight of the school system. There also has been some intermittent discussion of the contributions made to mayoral candidates by developers and other companies that would like to sell something to the city. Contributions made to Mayor Schoemehl became the object of a six-part series in the *St. Louis Post-Dispatch* in May 1986. Schoemehl appeared to have perfected the art of building a campaign war chest by receiving somewhere in the neighborhood of $1.5 million for his 1986 reelection effort. At least for St. Louis mayoral elections, this was an unprecedented amount of money.

10. *St. Louis Post-Dispatch* (July 7, 1988; July 24, 1988).

11. For examples of this line of reasoning see M. Gottdiener, *The Decline of Urban Politics* (Beverly Hills, Calif.: Sage, 1987) and Ira Katznelson, *City Trenches: Urban Politics and the Patterning of Class in the United States* (Berkeley: University of California Press, 1983).

12. Norton Long, *The Polity* (Chicago: Rand McNally, 1962), pp. 135 and 185.

13. Daniel Monti, *A Semblance of Justice: St. Louis School Desegregation and Order in Urban America* (Columbia: University of Missouri Press, 1985).

14. Ray Breun, "The Background for Public Education in St. Louis, 1812-1838," unpublished dissertation, University of Missouri—St. Louis, School of Education, 1987. Charles Glaab and A. Theodore Brown, *A History of Urban America* (New York: Macmillan, 1976). Richard Wade, *The Urban Frontier* (Chicago: University of Chicago Press, 1976).

15. Norton E. Long, "The City as a Political Community," *Journal of Community Psychology* 14 (January 1986): 79.

16. Gregory Squires, Larry Bennett, Kathleen McCourt, and Philip Nyden, *Race, Class, and the Response to Urban Decline* (Philadelphia: Temple University Press, 1987). Jo Darden, Richard Child Hill, June (Philadelphia: Temple University Press, 1987).

BIBLIOGRAPHY

Anderson, Martin, "The Sophistry that Made Urban Renewal Possible." In Jewel Bellush and Murray Hausknecht, eds., *Urban Renewal: People, Politics, and Planning*, pp. 52-66. Garden City, N.Y.: Anchor Books, 1967.

Baird, John. "LaSalle Park: Success Story of Corporate Involvement in Urban Renewal." Speech made at Cleveland State University on the occasion of Ralston Purina's reception of the George S. Dively Award for Corporate Leadership in Urban Redevelopment. February 4, 1984.

Baldassare, Mark. "Evidence for Neighborhood Revitalization: Manhattan." In John Palen and Bruce London, eds., *Gentrification, Displacement, and Neighborhood Revitalization*, pp. 90-102. Albany: State University of New York Press, 1984.

Baron, Richard. "Community Organizations: Antidote for Neighborhood Succession and Focus for Neighborhood Improvement." *Saint Louis University Law Journal* 21, no. 3 (1978): 634-663.

Beauregard, Robert. "Structure, Agency, and Urban Redevelopment." In Michael Smith, ed., *Cities In Transformation: Class, Capital, and the State* vol. 26, pp. 51-72, Urban Affairs Annual Reviews. Beverly Hills: Sage Publications, 1984.

_____. "Politics, Ideology, and Theories of Gentrification." *Journal of Urban Affairs* 7, no. 4 (Fall 1985): 51-62.

Bellush, Jewell, and M. Hausknecht, eds. *Urban Renewal: People, Politics, and Planning*. Garden City, N.Y.: Anchor Books, 1967.

Berry, Brian. "Islands of Renewal in Seas of Decay." In Paul Peterson, ed., *The New Urban Reality,* pp. 69-98. Washington, D.C.: Brookings Institution, 1985.

———— and J. Kasarda. *Contemporary Urban Ecology.* New York: Macmillan, 1977.

Boyer, Brian. *Cities Destroyed for Cash.* Chicago: Follet Publishing Co., 1973.

Boyer, Paul. *Urban Masses and Moral Order in America: 1820-1920.* Cambridge, Mass.: Harvard University Press, 1978.

Breun, Ray. "The Background for Public Education in St. Louis, 1812-1838." Unpublished dissertation, University of Missouri—St. Louis, School of Education, 1987.

Burris, Claudia. "Square Plans for Future Construction," *Square Talk* (St. Louis: Ralston Purina, Summer 1984).

Castells, Manual. *The City and the Grassroots: A Cross-Cultural Theory of Urban Social Movements.* Berkeley: University of California Press, 1983.

————. "Space and Society: Managing the New Historical Relationships." In Michael Smith, Ed., *Cities In Transformation,* vol. 26, pp. 235-260, Urban Affairs Annual Reviews. Beverly Hills, Calif.: Sage Publications, 1984.

Chancellor, Jesse M. "A Critique of the St. Louis Application to the Department of Housing and Urban Development's Public Housing Homeownership Demonstration Submitted by the Tenant Management Corporation of Cochran Gardens." Unpublished master's thesis, University of Missouri—St. Louis, 1986.

Checkoway, Barry. "Large Builders, Federal Housing Programs, and Postwar Suburbanization." In W. K. Tabb and L. Sawers, eds., *Marxism and the Metropolis,* pp. 152-173. New York: Oxford University Press, 1984.

Chernoff, M. "Social Displacement in a Renovating Neighborhood's Commercial District: Atlanta." In S. Laska and D. Spain, eds., *Back to the City,* pp. 214-219. New York: Pergamon Press, 1980.

Cicin-Sain, Biliana. "The Costs and Benefits of Neighborhood Revitalization." In Donald Rosenthal, ed., *Urban Revitalization,* vol. 18, pp. 49-75, Urban Affairs Annual Series. Beverly Hills, Calif.: Sage Publications, 1980.

Clavel, Pierre. *The Progressive City.* New Brunswick, N.J.: Rutgers University Press, 1986.

Clay, Philip. "Urban Reinvestment: Process and Trends." In P. Clay and R. Hollister, eds., *Neighborhood Policy and Planning,* pp. 21-33. Lexington, Mass.: Lexington books, 1983.

Crenson, Matthew, *Neighborhood Politics.* Cambridge, Mass.: Harvard University Press, 1983.

Cybriwsky, Roman. "The Fashioning of Gentrification in Philadelphia." *Urban Resources* 3, no. 3 (Spring, 1986): 27-32.

Darden, Joe, Richard Child Hill, June Thomas, and Richard Thomas. *Race and Uneven Development.* Philadelphia: Temple University Press, 1987.

Davies, Clarence, *Neighborhood Groups and Urban Renewal.* New York: Columbia University Press, 1966.

DeGiovanni, F. "An Examination of Selected Consequences of Revitalization in Six U.S. Cities." In John Palen and Bruce London, eds., *Gentrification, Displacement, and Neighborhood Revitalization,* pp. 67-89. Albany: State University of New York Press, 1984.

———— and N. Paulson. "Household Diversity in Revitalizing Neighborhoods." *Urban Affairs Quarterly* 20, no. 2 (December 1984): 211-232.

Denzau, Arthur, and Charles Leven. *Report on Alternative Revenue Sources: Local Revenue Generation,* report to the St. Louis Board of Education's Community Advisory Committee, Washington University, 1985.

Downs, Anthony. "Using the Lessons of Experience to Allocate Resources in the Community Development Program." In Jon Pynoos, Robert Schafer, and Chester Hartman, eds., *Housing Urban America,* pp. 522-535. New York: Aldine Publishing Company, 1980.

Eisman, Eugene. "Leveraging Maximizes the Effectiveness of State and Federal Housing Program Funds." In David Listokin, ed., *Housing Rehabilitation,* pp. 284-293. New Brunswick, N.J.: Center for Urban Policy Research, 1983.

Elliot, Brian, and David McCrone. "Austerity and the Politics of Resistance." In Ivan Szelenyi, ed., *Cities in Recession,* pp. 192-216. Beverly Hills, Calif.: Sage Publications, 1984.

Fainstein, Susan, and Norman Fainstein. "Economic Restructuring and the Rise of Urban Social Movements." *Urban Affairs Quarterly* 21, no. 2. (December 1985): 187-206.

Farley, John. "Metropolitan Housing Segregation in 1980: The St. Louis Case." *Urban Affairs Quarterly* 18, no. 3 (March 1983): 347-359.

Feagin, Joe. *The Urban Real Estate Game.* Englewood Cliffs, N.J.: Prentice-Hall, 1983.

_____. "The Corporate Center Strategy: The State in Central Cities." *Urban Affairs Quarterly* 21, no. 4 (June 1986): 617-628.

_____ and Mark Gottdiener. "The Paradigm Shift in Urban Sociology." *Urban Affairs Quarterly* 24, no. 2 (December 1988): 163-187.

Fischer, Claude. *The Urban Experience.* New York: Harcourt, Brace, and Jovanovich, 1976.

Fleishman, Joel. "Not without Honor: A Prophet Even in His Own Country, A Case Study of the Resolution of the St. Louis Public Housing Tenant Strike of 1969." Mimeograph, New York: Ford Foundation Dispute Resolution Project, 1979.

Friedland, Roger. "The Politics of Profit and the Geography of Growth." *Urban Affairs Quarterly* 19, no. 1 (September 1983): 41-54.

Gale, Dennis. "Neighborhood Resettlement: Washington, D.C." In S. Laska and D. Spain, eds., *Back to the City,* pp. 95-115. New York: Pergamon Press, 1980.

_____. *Neighborhood Revitalization and the Postindustrial City.* Lexington, Mass.: D.C. Heath and Co., 1984.

Gans, Herbert. *The Urban Villagers.* New York: Free Press, 1962.

_____. "American Urban Theories and Urban Areas: Some Observations on Contemporary Ecological and Marxist Paradigms." In Ivan Szelenyi, ed. *Cities in Recession,* pp. 278-308. Beverly Hills, Calif.: Sage Publications, 1984.

Glaab, Charles, and A. Theodore Brown. *A History of Urban America.* New York: Macmillan, 1976.

Goodman, Allen. "Neighborhood Impacts on Housing Prices." In Ralph Taylor, ed., *Urban Neighborhoods: Research Policy,* pp. 123-143. New York: Praeger, 1986.

Gordon, David. "Capitalist Development and the History of American

Cities." In Larry Sawers and William Tabb, eds., *Marxism and the Metropolis*, pp. 21-53. New York: Oxford University Press, 1984.

Gottdiener, Mark. *The Decline of Urban Politics.* Beverly Hills, Calif.: Sage Publications, 1987.

Greer, Scott. *Urban Renewal and American Cities.* Indianapolis: Bobbs-Merrill Company, 1965.

Guze, Samuel B. "The State of the Medical Center." *Outlook Magazine* (Summer 1984), pp. 20-23.

Hanson, Royce, ed. *Rethinking Urban Policy: Urban Development in an Advanced Economy.* Washington, D.C.: National Academy Press, 1983.

Harris, Nini. "The Rebirth of LaSalle Park." *St. Louis Commerce* (September 1983), pp. 25-27.

Hawley, Amos. *Urban Society: An Ecological Approach.* New York: Ronald Press, 1971.

Hays, R. Allen. *The Federal Government and Urban Housing.* Albany: State University of New York Press, 1985.

Henig, Jeffrey, *Neighborhood Mobilization.* New Brunswick, N.J.: Rutgers University Press, 1982.

_____. "Collective Responses to the Urban Crisis: Ideology and Mobilization." In M. Gottdiener, ed., *Cities in Stress: A New Look at the Urban Crisis,* vol. 30, pp. 221-245, Urban Affairs Annual Reviews. Beverly Hills, Calif.: Sage Publications, 1986.

Hill, Richard Child. "Market, State, and Community: National Urban Policy in the 1980s." *Urban Affairs Quarterly* 19, no. 1 (September 1983): 5-20.

_____. "Transnational Capitalism and Urban Crisis: The Case of the Auto Industry and Detroit." In Ivan Szelenyi, ed., *Cities in Recession,* pp. 141-161. Beverly Hills, Calif: Sage Publications, 1984.

_____. "Urban Political Economy: Emergency, Consolidation, and Development." In Michael Smith, ed., *Cities in Transformation: Class, Capital, and the State,* vol. 26, pp. 123-137, Urban Affairs Annual Reviews. Beverly Hills, Calif.: Sage Publications, 1984.

Hochschild, Jennifer. *The New American Dilemma.* New Haven, Conn.: Yale University Press, 1984.

_____. *Race, Class, and Power,* Working Paper 10. National Conference on Social Welfare, Washington, D.C., 1983.

Hook, Janet. "Selling the Idea of Virtue to an Amoral Society." *Chronicle of Higher Education* (March 9, 1983).

Hudson, James. "SoHo: A Study of Residential Invasion of a Commercial and Industrial Area." *Urban Affairs Quarterly* 20, no. 1 (September 1984): 46-63.

Judd, Dennis. "Electoral Coalitions, Minority Mayors, and the Contradictions in the Municipal Policy Agenda." In M. Gottdiener, ed., *Cities in Stress: A New Look at the Urban Crisis,* vol. 30, pp. 145-170, Urban Affairs Annual Reviews. Beverly Hills, Calif.: Sage Publications, 1986.

_____ and Randy Ready. "Entrepreneurial cities and the New Politics of Economic Development." In George Peterson and Carol Lewis, eds., *Reagan and the Cities,* pp. 209-248. Washington, D.C.: Urban Institute Press, 1986.

Kantor, Paul. "The Dependent City: The Changing Political Economy of Urban Economic Development in the United States." *Urban Affairs Quarterly* 22, no. 4 (June 1987): 493-520.

Karp, David, Gregory Stone, and William Yoels. *Being Urban.* Lexington, Mass.: D.C. Heath and Company, 1977.

Kasarda, John D. "The Implications of Contemporary Redistribution Trends for National Urban Policy." Unpublished paper, University of North Carolina, 1980.

_____. "Entry-Level Jobs, Mobility, and Urban Minority Unemployment." *Urban Affairs Quarterly* 19, no. 1 (September 1983): 21-40.

_____. "Urban Change and Minority Opportunities." In Paul Peterson, ed., *The New Urban Reality,* pp. 33-68. Washington, D.C.: Brookings Institution, 1985.

_____. "Urban Industrial Transition and the Underclass." *The Annals* 501 (January 1989): 26-47.

Katznelson, Ira. *City Trenches: Urban Politics and the Patterning of Class in the United States.* Berkeley: University of California Press, 1983.

Keating, Dennis. "Urban Displacement Research: Local, National, International." *Urban Affairs Quarterly* 21, no. 1 (September 1985): 132-136.

Keyes, Langley. *The Rehabilitation Planning Game* Cambridge: MIT Press, 1969.

Kinsella, Timothy. "The Future of Downtown as a Center for Business Knowledge Activity: A Review of the Literature in the Context of Organizational Theory." *Economic Development Quarterly* 1, no. 3 (August 1987): 279-292.

Kirby, Andrew. "Nine Fallacies of Local Economic Change." *Urban Affairs Quarterly* 21, no. 2 (December 1985): 207-220.

Kleiniewski, Nancy. "From Industrial to Corporate City: The Role of Urban Renewal." In W. K. Tabb and L. Sawers, eds., *Marxism and the Metropolis,* pp. 205-222. New York: Oxford University Press, 1984.

Krumholz, Norman. "Recovery: An Alternative View." In Paul Porter and David Sweet, eds., *Rebuilding America's Cities: Roads to Recovery,* pp. 173-190. New Brunswick, N.J.: Center for Urban Policy Research, 1984.

Land Clearance for Redevelopment Authority. "LaSalle Park Urban Renewal Plan." Mimeograph, St. Louis Land Clearance for Redevelopment Authority, 1969.

———. "Annual Report for 1974." Mimeograph, St. Louis Land Clearance for Redevelopment Authority, 1974.

Lee, Barrett, and Paula Mergenhagen. "Is Revitalization Detectable? Evidence from Five Nashville Neighborhoods." *Urban Affairs Quarterly* 19, no. 4 (June 1984): 511-538.

Lees, Andrew. *Cities Perceived: Urban Society in European and American Thought, 1820-1940.* New York: Columbia University Press, 1985.

LeFaivre, M., and N. Smith. "A Class Analysis of Gentrification." In J. Palen and B. London, eds., *Gentrification, Displacement, and Neighborhood Revitalization,* pp. 43-64. Albany: State University of New York Press, 1985.

LeGaters, Richard, and Karen Murphy. "Austerity, Shelter, and Social Conflict in the United States." In W. Tabb and L. Sawers, eds., *Marxism and the Metropolis,* pp. 123-151. New York: Oxford University Press, 1984.

Levine, Marc. "Downtown Redevelopment as an Urban Growth Strategy: A Critical Appraisal of the Baltimore Renaissance." *Journal of Urban Affairs* 9, no. 2 (1987): 103-124.

———. "Economic Development in Baltimore: Some Additional Perspectives." *Journal of Urban Affairs* 9, no. 2 (1987): 133-138.

Light, Ivan. *Ethnic Enterprise in America: Business and Welfare among Chinese, Japanese, and Blacks.* Berkeley, Calif.: University of California Press, 1972.

Lindsay, Almont. *The Pullman Strike.* Chicago: Phoenix Books, 1967.

Lipsky, Michael. *Protest in City Politics: Rent Strikes, Housing, and the Power of the Poor.* Chicago, Ill.: Rand McNally, 1970.

London, Bruce, Barrett Lee, and S. Gregory Lipton. "The Determinants of Gentrification in the United States: A City-Level Analysis." *Urban Affairs Quarterly* 21, no. 3 (March 1986): 369-388.

Logan, John, and Harvey Molotch. *Urban Fortunes: The Political Economy of Place.* Berkeley, Calif.: University of California Press, 1987.

Long, Michael. "Measuring Economic Benefits from Gentrification." *Journal of Urban Affairs* 18, no. 4 (Fall 1986): 27-39.

Long, Norton. *The Polity.* Chicago: Rand McNally, 1962.

_____. "The City as a Political Community." *Journal of Community Psychology* 14 (January 1986): 72-80.

MacIntyre, Alasdair. *After Virtue.* Notre Dame, Ind.: University of Notre Dame Press, 1981.

Maher, T., A. Haas, B. Levine, and J. Liell. "Whose Neighborhood? The Role of Established Residents in Historic Preservation Areas." *Urban Affairs Quarterly* 21, no. 2 (December 1985): 267-281.

Mandleker, Daniel, Gary Feder, and Margaret Collins. *Reviving Cities with Tax Abatement.* New Brunswick, N.J.: Rutgers University Press, 1980.

Marciniak, Ed. *Reclaiming the City.* Washington, D.C.: National Center for Urban Ethnic Affairs, 1986.

Meehan, Eugene. *Public Housing Policy: Convention versus Reality.* New Brunswick, N.J.: Center for Urban Policy Research, 1975.

_____. *The Quality of Federal Policy: Programmed Failure in Public Housing.* Columbia: University of Missouri Press, 1966.

Midtown Medical Center Redevelopment Corporation. "Proposal for Redeveloping the Midtown Medical Center Area." Unpublished report, Midtown Medical Center Redevelopment Corporation, 1977.

Mitchell, J. Paul, ed. *Federal Housing Policy and Programs.* New Brunswick, N.J.: Center for Urban Policy Research, 1985.

Molotch, Harvey. "The City as a Growth Machine: Toward a Political Economy of Place." *American Journal of Sociology* 82, no. 2 (September 1976): 309-332.

_____ and John Logan. "Urban Dependencies: New forms of Use and Exchange in U.S. Cities." *Urban Affairs Quarterly* 21, no. 2 (December 1985): 143-169.

Mollenkopf, John. *The Contested City.* Princeton, N.J.: Princeton University Press, 1983.

Monkkonen, Erick. "The Sense of Crisis: A Historian's Point of View." In M. Gottdiener, ed., *Cities in Stress: A New Look at the Urban Crisis,* vol. 30, pp. 20-37, Urban Affairs Annual Reviews. Beverly Hills, Calif.: Sage Publications, 1986.

Momeni, Jamshid, ed. *Race, Ethnicity, and Minority Housing in the United States.* New York: Greenwood Press, 1986.

Monti, Daniel. *A Semblance of Justice: St. Louis School Desegregation and Order in Urban America.* Columbia: University of Missouri Press, 1985.

_____. "A Bit Less Separate and Still Not Equal." *Metropolitan Education,* no. 4 (Spring 1987): 53-69.

Moynihan, Daniel P. "Toward a National Urban Policy," in Daniel P. Moynihan, ed., *Toward a National Urban Policy,* pp. 3-25. New York: Basic Books, 1970.

National Council for Urban Economic Development. "Establishing and Operating Private Sector Development Organizations: A Technical Guide Based on Model Approaches." Washington, D.C.: U.S. Department of Housing and Urban Development, 1984.

Nachmias, Chava, and John Palen. "Neighborhood Satisfaction, Expectations, and Urban Revitalization." *Journal of Urban Affairs* 8, no. 4 (Fall 1986): 51-61.

O'Connor, Carol. *A Sort of Utopia: Scarsdale, 1891-1981.* Albany: State University of New York Press, 1983.

Orfield, Gary. "Ghettoization and Its Alternatives." In Paul Peterson, ed., *The New Urban Reality,* pp. 161-196. Washington, D.C.: Brookings Institution, 1985.

Palen, John, and Chava Nachmias. "Revitalization in a Working-Class Neighborhood." In John Palen and Bruce London, eds. *Gentrification, Displacement, and Neighborhood Revitalization,* pp. 128-139. Albany: State University of New York Press, 1984.

Perry, David. "Structuralism, Class Conflict and Urban Reality." In Michael Smith, ed. *Cities In Transformation: Class, Capital, and the State,* vol. 26, pp. 219-231. Urban Affairs Annual Reviews. Beverly Hills, Calif.: Sage Publications, 1984.

Perry, Stewart. *Communities on the Way.* Albany: State University of New York Press, 1987.

Peterman, William, and Sherrie Hannan. "Influencing Change in Gentrifying Neighborhoods: Do Community-Based Organizations Have a Role?" *Urban Resources* 3, no. 3 (spring 1986): 33-36.

Peterson, Paul. *City Limits.* Chicago: University of Chicago Press, 1981.

————. "Technology, Race and Urban Policy." In Paul Peterson, ed., *The New Urban Reality,* pp. 1-32. Washington, D.C.: Brookings Institution, 1985.

Piven, Frances Fox, and Richard Cloward. "The New Class War in the United States." In Ivan Szelenyi, ed., *Cities in Recession,* pp. 26-45. Beverly Hills, Calif.: Sage Publications, 1984.

Pratter, S. Jerome, and William Conway. "Washington University Medical Center." In National League of Cities, ed., *Dollars from Design,* pp. 35-39. Washington, D.C.: National League of Cities, 1981.

President's Commission for a National Agenda for the Eighties, *Urban America in the Eighties.* Washington, D.C.: U.S. Government Printing Office, 1980.

Reiss, Albert. *Louis Wirth: On Cities and Social Life.* Chicago: University of Chicago Press, 1964.

Sanders, Heywood. "Urban Renewal and the Revitalized City: A Reconsideration of Recent History." In Donald Rosenthal, ed., *Urban Revitalization,* vol. 18, pp. 103-126. Urban Affairs Annual Reviews. Beverly Hills, Calif.: Sage Publications, 1980.

————. "The Politics of Development in Middle-Sized Cities: Getting from New Haven to Kalamazoo." In Clarence Stone and Heywood Sanders, eds., *The Politics of Urban Development,* pp. 182-198. Lawrence: University of Kansas Press, 1987.

Sawers, Larry. "New Perspectives on the Urban Political Economy." In William K. Tabb and Larry Sawers, eds., *Marxism and the Metropolis*, pp. 3-20. New York: Oxford University Press, 1984.

Schill, Michael, and Richard Nathan. *Revitalizing America's Cities*. Albany: State University of New York Press, 1983.

Sennett, Richard. *The Fall of Public Man*. New York: Vintage Books, 1978.

Smith, Michael. *The City and Social Theory*. New York: St. Martin's Press, 1979.

_____ and Dennis Judd. "American Cities: The Production of Ideology." In Michael Smith, ed., *Cities in Transformation: Class, Capital and the State*, vol. 26, pp. 173-196, Urban Affairs Annual Reviews. Beverly Hills, Calif.: Sage Publications, 1984.

Smith, Neil, and Michael LeFaivre. "A Class Analysis of Gentrification." In John Palen and Bruce London, eds., *Gentrification, Displacement, and Neighborhood Revitalization*, pp. 43-64. Albany: State University of New York Press, 1984.

Spain, Daphne, and Shirley Laska. "Renovators Two Years Later: New Orleans." In John Palen and Bruce London, eds., *Gentrification, Displacement, and Neighborhood Revitalization*, pp. 103-127. Albany: State University of New York Press, 1984.

Squires, Gregory, Larry Bennett, Kathleen McCourt, and Philip Nyden. *Race, Class, and the Response to Urban Decline*. Philadelphia: Temple University Press, 1987.

St. Louis Development Program Staff. "History of Renewal for St. Louis, Missouri." Mimeograph, St. Louis Plan Commission, 1971.

St. Louis Development Authority. "Brief Facts on St. Louis Redevelopment Authority." St. Louis: St. Louis Redevelopment Authority, 1984.

Steinberg, Stephen. *The Ethnic Myth: Race, Ethnicity, and Class in America*. New York: Atheneum, 1981.

Steinberger, Peter. *Ideology and the Urban Crisis*. Albany: State University of New York Press, 1985.

Sternlieb, George, and James Hughes. "The Uncertain Future of the Central City." *Urban Affairs Quarterly* 18, no. 4 (June 1983): 455-472.

Stone, Clarence. "The Study of the Politics of Urban Redevelopment." In

Clarence Stone and Heywood Sanders, eds., *The Politics of Urban Development,* pp. 3-24. Lawrence: University of Kansas Press, 1987.

Suttles, Gerald. *The Social Construction of Communities.* Chicago: University of Chicago Press, 1973.

Swanstrom, Todd. "Urban Populism, Fiscal Crisis, and the New Political Economy." In M. Gottdiener, ed., *Cities in Stress: A New Look at the Urban Crisis,* vol. 30, pp. 81-109, Urban Affairs Annual Reviews. Beverly Hills, Calif.: Sage Publications, 1986.

———. "The Limits of Strategic Planning for Cities." *Journal of Urban Affairs* 9, no. 2 (1987): 135-158.

Szelenyi, Ivan. "Urban Policies of the New Right—Critical Responses." In Ivan Szelenyi, ed., *Cities in Recession: Critical Responses to the Urban Policies of the New Right,* pp. 1-25. Beverly Hills, Calif.: Sage Publications, 1984.

Tabb, William. "A Pro-People Urban Policy." In W. Tabb and L. Sawers, eds., *Marxism and the Metropolis,* pp. 367-382. New York: Oxford University Press, 1984.

———. "The Failures of National Urban Policy." In W. Tabb and L. Sawers, eds., *Marxism and the Metropolis,* pp. 255-297. New York: Oxford University Press, 1984.

Taub, R., D. Taylor, and J. Dunham. *Paths of Neighborhood Change: Race and Crime in Urban America.* Chicago: University of Chicago Press, 1984.

Team 4, Inc. "Citywide Implementation Strategies: The Draft Comprehensive Plan." St. Louis: Team 4, Inc., 1976.

Thomas, June Manning. "Redevelopment and Redistribution." In Paul Porter and David Sweet, eds., *Rebuilding America's Cities: Roads to Recovery,* pp. 143-159. New Brunswick, N.J.: Center for Urban Policy Research, 1984.

Tobin, Gary, ed., *Divided Neighborhoods: Changing Patterns of Racial Segregation.* Beverly Hills, Calif.: Sage Publications, 1987.

Tobin, Gary, and Dennis Judd. "A Multi-Year Study of Demographic Change in Three Revitalization Projects in St. Louis," paper presented at the annual meeting of the Association of Collegiate Schools of Planning, New York City, October 19, 1984.

"Urban Decay in St. Louis." St. Louis: Institute for Urban and Regional Studies, Washington University, 1972.

"Analysis of the 1970 and 1980 U.S. Census—City of St. Louis." St. Louis Community Development Agency, 1983.

Urban Land Institute. "Project Reference File: Washington University Medical Center Redevelopment, St. Louis, Missouri." Washington, D.C.: Urban Land Institute. October-December 1980.

Velez-Ibanez, Carlos G. *Bonds of Mutual Trust.* New Brunswick, N.J.: Rutgers University Press, 1983.

Varady, David. *Neighborhood Upgrading: A Realistic Approach.* Albany: State University of New York Press, 1986.

Wacquant, J.D., and William Julius Wilson. "The Cost of Racial and Class Exclusion in the Inner City." *The Annals* 501 (January 1989): 8-25.

Wade, Richard. *The Urban Frontier.* Chicago: University of Chicago Press, 1976.

Ward, Richard, and Jack Pyburn. "Can Doctors Heal the City?" *Practicing Planner* (September 1977): 35-37.

Ward, Richard. "Neighborhood Strategy Application." Unpublished report, Team 4, Inc., 1978.

Ward, Richard, Robert Lewis, and S. Jerome Pratter. "St. Louis." In Rachelle Levitt, ed., *Cities Reborn,* pp. 147-203. Washington, D.C.: Urban Land Institute, 1987.

Warner, Raynor, Sibyl McCormac Groff, and Ranne Wanner. "Ralston Purina Company." In Frank Stella, ed., *Business and Preservation,* pp. 156-158. New York: Publishing Center for Cultural Resources, 1978.

Warren, Donald. *Black Neighborhoods: An Assessment of Community Power.* Ann Arbor: University of Michigan Press, 1975.

Washington University Medical Center Redevelopment Corporation. "Revised Development Plan." St. Louis: Washington University Medical Center Redevelopment Corporation, 1985.

Weiss, Marc. "The Origins and Legacy of Urban Renewal." In J. Paul Mitchell, ed., *Federal Housing Policy and Programs,* pp. 253-276. New Brunswick, N.J.: Center for Urban Policy Research, 1985.

_____. *The Rise of the Community Builders.* New York: Columbia University Press, 1987.

White, Michael. "Racial and Ethnic Succession in Four Cities." *Urban Affairs Quarterly* 20, no. 2 (December 1986): 165-183.

Wilson, William Julius. "The Urban Underclass in Advanced Industrial Society." In Paul Peterson, ed., *The New Urban Reality,* pp. 129-160. Washington, D.C.: Brookings Institution, 1985.

_____. *The Truly Disadvantaged: The Inner City, the Underclass, and Public Policy.* Chicago: University of Chicago Press, 1987.

Wolman, Harold. "The Reagan Urban Policy and Its Impacts." *Urban Affairs Quarterly* 21, no. 3 (March 1986): 311-335.

Worthy, William. *The Rape of Our Neighborhoods.* New York: William Morrow and Co., 1976.

Wright, Gwendolyn. *Moralism and the Model Home: Domestic Architecture and Cultural Conflict in Chicago, 1873-1913.* Chicago: University of Chicago Press, 1980.

Yago, Glen. "Urban Policy and National Political Economy." *Urban Affairs Quarterly* 19, no. 1 (September 1983): 113-132.

_____. "Urban Transportation Policy for Whom? Determinants and Consequences of Transit Change in the United States and Germany." In Ivan Szelenyi, ed., *Cities in Recession: Critical Responses to the Urban Policies of the New Right,* pp. 99-140. Beverly Hills, Calif.: Sage Publications, 1984.

INDEX